Nomadic Life For All Ages

Volumes I/II/III
Plus: Life on the Road: HOW they do it, WHY they do it

Published in the United States

Copyright © Norm Bour, 2023

All rights reserved. No part of this book may be reproduced in any form without permission in writing from the author. Reviewers may quote brief passages in reviews.

ISBN: 9798390485651

LCCN: TK

Cover art: Boza Karic

DISCLAIMER

No part of this publication may be reproduced or transmitted in any form or by any means, mechanical or electronic, including photocopying or recording, or by any information storage and retrieval system, or transmitted by email without permission in writing from the author.

Neither the author nor the publisher assumes any responsibility for errors, omissions, or contrary interpretations of the subject matter herein. Any perceived slight of any individual or organization is purely unintentional.

Brand and product names are trademarks or registered trademarks of their respective owners.

Dedication

In the movie, La La Land, the female lead, Mia, played by Emma Stone, auditions for a movie role, and is asked by the casting agent to "tell us a story." After years of trying to succeed as an actress, she is not overly optimistic about her chances, so shares a story about her aunt who lived in Paris and took many chances. Mia sang, "Audition (The Fools Who Dream)," with so much sincerity, heart, soul, and pain, that she got the role.

When I sat in the dark theater in January 2017 and heard that song I cried.

I cried because the song was dedicated to the Fools who Dream, and I considered myself one of them. I dreamt about living a life better than I was. I **dreamt** about making a difference and helping people. The frustration I felt after years of trying to "make it," came through those tears, and even though I had created a good life, I knew there was more.

I wanted to be like Mia's aunt—to take chances; to live abroad; to live life to the fullest, and if things didn't work out, she'd just try it again. And "a little madness was key…"

Her aunt was her inspiration, to dream.

She told Mia that she once jumped into the Seine River in Paris. She leapt without looking, the water was freezing, and she caught a cold. Yet, she would do it again because SHE was a dreamer. Like Mia. And like Me.

This book is dedicated to all of you who dream to see the world, and wish to do it, and especially to those that have taken those first steps to live life to the fullest.

You are not Fools. You are Dreamers and Doers.

Thanks!

Along our journey we have met many people from many different countries. All different, yet all the same. Some of them shared their stories and lessons which helped us along the way, and many became friends.

I also was fortunate to get help from other nomads and travelers, podcasters, and writers, and I thank you all here:

Interviewees:
Dave Hailwood
Austyn Smith
Sundae Bean
Tiffany Parks
Becky Gillespie
Mary Anne and Ricardo Machado
Jens Hoffmann

For strategic help with figuring stuff out...
Mike Wedaa
Chris Von Nieda
Christopher Trela

And for those that shared their *testimonials*. Thank you!
Robin Draper and Mike Davis
Ehren and Eva Boren
Paul Rosner
John McGann
Ginger Scalone

And last, but not least, I want to thank my wife, Kat Plumley, my "big brave dog," who has stepped up innumerable times over the years and confronted her fears.

Foreword

"**Nomadic Life**" is an essential read for anyone contemplating an extended trip outside their home country and wondering how to do it frugally and without lugging suitcases from town to town. Norm has taken the plunge to live life not as a tourist but a nomad who is exploring, discovering, and enjoying countries, communities, and the people who inhabit them. As he explores, he shares his discoveries with the reader to encourage others to not be afraid to take the wanderlust plunge.

Part travelogue and part personal diary, "Nomadic Life" offers titbits of important information, including how to deal with visa restrictions and what to do without one, to what cuisine you can expect to find, to how much an Air BnB costs in Croatia, to what to expect during the annual Valencia "fires."

The chapters are laid out in short bites, making the book not only easy to read, but hard to put down. Norm has also included a handful of photos—enough to complement his words without making this a photo-essay.

And, perhaps unintentionally, Norm reveals a lot about himself in the process, making this not only a fun read, but a personal one too. "Nomadic Life" should encourage those considering a similar foray into the international unknown. And who knows, you may just bump into Norm while you're out there enjoying your own personal discoveries of the many fascinating and diverse places to live.

Christopher Trela
Author of "Newport Beach: Celebrating a Century"
Professor of Public Relations, Chapman University
Lifestyle Editor, Newport Beach Independent
Newport Beach, Ca.

Table Of Contents

Introduction 11
Entry I, 02.17.19/ Every Journey Starts With a First (6000 mile) Step… 17
Entry 02, 02.20.19/ The Purging Process 18
Date: 02.23.19/ The Visa Issue 21
Date: 03.10.19/ Spain, Valencia & Las Fallas (part I) 23
Side trips worth considering in Spain: Toledo/ Seville/ San Sebastian/ Sagunto.26
Date: 04.03.19/ Next stop: Goodbye, Spain; Hello Italy! 31
Date: 04.16.19/ Being Open to New Experiences and New Relationships: The Amazing Amalfi Coast 34
Date: 04.20.19/ Learning to Love Train Travel 36
Date: 04.26.19/ Getting from A to B in Five Easy Steps 38
Date: 05.08.19/ How to Do this "Travel Thing" Better! 40
Date: 05.12.19/ Understanding Train Schedules in 5 Minutes 42
Date: 05.19.19/ Next stop: Welcome to Croatia! 44
Date: 06.15.19/ Motorcycles in Europe 46
Date: 06.29.19/ Observations & Insights from Croatia 48
Date: 07.08.19/ Size Matters (video). 50
Date: 07.18.19/ Review of Three Croatian Locations (published story) ... 52
Date: 07.22.19/ Borders Crossings: A Fact of Life 54
Date: 07.27.19/ Money Makes the World Go Around: Currencies 56
Date: 07.30.19/ Krakow, Poland: NOT Part of Our Plan! 58
Date: 08.05.19/ Eurail Passes: Worth it, or a Waste of Money?? 59
Date: 08.08.19/ What a 24 hour Travel Day Looks Like… 61
Date: 08.15.19/ Next stop: Impressions of Romania 63
Date: 08.19.19/ Things We Have Missed---and Others We 65
Date: 08.26.19/ Final Thoughts on Romania 68
Date: 09.01.19/ The Importance of Being Flexible 70
Date: 09.07.19/ 14 Cities in 49 days 72
Next chapter(s): 73

Life on the Road: HOW They Do It; WHY They Do It 74

End of Part I

Introduction 88
Date: 09.24.19/ The Bubbles of Comfort Zones 89
Date: 10.16.19/ Travel Angels… 91
Date: 10.19.19/ The Significance and Singularity of *ONLY* Things 94
Date: 10.23.19/ Next stop: Waking in a New City- and a New Adventure! ...96
Date: 10.26.19/ An Island of Contrasts…..97
Date: 11.04.19/ Living Like a Local 98
Date: 11.09.19/ WHY Six Weeks? 99
Date: 11.16.19/ History from a Personal Perspective 101
Date: 11.23.19/ The Importance of Flexibility..102
Date: 11.28.19 (Thanksgiving Day)/ American Holidays Outside America 104
Date: 12.07.19/ Next stop: The Misconceptions- and Realities- of Tunisia 107
Date: 12.14.19/ Trying to "Control" Travel Plans: Sometimes...Shit Happens 110
Date: 12.21.19/ Next stop: The Realities of Island Living 112
Date: 12.29.19/ Santorini from Top to Bottom 114
Date: 01.03.20/ Next stop: Singapore: "You will LOVE it!" 117
Date: 01.12.20/ 30 Days in Bangkok (about 27 days too long…) 120
Date: 01.18.20/ Lessons Learned: Time Lost, Money Wasted, Health Jeopardized; New Experiences to Share 122
Date: 01.27.20/ A NEW View of Thailand! 125
Date: 02.02.20/ Next stop: Vietnam: A Whole New World......................127
Date: 02.11.20/ A Tale of Three Cities: Chaotic, Busy and Normal… 129
Date: 02.17.20/ One Year After Leaving the US:
The Top 10 Memories and Experiences..131
Date: 02.25.20/ Thailand: Land of Many "Firsts" 135
Date: 03.02.20/ Next stop(s): Leaving Cambodia, Thailand, etc….........137
Date: 04.11.20/ Places We ALMOST Visited! 139
Date: 04.18.20/ To Cook or Not to Cook 141
Date: 05.09.20/ Next stop: Why I Got SOLD on Mexico! 143
Date: 05.23.20/ Cenotes: So Much Fun 146
Outside Media Links………………………………………………………... 147
Date: 07.18.20/ Is it Time to Consider Leaving your Country?................148
Date: 08.11.20/ Top Ten (10) Most *AMAZING* Places We have Been; 10 Most *MEMORABLE* Places We have Been..150
Date: 08.15.20/ When Something Bad Happens in a Foreign Country ...155
Date: 08.30.20/ Do These Things When You Can;
You May Not Have Another Chance 157

End of Part II
Life on the Road: HOW They Do It; WHY They Do It (part II)................156

Dedication..174
Date: 10.10.20/ What I Miss About California: Earthquakes!...................175
Date: 11.21.20/ The Good Old Days of Traveling!...................................178
Date: 12.19.20/ Exploring Mexico One Island at a Time 180
Date: 01.02.21/ The New Year is Here; Embrace it!................................182
Supplemental (article)..184
Date: 02.17.21/ Two Years Later...and Counting 185
Date: 03.17.21/ The LAST Year-and This New One................................187
Date: 04.05.21/ Is It Time to Start Traveling Again?................................189
Date: 05.14.21/ An Insider's Guide to Learning Inside Secrets 191
Date: 05.21.21/ Acapulco Report: Worth it or Not?.................................193
Date: 06.26.21/ You Can't Take It With You?..195
Date: 07.04.21/ Travel(ing) Younger is BACK!..197
Date: 07.09.21/ The Bohemian Lifestyle, Part I 199
Date: 07.16.21/ The Bohemian Lifestyle, Part II
(PLUS Bonus Feature on Nude Beaches 101)..201
Date: 07.28.21/ How Your Life Can Change over Five Years 204
Date: 07.31.21/ Parting Thoughts of Mexico: Time to Move on
(Mar 2020-July 2021) 496 days 205
Date: 08.03.21/ New "Firsts": Continent, Country, Hemisphere,
Living at 9,000 ft Elevation!...207
Date: 08.15.21/ Next stop: Ecuador on Two Wheels 209
Date: 08.24.21/ 12 Interesting Things About Ecuador 211
Date: 09.09.21/ Next stop: Peru Travels, Parts I & II...............................213
Date: 09.13.21/ Peru Travels, Part III (Machu Picchu and Beyond) 216
Date: 09.17.21/ Six Weeks in South America (Overview).......................219
Date: 10.01.21/ Next stop: Amazing Dubai..222
Date: 10.15.21/ Next stop: Croatia Feels Like Home...............................224
Date: 10.26.21/ Decisions, Decisions: Where to Next? (Hint: Gobble, Gobble!) 226
Date: 11.06.21/ Are You Eligible for an EU (European Union) Passport? 228
Date: 11.21.21/ Our First Ferry Trip to the island of Hvar 230
Supplemental (article)..232
Date: 12.10.21/ Next stop: Goodbye Croatia, Hello Turkey 235
Date: 12.28.21/ Settling Down, but not Settling: 2021 Review.................237
Date: 01.10.22/ Checking Off the Boxes in Turkey..................................239
Date: 01.20.22/ Tea! For all the Tea in Turkiye??....................................241
Date: 02.03.22/ Residency in a Foreign Country: Yes or No?.................243
Date: 02.17.22/ Three Years & Counting (part I) 245
Date: 03.01.22/ Three Years & Counting (part II) 247

Date: 03.23.22/ 1600 Kilometers (994 miles) from Bucharest,
Romania to Antalya, Turkey: on a Motorcycle 249
Date: 04.02.22/ The Affordability Factor of Traveling 251
Date: 04.17.22/ Our 21 Day Beta Test Road Trip 253
Date: 04.25.22/ What Makes a GREAT AirBNB/ Hotel Room Great? 258
Date: 05.03.22/ Our 21 Day Beta Test Road Trip (part II) 260
Date: 05.14.22/ Istanbul! 263
Date: 05.22.22/ The BEST Ruins I Have Ever Visited 266
Date: 06.05.22/ One City, Two Airports 269
Date: 06.16.22/ 14 flights, 31 days (part I) 271
Date: 07.05.22/ One Missed Bus Can Mess up Everything!!
(14 flights, 31 days, part II) 273
Date: 07.21.22/ A Travel Younger Reality Check: Traveling Older 275
Date: 08.05.22/ A Funny Thing Happened on the Way to Greece:
Government Bureaucracy 277
Date: 08.15.22/ A Sense of History 279
Date: 10.11.22/ My Many "Firsts" in Greece 281
Date: 10.26.22/ The Differences Between Turkey, Greece, Bulgaria, & Romania ... 284
Date: 11.09.22/ Are You a Tourist or a Traveler? Plus Residency Vs. Citizenship…287
Date: 11.19.22/ Our 87 Days in Greece 289
Date: 11.28.22/ Next stop: Getting Situated in a New Place 291
Date: 12.11.22/ Medical Expenses Overseas 293
Date: 12.28.22/ How SAFE Are Other Countries in the World? (beside the US) 295
Date: 01.18.23/ Indispensable Items to Carry when Traveling 297
Date: 02.06.23/ 27 Days in Israel, part I (Jan 23-Feb 1) 299
Date: 02.14.23/ 27 Days in Israel, Part II (Feb 3-Feb 11) 302
Date: 03.01.23/ 27 Days in Israel, part III (Feb 12-Feb 18) 305
Date: 03.01.23/ From Israel and On to Egypt (Feb 18-Feb 26) 309
Date: 02.24.23/ Egypt: Luxor 311
Date: 02.28.23/ Egypt: Aswan 312
Date: 03.04.23/ Return to Albania 313

The End (for now) March 2023

Introduction

Nomad(ic) Life for All Ages (formerly Traveling the World Six Weeks at a Time, Volumes I & II). On February 17, 2019, my life changed. After living in the United States since 1954, and California since 1981, I decided that there was nothing tying me to either place. At the age of 64 I sold or gave away everything I had except for whatever fit in a 28-inch suitcase and a backpack, and my (then) girlfriend (and now wife), Kathleen, and I left for Valencia, Spain.

There were many things that brought us to this place, but the primary driver was that we wanted to live *life*, not just go through the motions of day-to-day existence. We had a terrific life where we were, but I visited Europe for the first time in the summer of 2016, and spent 19 days visiting several different countries. Even though I was overwhelmed and intimidated by the unknown, I saw and experienced things that changed my life. The most important difference between life in the US and overseas was that the people I met and spoke with *enjoyed life to the fullest*. They lived a slower pace, enjoyed socializing with each other, and travelled with ease from one country to another. They were granted lengthy vacations of up to six weeks, and *they took every day*!

In the US, 3000 miles wide coast to coast, we travel from one state to the next effortlessly. No border crossings or passport controls; no changes in currency, and no change of languages- though accents and attitudes can certainly vary!

The "young" people I saw traveling overseas inspired me as they took everything in stride. They negotiated buses and trains and trolleys, and seemed to have no problem with language barriers or changes in currency. Overall they were very friendly and welcoming and willing to help an American in need.

When I returned to the US I decided that I wanted MORE and promised myself to return for more visits. I never had an interest in international travel, which is ironic since my mother was born in Hungary and always wanted to take me, but after my initial visit I tried to understand the reality of living and traveling outside the US. I downloaded some travel apps on my phone and kept track of "good deals," the ones I could not pass up.

I found one of those deals that allowed me in April 2017 to visit Iceland for about $200 round trip airfare from Miami, which I thought was crazy cheap. I had business in Florida, so the distance to Iceland was reasonable, and I spend just four days visiting that spectacular country.

Not long after I saw another deal too good to pass up, so I jumped on it. I had no plan to speak of, but a round trip ticket from Los Angeles to Barcelona, Spain for $389 was way too tempting. Granted, the trip was in January, off season, but I checked the temperature averages and found them very doable.

I booked it in summer, 2017, with a January 2018 departure and counted the days till I left. During that time I fantasized and visualized what it would be like to do this more often, and especially to actually *move* there and travel through Europe as easily as we travel the states.

Fast forward a few months when I met Kathleen in November, 2017.

I had no idea our first date would develop into a relationship, and when I told her I was going to Barcelona in six weeks, and had dreams of spending more time there, I asked her what she thought about that. Her response: "I have always wanted to travel the world and stay at many places for just enough time to get a feel for it."

With that common bond I invited her to join me in Barcelona, and that is how this adventure started.

We flew to Barcelona, and also added a side trip to Nice, France. The weather was cooperative in both countries and in Nice we rented a motorcycle and traveled the coast into Monaco—just like in the movies! And it was breathtaking.

Lodging was inexpensive, especially compared to US prices, just $45 USD per night at a Barcelona AirBNB, and $35 per night in Nice. Both were in terrific locations, and we joked that it would be cheaper to live in Europe than it was in Orange County; what started as a jest suddenly started looking very possible.

As it turned out, the stars aligned as a company that I worked with in the US decided that they would hold their first international event just six months later- in Barcelona. That event location was moved to Madrid and the date was set for August (2018), so Kathleen and I decided we would take that three day event and expand it. Initially for four weeks, then six weeks, and off we went on August 5, 2018, first staying in the Barcelona area, and then 20 days in other parts of Spain. We lodged in several locations, loved them all, then attended my event in Madrid and went onward to Portugal.

Portugal was even better, especially the southern Algarve region, and we took buses and trains around both Portugal and Spain and finished our journey on the island of Menorca, one of the Balearic Islands off the coast of Spain.

I called Menorca, "*the land that time forgot*," since it seemed to be mired in the 1970's, with no high rise hotels or timeshares. There was little tourism and was very calming, and was mostly agricultural with breathtaking beaches and coastlines. It left us with a mystical feeling that resonated with both of us.

During our entire journey, there was one question continuously on our minds: **Can We Do *This*?**

"**This**" meant, ***can we leave everything we've ever known behind***? Can we sell everything we have, travel just with a suitcase and backpack, and leave the US?

I had no attachments anywhere and could work remotely as long as I had internet access; I could be one of those **Digital Nomads**, like the Millennials! Kathleen's kids were in their forties and childless, so nothing kept her tied down, either.

But we had to decide: where do we want to "***live***?"

And in this context it meant, ***in which country do we apply for residency***? As American citizens we were generally limited to 90 days in any one country, OR 90 days in the European Union collectively. (See my Special Report called "<u>Winning the Schengen Chess Game</u>)

Our first attempt at residency in Spain was a bust, and initially we were disappointed, but decided it was for the best, and later said, "Screw the visa!" We'll just move when and where we want and stay ahead of visa restrictions.

And that's what we did.

From September 2018 when we got back to California after our six week trip, until February 17, 2019, when we left, our focus was on unloading what we had and deciding what to keep. That purging process is described in detail as you read on...

We sold everything of value, emptied our closets of any clothes we did not want to take, and purged records and books and pictures and furniture and everything else you find in most American homes.

STUFF.

We left with two suitcases, which we actually purged ***again*** the night before leaving, and over the first few months got rid of more than half of what we left with. We learned to travel lightly, quickly, and with minimum luggage. We learned how to use mass transit, change currency, and deal with everyone around us speaking in a tongue we could not understand!

We learned to travel like Millennials.

These young people, aged 23-38 (in 2019), travel easily because they are not afraid of the unknown, and carry in their pockets the best travel device ever invented: our *Smartphones*.

There are apps for almost everything you need for life on the road, including various forms of transportation (trains, buses, airlines, ferries, taxis), lodging (AirBNB, Hotels & Bookings.com), currency and language conversion, and our fave, Google Maps. The days of getting lost are *not* gone, but they are severely reduced. There are still challenges, but with co-shared cars from resources like Uber and Bolt, you have access to transportation from your train, plane, or bus, to your lodging. We have stayed at over 150 AirBNB rooms, and like it because we can dial in the location, bedroom count, and price we want, and book a room on the fly. They are (usually) cheaper than hotels, especially for longer stays, plus you have access to kitchens (again, usually), and are more personal than a hotel.

Our travels have had challenges, and we found that trying to cram too many locations in too short a period led to stress, frustration, and jeopardized Kathleen and my relationship and communication. **Less is more; quality over quantity,** has been our policy, and we try to stay in each location for at least four weeks, with six weeks being ideal. When we stay more than 30 days we can usually negotiate a significant discount for lodging, plus we try to limit the travel days since they *are* the most stressful and expensive.

UPDATED: 2023

Our "six week agenda" was severely challenged in 2020, due to COVID, and later extended when we got residency in Turkey. That allowed to stay there 24 months. We plan to stick with that six week schedule now that we've been doing this for almost five years. Less can be more—and better.

Our Travel Younger blogs start from the day we left the US, and these 150 plus blog postings allowed me to share and put a lot of things in perspective, along with comparing and contrasting the pros and cons of our new lifestyle. Among other things, here are some insights to be gained:

- ✓ Understanding the process of leaving your home country to become an expat--both the logistics as well as the emotional and psychological aspects
- ✓ How to pack and buy and purge to take only what you need (since you'll be carrying it with you!)
- ✓ Where do you go, how long can you stay, and do you need a visa?
- ✓ Along those lines, how to deal *without* a visa
- ✓ The best travel apps, airlines, and ways to get around
- ✓ Communication and phones! The best and easiest tools

- ✓ How to find other "friends," and being open to other travelers--and locals
- ✓ Understanding, appreciating, and using trains, buses, metros, and transit maps
- ✓ The **best** ways to exchange currency and get cash
- ✓ Is a Eurail pass worth it?
- ✓ Europe, Asia, South America, Middle East; so many destinations!
- ✓ How sustainable is the nomadic lifestyle?

Our journey continues into 2023, when this is re-published, and shares many lessons continually learned not just by us, but by others as well.

We have been asked, "When will you return to the US, or how long will you continue to do this?"

The answer to the first question is, "probably never," and the answer to the second is, "as long as it's still fun!" As I update this in 2023, it still *is* fun.

Herein are some links for videos and articles that I have created over the years. Our fans and followers have grown and there are dozens of people who have/are followed/following in our footsteps.

We are proud of that. Maybe you will join us?

Norm Bour, Travel Younger
norm@TravelYounger.com

UPDATED: 2023

Since my thoughts and feelings when we left the US were very raw, personal, and close to my memory, I left most of those entries intact. The others are a combination of experiences from back then, as they happened, and some are combined to offer lessons from the past four plus years.

Being nomads is now part of Kathleen's and my life. Oh, one big thing that DID change is that we married on June 17, 2022, in Columbus Ohio during one of our rare trips back to the US. I occasionally returned for business, but Kat had no desire to join me or go back. The question I posed before I started this update was, "Will we ever return?" and after all these years, nomadic travel has become our norm, so they answer is (still) probably, "no."

Our journeys got sidetracked in March 2020, as we got waylaid by COVID and were stuck in Mexico for 15 months, and our stay in Turkey beginning in December 2021 was also modified due to our (two-year) legal residency status. Those lessons are coming.

At the beginning we did things "according to plan," staying in new places for six weeks or so at a time. That agenda has become very flexible and our intension *is* to return to longer stays, less travel. We are older, and travel can be a bit more challenging. The author, Chaucer, (plus the Rolling Stones) said, "Time waits for no man," and that is very true. Climbing and packing and keeping track of things does become more difficult over the years.

I hope you enjoy what you are about to read. Some people are inspired by us and say, "Man, you are living my dream life!" and there are those that think we are crazy...but truth is, it may be skewed by envy since this life is not for everyone, nor should it be.

Since we have no plans to ever live in the US, many ask if politics or government actions keep us away. We are still patriots and will always be Americans, but the US we remember is no more. **Freedom**? It's just a word, but in our eyes, we feel that we have *more* freedom outside the US than within. More to come on that, too...So keep reading future possible nomad!

Entry I, 02.17.19/ Every Journey S With a First (6000 mile) Step...

As I sit here at Los Angeles airport, after 64 years, 8 months, and 2 days of living in the United States, I am leaving to become an expatriate. I'm not leaving to get away from anything, but to go towards something new and adventurous.

Welcome to the first entry of TravelYounger.com.

This will be more than a travelogue, as I will share the thought processes that goes through my mind to boldly move on with no specific termination date. Many have asked, "**When are you returning?**" and the answer is, "**We do not know**," but I do know that there is a big world to explore, and so far I have only seen 16 countries; I look to double that over the next 12 months.

I also hope to inspire other Baby Boomers and even those not quite Baby Boomer age, and to inspire us all to **dream**, to **get out of our own comfort zone**, and **try something new**. Many people think that they cannot afford to travel, or it is too challenging, and I don't believe that is true...We can live more comfortably and enjoy life much cheaper outside the US than within.

After all, Millennials do it with ease, **so why can't we Boomers**?

The first six months are already planned, but after that, all we know is that we are heading towards warmer climates as next winter approaches.

I hope you find my journey enjoyable, and hopefully inspirational. Next stop, Spain!

Entry 02, 02.20.19/ The Purging Process

After two days in Spain I have been thinking about two major steps to consider when it comes to leaving your home country and becoming an ex-pat: (1) what to "*purge*," ie, leave behind, what to take, and (2) how do you legally stay in different countries?

Important Traveling Info

** The Purge, Part I (leaving things...)

The process of leaving is a challenging one. First, there is the realization that you may not have a "home" for a while. What you always had available, or took for granted, may change. One of the hardest steps is that process called getting rid of "*stuff*."

When traveling, less is more, but how do you know what you need? Clothing is the number one factor, since you want something comfortable that fits. But what about the things we/you have been collecting for years, including books, pictures, electronics, memorabilia, etc...? They all become less important.

As I sorted through old pictures and things, I had to ask myself, "*Do I really need these? Who will look at them after I am gone?*" In my case the answer was "no one" since I had/ have no biological kids or heirs. I am probably the exception, but if you do have kids/ family, you need to ask *them* what is important to *them*. In many cases the answer is, "None of it." Lots of times we keep things to "pass on," but if they don't want them, why bother?

I used that process with clothing and eliminated the majority of what I had. Kathleen was brilliant at helping me get rid of most of my clothes, and helping me buy things that fit; clothing that was light and comfortable, and would also pack well. When you travel to a specific location, you must be mindful of the climate(s) you'll encounter. It's a process, but it gets easier when you realize how *little* we need.

I started keeping a journal in 1981 and over the years collected 19 of them filled with memories, dreams, plans, relationships, and all my experiences over 38 years. My original thought was to keep them in storage at "home," but realized one day that I would probably *never read them again*, so why bother? Over those almost four decades I rarely reviewed them, so one day in a fit of, "what the hell," into the dumpster they went. I considered having a book burning ceremony at the beach, but time and rain killed that idea. **And I am glad they are gone**. My new life is here and now; the past is gone.

** The Purge, Part II (leaving people...)

Getting rid of "things" is easy compared to leaving behind people and those you love. Since I had no children or siblings, saying goodbye to my home country was not as difficult for me. How old are your kids? Do they still "need" you on a regular ongoing basis? Do you think about traveling with them? This is an individual decision, but on the other side of the age curve are parents, possibly elderly, maybe not. Knowing that you may be ***gone*** when they need you is a difficult emotional tug, so be sure you know how to stay in touch and handle the emotional void it may cause.

Fortunately, technology can make this process very easy, and your "telephone," may take on a whole new role. Here are some communication apps to consider (2023):

- ✓ WhatsApp (audio and video over data network). This is the most prevalent international communication app I found and you can communicate with almost any country from any anywhere. I have used WhatsApp for years and it is the de facto standard when communicating with new friends in different countries, as well as room hosts and hotels. You can call, text, message, even video chat, effortlessly.
- ✓ Skype, the original "free long distance calling" standard. Each party needs a Skype account, and I rarely use it, but you may be a fan.
- ✓ Viber, similar to WhatsApp. We see Viber less than we used to.
- ✓ Google Meet, which is becoming more popular for vid and audio calls.
- ✓ Signal, another a voice, text, and video app that many prefer since it is highly encrypted and less prone to "eavesdropping." WhatsApp is owned by Facebook (Meta), and some are adverse to using it or sharing private information. Signal is actually run by a non-profit foundation and focused on open source technology and free speech.
- ✓ Facetime, for Apple phones and iPads, but not practical for PCs or Android phones.
- ✓ Facebook Messenger. This is part of the Facebook app which allows you to share private messaging and also make audio and vid call.
- ✓ ZOOM, a great video recording app which I have used in business for many years. It's a standalone app across all platforms and is free to use for up to 40 minutes with three people or less online.
- ✓ Marco Polo, which is a fun way to send video messages to your friends and family and they can watch them at their leisure.

There may be more, but these are the main ones that we've found.

Next up: "Staying in a foreign country legally?"

Date: 02.23.19/ The Visa Issue

Deciding where to go is a personal decision and after spending six weeks in Portugal and Spain in Aug-Sept 2018, Kathleen and I had a hard time deciding where we wanted to go first and whether to apply for a residency visa. And there are many types.

The American passport is very strong, and we usually do not need a separate visa to visit another country. There are exceptions worldwide, and not every passport allows that same freedom. For example, an American can stay in Albania for up to one year, but most other passport holders are limited to 90 days, which is the most typical time allowance.

There are different visas for students, employees of companies that have them placed in Spain, plus those for entrepreneurs. "Digital Nomad visas" have become a big thing, and we will address those later, but the short story is, the world and many countries recognize that travelers are (1) more mobile than ever before, and (2) these new nomads usually are self-sufficient so don't use any national resources or services, and (3) they spend money! They use lodgings, eat, drink, create and attend events, and are sources of revenue.

Many countries offer "Golden passports/ Visas" for those buying real estate worth more than a certain price. In Spain we applied for the "Non-lucrative Visa," which is a name that says nothing about it, but requires that the applicant not seek employment or work in Spain, so we would not take anyone's job. Truthfully, getting a JOB overseas is a pain, unlikely, and very cumbersome.

This Non-lucrative visa is ideal if you have **provable** retirement income that would be received whether you work or not. In Spain they also wanted **assets**, about 30,000 euros worth when we applied in 2019, which is about the annual income of the average Spanish worker. These numbers always change and are indexed to some type of government statistic.

Getting residency is challenging in most cases, and takes patience and either professional guidance or good research skills. Some of the information is contradictory and there are many ex-pat Facebook groups in almost every country that can offer real-world experience.

Bureaucracy (and contempt for politicians) is the norm for much of the world--in fact **all** of the world, and is common everywhere. We initially started the residency

...pplication for **Portugal**, but stopped when we discovered that you needed "*passable language proficiency*" to apply for full-time residency after five years. That stopped us, and that is how we got to Plan B, Spain.

We spent dozens of hours and a fair amount of money to apply for Spanish residency, and had it been granted we would initially be approved for only one year, and then we would have to go through almost the same process *again*. We would be required to go to the local police department in our new location and complete the second step of getting the visa.

After one year (we would need to apply at least six months early), we'd have to do it all again to get an additional two year extension. Assuming we got *that*, we would need *another* two year extension and then, after five years, we could apply for official residency. This process is not for the impatient, or those resistant to paperwork, but residency *does* offer many benefits, including a Spanish passport and access to cheaper health care. After our denial from the Spanish embassy we decided to go another way, and said, **"Fuck the visa,"** and we became digital nomads.

For us we did not plan to reside in just **one country**, but only needed a visa that would allow us more than 90 days residency in **Europe**, which is controlled by the "**Schengen Zone**", and includes (currently) 27 countries that share common passport controls. Those in the EU can travel freely without time restrictions, and they can get a job, but we were not looking for a second home, unlike many others.

UPDATED: 2023

In 2023 Croatia joined the Schengen Zone, and that particularly bothered **us** since it was one of our very favorite countries, and a great "safe harbor" to reset our timetable. Aside from now being part of that large 27 country umbrella, there is uncertainty about how the euro dollar replacing the kuna will affect prices of traveling there.

We'll also explore the **Line of Descent citizenship for those who have family lineage from certain countries. As the son of a Hungarian citizen, I may be eligible for citizenship, and some countries will allow you to go back to grandparents and even great grandparents bloodlines to prove lineage. My application to become a Hungarian citizenship is in process, but they need one more document which I must get in the US.

If you can work or live anywhere and do not want to "settle down" in one spot, then traveling within visa guidelines and restrictions is a viable option. For us, we wanted to go everywhere that was warm, so that included many countries that are not part of the Schengen restricted areas.

Date: 03.10.19/ Spain, Valencia & Las Fallas (part I)

UPDATED: 2023

Spain was our first port of call and we lived in Valencia for six weeks. We had no idea about the chaos called Las Fallas, but we quickly found out. This is a major international event, so my recollections and memories follow.

This week all hell is about to break loose as Las Fallas (the Fires!) begins for real.

From March 15-19 (2019) (the feast of Saint Joseph, day of the father in the whole country), Valencia is given over to a carnival of bonfires, fiesta, fireworks, and a healthy dose of satire known as Las Fallas- the fires. The festival also signifies the end of winter, and you cannot escape the sounds (and smells) of fireworks as kids of all ages are igniting and throwing them.

Every afternoon at 2:00 p.m. fireworks erupts from a large square downtown and on corners throughout the city are colorful **ninots**, giant paper-mâché figures, some over 20 feet tall. They are all over town, like portable Rose Bowl floats. Most are still under wraps, but they satirize political figures, soap opera stars, or more exotic creatures from the movies. Some are grotesque, others playful, and all are larger than life and available for public viewing.

Oh, and get this:

On the final night they get **torched** in the streets. Holy crap!

We had no idea this festival existed, but when we were startled awake on our first Sunday morning at 0800 with sounds like warfare around us, we asked our host, "What is going on?" She was surprised that we had no idea! Sometimes you luck out, and that is what happened as we arrived just in time for this annual event which people from all around the world come to celebrate.

Las Fallas, part II

Las Fallas continues, with celebrating in the streets, and many are closed off to cars. Fireworks continues and the ninots are being unveiled!

These giants are all over the streets, and that is not an exaggeration, with some over 50 ft tall, with workmanship and craftsmanship that is spectacular. The whole town is in a festive mood and reminds me of the City of Pasadena during the Rose Bowl season.

Las Fallas, part III

All the ninots are now uncovered and throughout the city are hundreds of them. They are made from polyurethane and are usually whimsical with bright coloring and creative design.

I went to the Las Fallas Museum where they had samples from every year since it started over two centuries ago. Every year one ninot is offered a "pardon" and is not destroyed, like when the US President pardons a turkey for Thanksgiving. The museum offers the history, and shows how the designs have changed.

Along every block they sat, ranging from small to very, very large. The small ones are built by kids, and are amazing in their own right, but it's the big ones that blow you away. The crowds are getting worse as we reach the last night when fireworks destroy them all at midnight after turning off the streetlights.

Imagine the biggest, most dense crowd of partiers you've ever been in: now double it. That's what it was like today after the 2:00 fireworks show. You cannot move **against** the crowd and you can barely move **with** them! What it's like at midnight I'm not sure I want to experience! Roads remain blocked and driving must be a nightmare.

You can see them, and you can hear the sounds, but you cannot smell the smell of fireworks nor feel the heat. There are 340 or so of these statues all throughout the city of Valencia and they are all being incinerated tonight.

Las Fallas, part IV

The last night was everything I thought it would be: noisy, smelly, crowded, and lots of fun which continued long past when I finally got home about 0200. Row by row, street corner by street corner, the fire department would move their equipment, watering down the street signs, lamp posts and anything combustible as they strung firecrackers along the statues, and then finally, WHOOSH, up they went in flames!

.e bedlam.

First they started with amazing fireworks at EACH one, then hit the detonator. They all exploded, then the fire took over as it turned into a fireball, and in a few seconds the heat became oppressive

Then, finally... the Sounds of Silence.

Not a good night for anyone with PTSD since it was all very violent and chaotic, like a war zone during an airstrike. Anyone with fear of crowds or chaos would not do well, but by the next morning, all was back to normal. Streets were open, vendor booths and tents were gone, and it was business as usual.

Valencia was nice for six weeks and we had a great condo location along with good weather. The language barrier took some time for me to adjust to and to make things harder, **the Valencians have their own dialect**, which is not Spanish, but is local to the region.

Valencia is the third largest city in Spain after Barcelona and Madrid, but in those cities English was prevalent. Not so much here.

Keep that in mind with simple things we take for granted, like signing up for a yoga or exercise class. I planned to take some classes, but not understanding instructions would make that difficult, so I decided to stick to gym workouts, which I can do in silence and without conversation.

Side trips worth considering in Spain:
Toledo/ Seville/ San Sebastian/ Sagunto

I had a business event in Madrid for a few days and afterwards had a chance to explore other cities, including Toledo.

It's about 45 minutes south of Madrid, built on a huge rock, with streets that are small, narrow, and winding, and filled with shops selling swords, suits of armor (!), and knives everywhere! I did some investigation and here's what I found.

More than 2,000 years ago, around 5th century B.C., Iberian blacksmiths forged Toledo swords with a special iron blade. They were so tough and durable that they were the weapon of choice for that elephant riding conqueror known as Hannibal. He beat the Romans with these mighty swords, Rome got the hint, and also adopted them, and their fame grew.

Toledo is a thriving city of 83,000 and the capital of the region, so houses government and political offices. The famous painter, El Greco, hailed from there and the civilizations of Arabs, Jews and Christians all tried to grab their share over the centuries. That adds for an interesting mix of crosses, menorahs, and Arab symbolism throughout the town.

Is Toledo worth visiting?

A big thumbs up from me since it is an easy and cheap bus ride from Madrid and a nice getaway.

Side trips: Seville

After two weeks of our new life abroad, I finally had my first WOW day, courtesy of the city of Sevilla (Seville), Spain.

was an impulse decision, but since we were already in Madrid, and there was no rush to get back to our home base in Valencia, we decided to use our Eurail pass and go somewhere else. That somewhere else was Sevilla, a little over two hours train ride south of Madrid.

A note about these high speed trains. They are amazingly comfortable, and generally have electrical outlets, wifi, and food. They zip along at 250-300 kph and time just whisks on by-- as does the scenery--which was beautiful. Our return trip to Valencia was effortless, and reinforced my love of trains in Europe.

In Sevilla the sense of history was breathtaking.

Christopher Columbus left here just before he hit the road, or in this case, the ocean, to discover the US. When he returned he was the Golden Boy, and for about a century afterwards, a lot of money poured into the town. There was a period of massive construction, then the money went elsewhere, and there was little built for some time. We especially loved the Seville Castle and the Alcazar at night, which were beautiful.

Our first impressions were reinforced as I got to go through the oldest continuously occupied palace in all of Europe, called Alcazar. The original palace was built in the 1200s and has been continually upgraded and remodeled, not unlike houses everywhere. Two things blew my mind.

One was standing in the bedroom of the young son of Queen Isabella and King Ferdinand. It was a spectacular room, and being in the room of the king and queen who sent Columbus to America made me ponder *true history*.

The **second** mindblower was viewing the *first painting* that showed the brand new country that Mr. Columbus discovered. It shows the Virgin Mary with Columbus on one side and King Charles on the other. At the bottom are pictures that represented the three ships that he sailed to America.

Reflections of history:

My trips to Europe over the last few years have put history in a whole new perspective. California is just a few hundred years old; East coast history, a bit longer, but when you stand inside a castle that's over 1000 years old or visit catacombs that are two millennia old, it provides a new scale of the timetable of recorded history.

We came across this large **wooden** structure called Metropol Parasol, and for three euros you can take an elevator to the roof and see amazing views. It's located at La Encarnación, which was officially ground zero for the city when it was founded in the 1200s. That is 800 years ago which is staggering, and this is where the original occupants, the Moors, laid ground, followed by the Catholics and the Christians.

Sevilla vs. Valencia

The differences between Valencia and Sevilla are noteworthy. Valencia felt like an industrial (real) town with real-world people, and not as much as a tourist destination. Most of the shopping districts did not have that feel either, but Sevilla truly felt like a holiday destination where fashion and shoes rule!

In hindsight we wished that we had made *Sevilla* our home base instead of Valencia, but **that is how we learn what works and what does not**. We stayed for two days and planned to return for longer, and that is what this journey is all about; to find those places that we like and want to spend more time in, and to eliminate the others.

This is not a scary (ad)venture, but **there is** a learning curve. Technology makes this amazingly effortless, and for those of you who think that it's beyond your skill set, think again.

Side trips: San Sebastian

It's interesting how you can "feel" the energy of a city.

When we got to Valencia, neither Kathleen nor I were wowed. It's a nice town, had great restaurants and cathedrals and other attractions, but nothing that gave us the warm and fuzzies. Seville on the other hand- lots of energy; good Feng Shui. We were there for just two days, but gave it very high marks and will return again; San Sebastian is that and more.

The more is the ocean, mountains, and the amazing history in one of the food capitals of the world! This town, also called **Donostia**, which is the Basque name for San Sebastian, has a history that goes back over 25,000 years and the lineage and genetic makeup of the people is amazingly pure. There are families that can legitimately claim to go back thousands of years.

...ated on the Bay of Biscay, and just 20 km from the French border, this town is magical, and we felt it as soon as we left the train station to walk to our room. We stayed in the heart of "Old Town" and were within a 15 minute walk of more restaurants than you could visit in several months! The population is normally about 200,000, but from what we were told, this is not the place to be in summer as the population increases exponentially.

OK, foodies, here's news for you.

Tapas are a well-known Spanish food style, small dishes, and usually very affordable. Here they call them ***pintxo*** and they include every exotic seafood that you could imagine, along with meats as well. They are usually served on a small piece of bread roll, some of the tastiest bread I ever ate. We hit the streets Thursday night, which is their local night out, and on the bar sat, 20, 30 different types of pintxos. OMG, and so tasty! Beers and wine are about $2.00 USD, about the same for the pintxos, so you can get your fill for not a lot of money.

We took a funicular (built in 1912) to the top of Mount Igueldo, and from there you could see the entire bay, the city, and beyond, which was breathtaking. At the top was a tower, La Farola, which was constructed before America was a country, along with an amusement park which was closed while we were there, but in summer must be spectacular.

San Sebastian: huge thumbs up and a highly recommended place to visit, plus the train routes connect from almost any major city in Spain.

Side trips: Sagunto

We thought it was just a sleepy whistle stop on the railroad track from Valencia to Barcelona, but they had this really cool castle on the hill, so we decided a day trip was in order. And so glad we did. What appeared to be a quiet little burb is a thriving town of 65,000 people with an amazing history.

The name is Sagunto today, but the Romans called it "Saguntum" and the Iberians called it "Arse." Go ahead, I laughed, too. The castle is 2000 years old and as they usually do with castles, it's built waaaay up on top of a big hill. They appreciated views back then, too, plus it helped defend the castle. There's a theater built from the rock of the mountain which has been there since day one, but it's been modernized and can hold 6000 attendees, and it was very cool walking through hallways that were built in the first century and wondering what it was like back then.

Hannibal the conqueror conquered this town, too, and allowed Rome to be granted a favored status, so Sagunto has a long history behind it. The castle is divided into seven sections and is almost a kilometer long, plus the views were amazing.

As cool as the castle and theater were, the city was, too. Walking into town for lunch we found a multi-block long street fair with lots of unique offerings, from shoes to clothing, and even underclothes for sale. I got some workout pants for eight euros, Kat found a scarf for three, and once again we concluded that prices are great in Spain, as is train fare. Sagunto is about 30 minutes, 20 km. from Valencia and for two people, round trip, the price was $18 USD.

Date: 04.03.19/ Next stop: Goodbye, Spain; Hello Italy!

As we finish up the first leg of our Worldwide Adventures, Valencia and Spain are now memories with some memorable things to take with us.

1) Las Fallas, the Fires, probably the loudest, most irritating, but fun event I've ever been to! It pushed our envelope of annoyance and patience, with firecrackers popping at our feet just walking through the streets. Very, very crowded streets. The ninotes were breathtaking, and seeing them burn was exciting and heart-breaking as well.

2) we used Valencia as a home base with several side trips, including Sevilla, which Kat and I both loved. Very pedestrian friendly, lots of good energy, very clean, plus amazing history. A place to return to, including...

3) San Sebastian. Again, history by the water with amazing views, coastline, castles, towers, etc...Oh, and food! One of the gastronomical capitals of the entire world. It's weird to think that you get cynical and tired of cathedrals and churches, but they all do look similar. Although still worth touring.

Spain is now behind us, and between this trip and the last, I think I know it better than any country outside the US. We have been to all four borders, used their rail system extensively and visited many of their major cities. I give high, high marks to Spain as a place to visit and possible move to if you are looking for a laid back, affordable lifestyle. Now: Italy.

We arrived in Rome and had just a few hours to do a quick walk before our train to Tivoli. Even so, in just that time we saw the Colosseum and Forum, which gave me pause and brought on old emotions, since the last, and only time I had been there, was in 1995 when my ex-wife and I chaperoned my stepdaughter's high school trip. That was our only international trip, and that marriage and relationships are memories, just like the trip itself.

There is amazing history here, equaled maybe only by Greece, which will be coming up in a few months. When you walk the same ground Caesar and Nero and a host of different historical figures have walked, plus millions of people walking those *same* steps, it brings perspective of how long history is- and how short a time *we* are here.

When we contemplated doing this adventure we questioned if we really **could** do. And had we not made this leap I would be remorseful the rest of my life. Yes, there are long days, inconveniences, and delayed trains along with late planes, and bad meals as well as good, but the experiences of the places we've been to in less than eight weeks leaves me wanting more.

Now we're in Tivoli, a "medieval" town about 20 km from Rome, just a 30 minutes train ride, for just three euros. This town has **real** history since it predates the city of Rome and the Roman Empire which ruled most of the known world for centuries. The town itself was founded in 1215 BC, 1000 years before Christ, and what the city must have looked like back **then**, when statues and pillars were new and clean and not aged by twenty centuries along with war and pollution, boggles my imagination. There are several "villas," ie, attractions here, and so far we have only seen one.

Tivoli: The City of the "Three Villas"

We have started to explore the three villas of Tivoli: **Villa Gregoriana, Villa d'Este**, and **Villa Adriana** (also known as *Hadrian's Villa*), and they are all so different.

Gregoriana is the *Villa of Waterfalls*, whereas d'Este should be labelled the *Villa of Fountains*, since it has more than I have ever seen in one location-- fifty one of them per Wikipedia--and each one more magnificent than the other.

Gregoriana remains my fave since it is so unique. Between natural cliffs, man-made and natural waterfalls, foliage to light up your eyeballs, and a lot of climbing up and down ridges—it just took my breath away. As we walk to our favorite cappuccino spot most mornings, we cross over the Gregoriana bridge, which is 2000 years old and overlooks the park. I cannot cross that bridge without stopping and peering over the edge and thanking God for his creation. But back to d'Este, which we visited today.

Villa d'Este

This is a 16th century estate and a UNESCO world heritage site, with more than 4.5 hectares (11 acres) with fountains of all sizes. There is a large interior palace with many tapestries and paintings, but the grounds are where the action is.

ountain of Europa- spectacular; The Hundred Fountains- about 200 feet of ...id fountains, and the Fountain of Rometta, with its many tiers and levels of water treatment and landscaping, are all jaw dropping. And by the way, there are no pumps to be found; these are all fed by gravity.

Date: 04.16.19/ Being Open to New Experiences and New Relationships: The Amazing Amalfi Coast

Part of the adventure and fun of traveling is meeting new people and there are many reasons to stay **open** and inviting to strangers that may become friends.

A few days ago while walking in the street I heard a couple speaking English, not that common here in Tivoli. We had a brief conversation, compared backgrounds, and decided to meet for coffee the following morning. That was followed by a few other meals and we found that Chad and Eileen Rider were similar in age and mindset and we all clicked. One Saturday morning they were ready to leave the town, and we met for coffee to bid our goodbyes as their plan was to drive south to the Amalfi Coast. Kathleen had been there before, I had not, but we both wanted to go. I jokingly said, "You have a four-seater car don't you?," and after an excited, "Yes, please join us!" reply, Kat and I hurriedly packed a bag and were off on a Road Trip in less than an hour.

The ride through the central part of Italy was picturesque as was the entire trip to the amazing Amalfi Coast. We found a great hotel, Hotel Bellavista, in the lovely city of Praiano along the coast, which offered a great view along with the sound of the surf in front, plus a panorama of lemon trees from our room to the beach.

We awoke in the morning to the sound of roosters crowing and concluded that even though this part of the coast was tourist focused, it did not feel "touristy." That means, not a lot of gift shops or vendors hawking everything under the sun.

After breakfast, which was included with our room, we headed north and spent the afternoon in the beautiful city of Positano, which is spectacular beyond belief- or words. It offered cliffs several hundred feet high just dropping into the sea with just a road and a city in between. It was almost Easter and the crowds were reasonable, but we were warned that in summer it is bumper to bumper traffic. The best way in? Via boat, they suggested. So noted.

We decided to spend night number two in Sorrento, which has a great reputation as well. Though not as over the top majestic as Positano, Sorrento felt like a "real city" with real people and real commerce. Again, great cliffs, but not as much BEHIND

.y, but in front, dropping into the ocean. A particular highlight was Mount Vesuvius, splayed out before us in all its glory, even after half the mountain was destroyed in AD 79, which levelled the city of Pompei. Unfortunately we did not get to Pompei.

Important Traveling Info

The advantages of mass transit: The beauty (and convenience) of Europe and most of the world, is that mass/ public transportation is readily available and offers lots of benefits. We decided to spring for a ferry across the Gulf of Naples, which only took about 30 minutes on a turbo jet airfoil. It was magical; the sun was out, skies were clear, and Vesuvius was prominent in our camera lens. We took the high speed train to Rome from Naples, about 90 minutes duration, and then a quick regional train to Tivoli, and after less than six hours, we were back home.

But none of this would have happened if we were not open enough to (a) invite conversation with a stranger; (b) accept graciousness from those that wish to offer, and (c) be willing to accept and go with the flow. Four strangers in a car for four hours just days after meeting turned out to be an Adventure with a capital "A" and I believe the beginning of a long friendship.

NOTE: Today, in 2023, we remain in touch with the Riders and are helping them possibly become nomads, too...

Date: 04.20.19/ Learning to Love Train Travel

I never knew how much I liked trains (and train travel) until I started using them in Europe, and they have become my favorite and primary means of transportation.

As an American- and Southern Californian for decades- train travel was impractical and usually inaccessible. In S. Cal. it's all about cars: cars here, cars there, along with the hassle of owning a car and commuting for business or for pleasure. After living in Europe for over two months, here are some reasons I love trains:

Different types of trains...

1) They are usually comfortable. Just one trip, an overnighter from Madrid, SP to Lisbon, PT, was uncomfortable, primarily because sleep was a necessity, not a luxury, and this train went way too slowly and stopped way too often. But I learned the differences between high speed lines, regional trains, and commuters, and they all travel at different speeds and different itineraries. Most of my train trips have had comfortable seats, with electrical connectors for the necessities of entertainment, and sometimes with Wifi.

2) They are timely, as in, they leave on the minute (give or take) or when they say, and they usually arrive as planned or earlier. Of the 30 or so trains I have been on in the last several years, just one has been late, and that was because there was a car accident at one of the crossing gates. You gotta' respect that compared to plane travel, or the uncertainty of car traffic.

3) They are affordable, some more than others. Tivoli is about 19 km east of Rome and a 35 minute train ride- assuming we take the ***direct*** line, without extra stops, which can delay it by double. The price of this trip, one way? Three euros. Mind you, that is ridiculously cheap, but here's another example. The high speed line we took recently from Naples to Rome was about 1 hr., 45 minutes, and cost $45.

And reason #4, harder to quantify, but one that elicits an emotional feel, is the romanticism of trains. They have a history of hundreds of years and we have seen many movies filmed in and around and about trains. You get on a train and you recreate what passengers have been doing for 150 plus years. Now we do it faster, as fast as 300 kph, and on magnetic cushions.

er benefit, we'll call it #5, is that in today's app driven world, we can find and book a train on the spot, without having to use a ticket machine, speak to a non-English speaking civil servants, or read undecipherable train schedules in another language. My favorite app for trains is www.omio.com, and it's easy to use, plus I can learn how to get from point A to point B within seconds, book the trip, plus generate an e-boarding pass. I booked the trip we took from Naples to Rome while in the terminal and paid for it on the spot.

Date: 04.26.19/ Getting from A to B in Five Easy Steps

We talk about travel as though it's effortless. To get to Rome from Philadelphia you just take a flight and that's that. But it's not. In most cases there are multiple steps involved. Case in point. I left Tivoli, IT on a Wednesday to get to Philadelphia, PA, USA, and it took five separate steps and you have to know that going in. It usually works out, but there are some caveats.

Step I: Wednesday morning I took the 10:23 train from Tivoli to the Rome airport, about a 35 minute ride, but first I had to get *to* the airport and that happened via the train station at Roma Tiburtina train transfer. There was no DIRECT way to get to the airport unless you drove.

Step II: From Tiburtina station I had to take another train which took about 50 minutes and that got me to Rome Fiumicino airport. That's an easy ride and I got there about 90 minutes before take-off, which was very tight for an international flight. Why? Because going through check-in and security can be cumbersome and in many cases, including this one, I had to go through two security checkpoints.

Step III: I made the flight, and in about nine hours I was in Boston, ready for step #4. The timing worked out well since the flight was almost equal to the time zone change, so I started my journey Wednesday morning and finished it the same Wednesday 3,000 miles away.

Step IV: Another flight from Boston to Philadelphia, another tight timing dilemma with just a 90 minute window, which caused me to be anxious. Like security check-ins, you must leave time for immigration and passport control. The lines can be long, and it can, in some cases, take an hour to get through passport control. NOTE: I suggest a mobile app called **Mobile Passport** which is approved by the US government, and it can save time. Even better, I used my Global Pass for the first time and instead of a long 30 minute serpentine line, I was able to step to the Global Pass machines and be done in less than five minutes. Sweet!

Update 2023:

Global Pass has become very popular, and even though there is a backlog of appointments to get one, I highly recommend it. On a recent flight into the US there

...ore people in the Global Pass line than I have ever seen before, but it still cut processing time significantly. The machines offer facial recognition and prints out a receipt which you hand to the customs officer as you exit. It could not be more simple.

The Jet Blue flight from Boston was smooth and got me into Philly at the scheduled time. And finally, step #5, which involved renting a car to get to my destination. It was very easy to navigate these steps, and it takes time to get comfortable with the process. It's about practice, leaving enough time, and not getting nervous. Airlines recommend getting to the airport two hours early before your flight, and allow even more time for international travel. It's good advice and with free Wifi, lots of eating places, and ways to keep busy at the gate, you are better off having more time to kill than being stressed.

International flights can take 24 full hours of "real time," but you sometimes get that time "back" due to time zone changes.

I have taken many trips over multiple time zones and the question of "jet lag" is a common concern. This is nothing new, but I recommend you get on the SAME schedule as where you land as quickly as possible. That may involve a nap or staying up when you are tired, but I can usually adjust to an 8-10 hour time difference in two days with little after effects.

Date: 05.08.19/ How to Do this "Travel Thing" Better!

We have spoken about our "journey," ie, traveling the world six weeks at a time with no specific return date, and almost everyone says "Awesome," or something similar. Most people respect what we're doing and say they would like to do it (1) when I retire, (2) when I have enough money, (3) when the kids are gone, or (4) "someday. I don't like "someday" since that is similar to "when I get around to it," which usually never happens. So I started thinking of tips I to help you Travel Younger and to dip your toes in the water.

Cool stuff to know...

1) **You do not need to leave "*forever.*"** No one ever knows how long forever is, so how about "I will take a month long trip in (insert date here)," to, _____, just fill in the blanks. Do yourself a favor and DO NOT take just a weeklong vacation. It's nice, but not usually relaxing if you're traveling too far, and it does not offer you enough flavor of your destination. Two weeks is OK, but give yourself a solid month if possible. Determine **where** you want to go, **when** you want to go, and book a flight! You'll make it work. Most people in Europe get six weeks' vacation- and they TAKE THEM. American workers can usually get long vacations, but rarely use them, and *instead* let them accumulate- then they disappear. It's sad.

2) **You can afford it!** International travel is cheap compared to domestic travel and there are always bargains. Many "secondary" destinations do not have direct flights, so you may need to take two flights. Stay at AirBNBs. I cannot praise them enough and have stayed in several dozen over the years. Yes, sometimes you get a shitty location or a dirty unit, but do your research and plan for the best. You will usually get local advice from the host and having a kitchen is a huge savings of time and stress of always eating out. NOTE: Even years later, as I update this in 2023, international flights are still a bargain compared to US domestic flights. Travel has increased and carriers are still short staffed, so I recommend you plan and book your flights in advance as much as possible.

3) Here's tip #3. *It IS scary- but it's not*. It's just uncomfortable being around foreign speakers, using different currencies, and not knowing how to navigate. Been there, done that, and it's still intimidating to me sometimes. "All the fun is outside your comfort zone" is a great expression and it still holds true. In the US we think that

...HING revolves around America, but that is not reality. It's a big world and ...one has their own world revolving around themselves and their countries. It truly makes me appreciate our "place" in the world- and in the Universe! While traveling you will certainly get lost, maybe miss a connection, and will encounter bad weather. It's all OK, trust me.

Date: 05.12.19/ Understanding Train Schedules in 5 Minutes

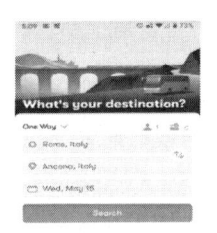

As I mentioned, train travel is a personal favorite of ours and usually available in most of Europe and much of the world. The learning curve to understand "schedules" is not that steep, though the intimidation factor is!

Here's the easy way to get around Europe or almost anywhere via train.

Important Traveling Info

Resources: Along with the Omio app, I also like Trainline. The Omio interface is better, and there are two steps involved in the process of getting a train: FINDING it, BOOKING it, and getting on the RIGHT train at the RIGHT station.

When booking, you must know **where** you are leaving from, which means the **station**, not just the city, and many towns have **several rail stations**. They come in many sizes, from long distance to regional to local, but once you start using these apps you will understand the ease of using QR codes to board.

Your app will identify which **STATION** is best even if you don't know, so pay attention. Getting to the wrong station after booking and paying your ticket is a bad start.

Using the app (picture) you can see that we plan to leave Rome Termini (one of their main stations) at 09:28, and arrive at Ancona, IT at 13:45 (1:45 p.m. in American speak) after a 4h17m ride. You can pretty much set your watch to it baring anything unusual. The cost: $22 USD, very reasonable.

Now, what happens when you GET to the station? How do you know what to look for?

If you look at the tote board picture the first thing you look for is the **TIME** of departure, since they're all sequential. NOTE: They will be in 24 hour time, so don't fight it; adjust. In most cases they won't post the track number until 20-30 minutes beforehand, but you should see several hours' worth of trips pending.

From there you look for your destination, which is USUALLY your city, but could be another further down the road. To double check, compare your train **NUMBER**

...e one on your app. If they match, you know you have the right train, plus ...eed to know which **PLATFORM** to use. Learn certain basic words in the language of that country, like "platform," which in Italy is "binario," which does not translate well. Don't fight this either! Case in point, the Termini station has at least 22 binario, 'cause I have been on #22.

TEST! (see board in picture)

If you plan to go to Venice (Venezia in Italian) on the 12:50 train, double check that you are booked on train AV8434 (check your app ticket) and you will depart on binario #1. Bear in mind that there are usually several train operators similar to our Amtrak and other trade names, like Union Pacific, CSX, etc... but they are not critical to know. You will also see a rolling screen after the arrival city which may indicate other stops on the way. Know in advance that you can get from A to B in varying amounts of time, so look for 1) anything that mentions "change", rather than a direct line, and also look for 2) the least number of stops. When you book online your charge will usually include the transferring train, but avoid it if you possibly can. Same thing with excessive stops. Smaller cities, overnight trains, or longer distances WILL involve transfers and many stops. Again, part of the process.

From Termini station in Rome to Tivoli can take 34 minutes direct, but 90 minutes with stops if you do not take the express train.

I hope this helps!

Date: 05.19.19/ Next stop: Welcome to Croatia!

Today it has been 90 days exactly since we left Los Angeles/ Orange County/ California/ the United States, on our Great Adventure.

So far Croatia is awesome, and even though some said that their food was not their favorite, we found it yummy! Quite affordable and very, very good. We are in a small village which is on the water and they are mostly locals.

We stand out.

One, as strangers because we don't look like workers or residents (plus they know everyone) and two, because I think they recognize that we are not Europeans. They don't go out of their way to be friendly, but if we smile and say "hello" they reciprocate, and so far English has become pretty common since their exit to freedom from Soviet rule back in 1991.

For decades they were under the Iron Fist of Soviet communism and freedom did not exist. Their lives must have been horrible, but as they found freedom they had to align somewhere, and that somewhere was the West, specifically the US. Many of the "young" understand and speak English and many of the shop keepers do as well, but the average resident here in our town, does not. Their Croatian language is different than Latin based ones, and it is hard to remember simple words like hello, thank you, and good morning.

In many countries a sign in front of a building can offer an educated guess as to what kind of business it is. Pictures help. Here, you could be looking at a butcher shop or a massage parlor and there is no way to know without pictures.

Croatia also operates on "normal" business hours, unlike Spain and Italy. In Spain, most businesses, including restaurants, closed mid-afternoon, and opened later, as late as 8:00 p.m. On Sundays, good luck finding an open grocery store! Italy was a less restrictive version of that with some businesses closing during the day, but Sundays were more American-like in hours. Here in Croatia, just a few closed during the afternoon, but most restaurants are open from 10:00 a.m. to as late as midnight.

countries in the world, corruption gets in the way of government and ...zation and when things break, it can take a long time to repair it. The "older" residents dress very old-fashioned and they carry a weariness about them, but the younger, under 40 or especially under 30 crowds, carry better energy. We have an easier time in restaurants since English is taught in schools and they know that tourism is a huge part of their economy.

Valencia had about 750,000 residents, and Tivoli, with about 50,000, was a very small town. Split, just a 15 minutes bus ride, has about 180,000, but we are in a smaller village just north.

Water is everywhere in this country! Many countries in the world have beautiful coastlines, and I must add Croatia to that list. In the span of just 138 km, about 90 miles, we have viewed some of the clearest water ever and the beauty of the rocks is incredible.

We went south to Makarska and north to Sibenik, and "live" about midway in between, a village called Kastel Kambelovac, just north of Split proper. The area south of Split is amazing with a huge block of rock along the inside coastline, and beautifully clear water on the other side. Going north is not as impressive as far as the big rocks, but the coves and inlets are incredible.

UPDATED: 2023

Things have changed in Croatia since I wrote this in 2019. They are now part of the Schengen Zone, and their currency is now the euro. They have been profiled and highlighted as being a hidden gem, and many are discovering that, so it is not as obscure as it was just a few years ago. They were the first country in Europe to offer a "digital nomad passport," and many have applied and received it. That offers a one year residency which is a huge benefit for those that are limited in the Schengen Zone.

Date: 06.15.19/ Motorcycles in Europe

Over the past year, Kathleen and I have rented motorcycles in Portugal, Spain, France, and Italy.

I never had much "respect" for scooters and was a motorcycle rider since 1974, and scooters used to be small, under powered and truthfully, looked wimpy. Vespa was the big brand that came out in the 60s and they became the "cool bikes" for the hip crowd. Entire clubs and groups formed around them and they still exist today. In the US scooters never made it big until the **bikes** got big. Now you can get a 650 cc bike powerful enough for almost anything you need to do, and Suzuki and BMW are prominent. Many "older" riders can handle a scooter much easier than a shift bike since they are automatic transmissions, ie, no clutch, and easier to balance and sit upon.

And Europe LIVES on two wheels!

They are small, affordable, both to buy and maintain, and with the cost of gas, they make sense. And parking is no problem with a bike. You can park on most sidewalks and many places offer dedicated bike parking. Why park your car up the hill and walk a half mile, when you can ride down to the shoreline? Driving a car in most European cities is a pain and can be dangerous. With a bike, much easier.

We recently rented a Piaggio Beverly, which is 300cc and adequate for two people. It is comfortable, but you wouldn't want to ride it more than 150 miles a day or so. Storage is abundant in most scooters since many have a tank bag on the rear and storage under the seat, including a safe area for your helmets. Carrying beach towels and changes of clothing are easy since you have room for that, and the added benefit is their agility so you can turn around and go back to see that amazing view you just passed.

The other benefits:

You immerse yourself in the scenery. In the US, cars are called "cages" and many biker riders disdain cars, and drivers, since they don't respect bikes. Most European drivers respect bikes since they may have a one too, or have kids that ride.

...bike in Europe is easy, but having a valid bike license from your state or ...y is helpful. Many countries only rent a 50-125cc size without a bike license, ... our 300cc bike required me to have one. The costs vary, but we've rented for about $20 per day to $40 per day. These are not usually long term commitments, but can be, and instead can be treated as a special treat. Another thing to look at is an "International Driver's License" which is required in some countries, including Spain, and is easy to get in the US. They cost about $20 and AAA offers them by just filling in a form and supplying two photos.

Date: 06.29.19/ Observations & Insights from Croatia

Croatia is impressive, and the water is amazing, warm, turquoise blue and full of life! Here are some unique aspects of life in Croatia should you want to check it out for yourself. Which you should...

The lifestyle:

Is very carefree, and even residents acknowledge that things happen at a pace that can be unpredictable. Sometimes people come into work late or don't come in at all, though we haven't seen that personally. There is a laisse faire attitude, and since we're at the beach we see the same people hanging out day after day. Just talking, BS-ing and enjoying life. I admire that and hope to live up to that standard!

Driving:

Most of the cars we see are pretty ratty, though there are more "nice" cars than we saw in Italy or Spain. Beemers, Mercedes and high end SUVs, and no one seems to look differently at others based on what they drive. We have seen no "road rage" or anything like that and there is a respect towards drivers I am not used to. If you're driving behind someone slower, you wait to pass them and move on. No one gives them the finger or shows annoyance, they just move along. I've noticed that on the bikes I've rented, too. People respect the bikes, make room for you, and I can pass just about anywhere! Parking is easy and I have never seen a ticket issued or a tow truck! It reminds me of the old west days where everyone took care of themselves, no one hassled other folks, and everyone got along. I see police cars, but they are more social than enforcing, and it seems that respect and common sense go a long way.

Safety and security:

Along with the sense of everyone watching out for themselves, they also watch out for each other. Petty crimes and theft are highly disdained by the residents, and I'm not sure how stiff the penalties might be. I can leave my helmet hanging from the handlebars of the bike and not worry about it being stolen, and so far no problems. I mistakenly left a pair of shoes sitting on the seat of the bike for several hours, and found them where I left them. Oh, and that bike was parked on the sidewalk of a commercial area which we could NEVER do in the states! I can virtually park this bike anywhere without worry. Weird.

And even though a LOT of beer is consumed here, I never see anyone drunk or disorderly. I rarely saw that in Spain or Italy either, and alcohol, which is everywhere, appears to be used moderately. Many men would start drinking in the street early, and beer seemed to be the "orange juice" of breakfast! In the six weeks we've been here I never saw anyone obnoxious and loud except once; and that was a college age American male showing off for the ladies. Whatever...

The people:

Croatia has only been free since 1991, just three decades, and the older generation is traditional, speak little English, and they dress in dark, drab colors. Meanwhile the 30 and under crowd are well travelled, are very respectful, and feel comfortable with English.

Until a few years ago I didn't even know where Croatia was, and had zero desire to visit. Now that I see how much these former eastern Bloc countries have to offer, it makes me want to see even more.

Date: 07.08.19/ Size Matters (<u>video</u>)
Time: 2:32

Everything in Europe is small!

Cars, grocery stores, and streets, outside, and rooms, kitchens, and bathrooms on the inside. In Spain and Italy we found almost ALL smaller European cars; not an American or German car in site, but in Croatia that has not been the case. We have seen our share of BMWs, Mercedes, and "normal" sized SUVs, and we found out that many people here make automobiles a priority- a sign of pride and stature. The owners may sacrifice in exchange for their status symbol, just like America. Streets are very narrow, and in some places only one car can pass at a time and you may need to move your side mirrors IN to avoid hitting a wall!

And grocery stores? There are some "larger" ones, but mostly we find local bodegas, similar to what you might find in the larger cities. There may be several within just one city block and the selection is usually limited—except for some things you find everywhere, like BEER, WINE, and CHOCOLATE- the three major food groups! Sometimes we have to guess what we are buying due to different languages/ terminology. What is body lotion/ crème/ gel in one country may be different in another.

As the video shares, the small interior room in your lodging takes some getting used to. King sized beds? Highly unlikely. Bathtubs? Very rare, and instead you will use a shower with a shower head that must be HELD to be used, a personal source of irritation for us. Sinks can be small and usually using a bathroom is a one person job with no room for two, ditto kitchens. Gas stoves are rare, and refrigerators are usually very small since getting a large one up a narrow staircase would be death defying. Microwaves are typical, but everything else is iffy, even coffee makers! In Spain and Italy a coffee maker was a standard item, but here in Croatia it's not.

In America, the land of wide open spaces, we have room for so many things except in the larger cities. In suburbia there is land to build upon, so everything expands to fill it up. It's a unique traveling environment, but I like it and recommend you try it too, even for a bit.

Date: 07.18.19/ Review of Three Croatian Locations (published story)

After 63 days in Croatia it is finally time to move on. We stayed at three different locations, all of them great in their own way, so I wanted to share the details for those that are interested in learning more. This country is so special, with amazing water, weather, and people, and the food is some of the best I've found! Our next 45 day journey starts today, but here's an overview of our stay here:

Leg #1: Kastel Kambelovac, just 20 minutes north of Split

We stayed in a very small one bedroom unit with a direct view of the channel, and a balcony where we ate as often as possible. When we arrived mid-May it was a bit sleepy with not much activity, and the weather was rainier and colder than usual, but within a few weeks got quite hot, in the nineties. The energy of the city also changed by mid-June, when it switched to summer. Within a few days people were everywhere, beaches were crowded, and the ocean was roped off to delineate safe areas as it became more bustling.

Split town, which was pretty easy to walk around when we arrived, also got busier, and we saw an increasing number of cruise boats. When we first got here we weren't that impressed, aside from the view and closeness of the water, but as we are now leaving we have become "part of the city." We have conversations with restaurant people, plus many some locals, and I can see that over time it could grow on us. Learning the language is highly unlikely beyond a few words, since it is difficult and different than anything we were used to.

Leg #2: Dubrovnik (the city of Plat, 10 minutes south)

We liked Dubrovnik Old Town, but it was crazy busy and hot in summer. We found some great places to enjoy the water, and the beauty of Croatia is that you merely have to take a ride along the coast, and when you see a place that looks good, you stop. Parking is never a problem and you can do it anywhere.

Leg #3, Lokva Rogoznica, a small village just south of Omis

As we rode into Omis the first time we were awed at the rock walls alongside the city, which were incredible, but our lodging was 20 minutes away via several switchbacks in a small village which looked deserted. It mostly was, but still had enough people to create good energy and our unit was outstanding.

A car was required to get there and we spent a lot of time at the beaches and in the town of Omis, plus did a great raft ride on the River Cetina.

After 63 days in Croatia, the question was, "Do we come back?" and the answer was a 1000% yes. For anyone who lives or spends time in Croatia, you get it, and for those that had no idea where it is (like me), put this country on your vacation plan and bucket list.

Date: 07.22.19/ Borders Crossings: A Fact of Life

There are many ways to cross international borders, and in the United States we have little opportunity to drive across a border unless we go NORTH to Canada or SOUTH to Mexico. In Europe, and other parts of the world, things are different, and you can cross several different countries within the span of a few hundred miles.

For our side trip to Dubrovnik, Croatia, from Split, I knew that we had to cross a 20 km stretch of Bosnia- Herzegovina, which is a weird thought to begin with. You cross into a small section of land and 15 minutes later exit back to the same country you left from. The city in between is called Neum and as we entered, we had to go through ONE border check exiting and ANOTHER as we crossed through what is called No Man's Land. Usually a border is just one crossing gate, but not here; one stop to enter, one to leave. Fortunately crossing into Montenegro was much easier.

UPDATED: 2023

A new bridge that connects Croatia with Croatia and eliminates that crossing into B-H was opened in July, 2022, and the new Pelješac bridge saves a lot of inconvenience.

That was weirdness #1.

Weirdness #2 was leaving Croatia, an EU country, but NOT part of the Schengen Zone (at that time), and crossing into Hungary. The bus stopped at the border, all our passports were collected, then we all had to exit the bus to retrieve them one at a time. There were only a dozen passengers, but it would have been worse with a full busload!

Over the last year we have ferried several times, including crossing into new international borders, and it's a piece of cake. Crossing borders via train is pretty easy too, especially if you stay within the EU, then it's a non-issue. But when you leave the EU and go to a non-Schengen country you get scrutiny. Train travel in Croatia is bad and to be avoided, and trying to book tickets online is impossible. We were told that the bus out of Hungary is better and cheaper than the train, so that's what we did. Those who know said that (1) train travel was much more effective in the central to northern parts of Europe, ie, Austria and north and (2) due to budgetary cuts many national railroads are NOT what they used to be, and some are now privatized. As much as we teach others, many teach us. We were told by some German travelers that trains were not well maintained there, nor were the tracks, all in the interest of saving money. Scary.

This blog was designed to teach everyone how to Travel Younger, like the Millennials, and they handle uncertainty better than those of us over 60, plus they can be more flexible. For example, we arrived in Vienna, Austria, on a Sunday afternoon at about 4:00 p.m., and had no room reservations. We also had very sketchy mobile service and no wifi, so we were stalled in our tracks. Mind you, that was NORMAL 20 plus years ago, but today we are victims of our Smart phones as well as beneficiaries. It all worked out, we got a great room, but many Boomers might not react well to the uncertainty, so we're trying to take that uncertainty AWAY by sharing our experiences.

Date: 07.27.19/ Money Makes the World Go Around: Currencies

Traveling has been a learning experience on SO many levels, and currency is one of them. The US dollar rules America, and the Euro rules MUCH of Europe, but not all. Converting dollars to euros is not much of a struggle and uses similar coinage.

Hungary, firmly planted in the EU, uses *forints* as their currency. That involved exchanging some form of currency, either euros (better) or dollars (harder), for forints, and every time you do that, you lose money on commissions and conversions. We us a benchmark of certain food items to benchmark the differences in costs of living in different countries. Those items include: (1) a cup of coffee, (2) a beer or a glass of wine, and (3) spaghetti.

Coffee is everywhere, but not all coffees are equal, which all coffee lovers understand. In Croatia, "white coffee" was the thing we loved, and just under $2.00; Hungary was more expensive by about $1.00, and Austria, even worse, about $4.00! The Czech Republic was cheaper than Austria, but still about $3.50. And I THOUGHT beer would be cheaper than it was.

From Hungary, very reasonable when it comes to expenses, we went to Vienna, Austria and got sticker shocked. Our normal commodities, beer, wine, and spaghetti, were all noticeably higher, as was the cost of our room. From Vienna it was on to the Czech Republic and another currency: the *koruna*, or crown as they call it. The food value was right in the middle between Hungary and Austria, and the COINS were heavy, like carrying lead in your pocket! Coinage can be a nuisance, since some are marked and easy to identify, but not all. Many times I held my hand out with loose change and had the merchant take the right amount. Trust and faith, and I think they are honest about it.

But what happens when you leave one country and have bills left over? It's a balancing act since you usually need SOME money at the departing station, bus, or train, and you usually need money at the arrival station. A fun fact: almost all "public bathrooms," called WC, or water closets, cost money. That can range from about $.50 to $1.00, so keep that in mind when you travel abroad. And most "new" arrival countries do not accept currency from the country you left, but some will.

To get cash it's best to use ATM machines and get money directly from your US bank, but there are commissions, possible gouging, and commissions can run up to 10%. That means you withdraw $500 and pay $50 in fees/ commissions to the bank that controls the ATM. My home bank, Wells Fargo, charges $5.00 for each withdrawal, which is reasonable, and I usually get larger amounts to avoid excessive usage. I always seek out an ATM machine connected to a bank, rather than at the airport or in a shopping area.

Date: 07.30.19/ Krakow, Poland: NOT Part of Our Plan!

Over the past few weeks we spent a short time in Zagreb, Croatia and Budapest, Hungary, where we stayed for three days. Budapest is a pretty large city and it was crowded but not overbearing.

Vienna was spectacular, but felt a bit "posed," if that is the right word. The buildings, the architecture- all beautiful- but it felt like a Hollywood movie set which was the same impression we got in Monaco. It was so perfect it was almost sterile. From there onward to Prague, also busy to the point it took away some of enjoyment. We have but ourselves to blame, going during July, but it was unpreventable this time. The city felt very authentic and even though the buildings and palaces were preserved, they retained their sense of realness.

Now we are in Krakow, Poland, which was NOT part of our original plan! Our intent was to train directly to Warsaw but since it was a six hour trip thought we'd break it up with a stay in between, and that in between is here. Even so, the train ride was almost the same length due to many stops, plus our train had a mechanical failure and they had to replace our engine car with another. That was weird as we were sitting still for almost an hour with no AC or access to working bathrooms, bit it's all part of the flow of traveling.

Krakow is the closest town to Auschwitz, so we extended our time HERE and cancelled Warsaw- with a stiff penalty. This is a mid-sized town, much smaller than Budapest, Vienna, or Prague and it has a genuineness that is intoxicating. Walking down the streets which are clean, but not pristine, busy, but not wall to wall people, and eating at some great spots with the best pricing since Croatia, made us stay a few extra days. I love my pastry, and I had what I believe is the BEST cherry turnover in all our travels- and that includes dozens of different places. It was about $2.00 and worth every morsel.

Krakow has a bit of an ominous history since it was so close to the horrific events taking place 70 km away, though they were faultless as to what was happening there.

Date: 08.05.19/ Eurail Passes: Worth it, or a Waste of Money??

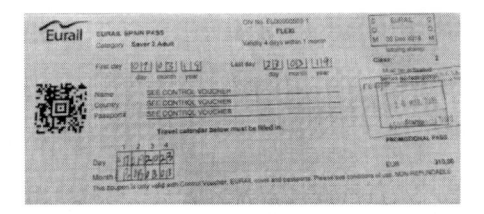

Eurail passes have almost a mystical history behind them. They been around for 60 years, and for decades they were "THE way" to visit Europe via train. For those *of a certain age* that maybe travelled Europe via the train in the "good old days" of the sixties and seventies (you know who you are), the Pass was a great way to get from one place to another. Using paper maps were the only way to travel back then, long before technology and Google Maps and various travel apps simplified the process.

The Eurail pass is a two sided system, one side for European Union (EU) members who get the Interrail Pass, and those outside the system, who get the Eurail pass. Americans pay more for these passes, but there is a downside, too, and sometimes the math works out in favor of the pass, but sometimes I think it's easier to travel without it. The biggest downside is the reservation of tickets process, or actually, the LACK of one.

With today's numerous travel and train apps, like Omio, Trainline, Rome2Rio, etc.. you can find many options to get from Point A to Point B, and they include using trains, buses and sometimes the combination of them. Over the past few weeks we've had to BUS several times since trains weren't an option, and so far we have been happy with FlixBus and LeoExpress. They both offer good sites which allow you to book and pay in advance, which removes any concerns of not getting a ticket.

With the train passes that is not an option.

We left Prague, Czech Republic, intending to go to Warsaw on the only direct train on that day, but since we could not book in advance we had to wait till we got to the station. And that train was sold out... Plan B involved hanging out at the train station for four more hours and taking a later train to a stop in between, then transferring to another direct train to Warsaw. That plan didn't work since the Plan B train had mechanical problems and was stagnant for over an hour while we waited for another engine to haul us. It all worked out (it usually does!) but timetables and expenses got pushed out including having to grab a bus instead and getting to our room much later than planned. Had we been able to book in advance this could have been averted.

Important Traveling Info

If at all possible, get your departing train ticket ASAP, even as you initially GET to that location. Better safe than sorry. Oh BTW, even when you use the Pass you still must pay to have a "reserved seat." That can run from a few dollars to as much as $10 per ticket which is on top of the initial cost.

Another downside to the Eurail pass: many national railways do not honor them AND sometimes the train trip is just too bloody long. A six hour train trip could be a four hour bus ride, so which is better?

The rail offers more room to stretch, plus bathrooms, and if you are lucky (we mostly were) you get electrical connectors and wifi, though that wifi can be spotty. Bus seats are not as comfortable and most of the long hauls DO have onboard water closets, but not all. Those without generally stop every two hours for a break and sometimes a driver change. And remarkably, sometimes the bus is significantly cheaper than the train EVEN WITH the discounted Eurail package. Most of the buses we found had electricity, and wifi is hit or miss.

I'm less a fan of the Eurail pass than I used to be, and you can get passes for specific countries or several of them, so compare those packages, too.

Date: 08.08.19/ What a 24 hour Travel Day Looks Like...

We've had a few 24 hour travel days, but they usually involved overseas flights and thousands of miles. But we had one when we went from Kosice, Poland to Brasov, Romania, a distance of just 400 miles, yet it took a whole day. The following is a real life journey and not for those who like to control things or lack patience...

We had tickets from Kosice via a two-part train trip. Part one was a four hour train to Budapest, followed by a few hours' layover, and then a 13 hour overnight train from Budapest to Brasov. But when we looked at our tickets we had some concern that the ticket only addressed part TWO of the journey and not part one. With some research we found out we could get a bus for just 15 euros each, and that bus got us to Budapest much earlier and allowed us a lot more wiggle room in Budapest. Sometimes spending a few dollars for peace of mind is worth it. We got to the Kosice train station about 2:00 for a 3:30 bus, allowing plenty of time to chill. When 3:30 rolled around, no bus arrived. Nor did it arrive at 4:00 or 4:30, but it finally did get there at 5:00, a full 90 minutes late, but still with enough time to catch our second leg in Budapest. These are the realities of mass transit and truthfully, it could happen with a car, too.

We got to the bus station 90 minutes late, then hauled buns over to the train station after a quick Uber transfer, and that extra wiggle room we hoped for was gone. No matter, we got on our sleeper car at 11:00, and ALMOST got in trouble since we did not complete our first leg that concerned us. Anyway, the train rolled, we got into our cozy bunks and were awakened by Hungarian passport control at 2:00 a.m. Usually this is taken care of when you get to your destination, but because we were leaving the EU and going to a non-Schengen area, they are more strict. We passed muster but were awoken AGAIN an hour later by the Romanian passport control. Let's just say that the process was a nuisance, but sleep still came after that.

A beautiful sunrise and morning made the trip enjoyable, except this train was so slow that we could almost have walked faster! It seems the Romania rail system is dated, along with the machinery, so they are always working on the tracks, which forces the trains to stop or go very, very slowly. Plus we sat dead on the tracks for about 45 minutes while they brought in a new engine (seems to be an issue we encounter), and the morning went very slowly. We finally did arrive in Brasov, Romania, about 2:00 that afternoon.

The Romanian train system- and much of Eastern Europe- cannot compare to the Western European train system. Spain and Italy, the ones we used the most, were light years ahead of many others.

Travel can be fun and adventurous, but it has risks and sometimes is too easy to do wrong. Missed connections can ripple and turn a peaceful day into a stressful one. Or so they say...

Date: 08.15.19/ Next stop: **Impressions of Romania**

We got to Brasov, Romania and it didn't take long to fall in like with it. The town is just the right size; large enough to keep us interested, but small enough to not be overwhelming. Of course food was one of the first things we looked for, not because we're foodies, but because we have so enjoyed the amazing quality of food here in Europe as we approach our SIX months anniversary of being on the road. And the food got a quick thumbs up and that has not changed, along with the noteworthy hospitality and friendliness of the people we have met.

In some places people are friendly, but phony. Not here. People on the street and especially those in the food and hospitality industry are amazing. Our AirBNB hosts have become friends and have been super helpful, teaching us new things in the area and finding new places to explore. They invited us to their home for a TRUE Romanian meal, so we're looking forward to that and we liked it here so much we are extending our stay an additional week.

A few days ago the country opened up as we rented a BMW GS750 motorcycle and now we can visit the many castles in the area (including the inspiration for Count Dracula!) and over the past few days we traversed what is called the most beautiful road in the world. Tours are great, but pricey and forces you to conform to the guide's agenda. Maybe we learn less, but we enjoy more and have more freedom to come and go as we please.

That beautiful road is called the Transfăgărășan highway and it is the most jaw dropping and exhilarating experience I have ever had. Views that made me speechless, plus waterfalls, bridges, tunnels, green fields, cows meandering along the road- wild burros, too- the list just goes on. We stayed in an area that is known for bear activity but saw none; not sure if that's a good thing or not!

After six months on the road we have developed a sixth sense of the places that have good energy and especially those worth returning to. A few towns in Spain, most notably Sevilla and San Sebastian, get high marks and we plan to go back there for our typical six week's stay. In Italy we were likewise awed by the Amalfi Coast, and several towns there. But we will NOT go back during holiday season, when all these areas turn into madness. Croatia, of course, will turn into a 90 day stay when we need to get out of the EU, and ironically Romania serves that same purpose. It is an EU member, but non-Schengen, so this would be an awesome safe haven. These two countries have a way of making your money go further. Food, both in restaurants and grocery stores, are silly cheap, and we had cappuccino on our journey to the Transfăgărășan for less than $2 US and our room was less than $50. These things offset the downside of not having a home. When people ask, "Where are you from?," we tell them the US and California, but that we really don't have a home anymore.

We decided that large towns (250K +) are NOT appealing to us and we enjoy the intimacy of smaller locations. As much as we love the water, we are finding Romania, with the hills and valleys and greenery to be almost as captivating.

Date: 08.19.19/ Things We Have Missed---and Others We Have Not

A few days ago was our six month's anniversary since we left America and became Traveling Nomads. We learned SO much about the world, ourselves, and each other, and I don't think I've ever known geography and different countries as well as I do today and even though we've been focused and traveling within Europe, we are still exploring "next steps."

Important Traveling Info

I put together a list of three different things:

- ✓ Things I have MISSED since we left,
- ✓ Things I have NOT missed,
- ✓ And the longest list, which includes things we've gotten used to.

The third item is the longest and brings to mind the "let it be" attitude since there are many things we cannot control in LIFE, and certainly not when you live a nomadic lifestyle.

Missed:

- I miss large grocery stores, where you can read every label and get what you want. For much of our travels we only had small bodegas, ie, neighborhood stores where you can get some basic things, but not all. At a few of our bases we DID find decent sized supermarkets, including here in Romania, which makes shopping (and eating) much easier.

- I miss the ease of getting in my car (which I no longer have) and going to the "fill in the blank." Market, beach, barbershop, you name it. In America we all (usually) have cars, so are mobile and everything is convenient. Life on the road is not so easy and things need to be planned since it involves some form of public transportation or an Uber, when they are available.

- I miss signs and movies and things I can read in English! We take this for granted, but over here much is illegible and beyond our comprehension. Most movies we find ARE in English with native language subtitles. Thank God for technology! When we were in Croatia for two months we were always shocked how UN-readable signs in front of businesses were. It could be a butcher shop, florist or whatever, and we had no idea.

- I miss having a decent selection of clothing to wear- and I'm a dude! Kathleen has a much greater challenge, but since we carry what we wear, we carry very little. This is easier in summer, but come winter we'll have to stock up, but we're moving towards warmer climates anyway. We have jettisoned half of what we LEFT with in February and concluded a while ago that it's easier and cheaper to buy new stuff than carry old. Kind of a forced wardrobe makeover!

What I DO NOT miss:

- Since I don't have a "home," I have few bills except for my credit card. No gas, electric, water, internet, etc... and accounting is much easier when you only have one bill to pay and to just keep an eye on one bank account.

- I don't have a car, and I really don't miss driving, especially Southern California driving. Rush hour traffic is mostly a thing of the past except for when we have access to a bike. Then we split lanes and pass the idling hoard!

- I am pleasantly ignorant of all the shootings and politics and crap that plague America. Since we left there have been several mass killings, but I don't follow any news feeds and catch up only when the need drives me- which is seldom. Maybe it's selfish, maybe it's closed minded, but I have a different form of stress now, and much of THIS stress I can control.

What I've GOTTEN USED to (this is more fun!)

Along with missing or not missing things, some things just ARE, desirable or not.

- Bus and train stations have PAY bathrooms, which can be awkward when you enter a new country and don't have their currency. Airports are still free, and no one calls these "bathrooms!" They are water closets, WCs, or toilettes. This is one you can't fight so you roll with it.

- Speaking of...exchanging currency and using a currency calculator. Many of our countries use Euros, but Hungary, Poland, Slovakia, Croatia, and Romania all use their own currency. That means a quick lesson in currency conversion and value vs the US dollar.

- Since menus in different languages can be difficult to read, many times we order via pictures, which is an adventure in itself. Some places have "English" menus, but not all, and when they DO, many times the prices are higher!

- Our time zone differential to the west coast of America has ranged from 9-10 hours. This is a fact of life and time, and we have to adjust accordingly, since it is impossible to fight! In one sense it's cool since I check my mail in the morning and don't really need to check it till the end of the day. In between the rest of America is sleeping.

- Uncertainty over mass transit, primarily buses and local transport. Trains I've gotten hip to, but bus stations are busy beehives and you have to be on top of things to be sure you're at the right platform for your ride.

- Hand held shower heads SUCK, but they are the standard over here. Most can be manually removed, some can be aimed, but not all. Regardless, the shower head thing and the SIZE of the showers take getting used to. There are few downsides to being short, but some of the showers we had could not handle anyone over 6 feet, so you tall people have my sympathy.

- The 24 hour clock has become almost second nature, but I keep MINE on a 12 hour schedule. When someone says "1800 hours" I can do that calculation MUCH faster than before.

- Along those lines, metric is becoming easier, especially speed, ie, KPH vs. MPH. It's kind of cool since a sign that says 100 km to Nirvana is really only 2/3 that far! The volume conversions, ie, liters, have been more challenging, but meters and derivatives are not too bad.

- And the last one, a pet peeve for Kathleen and myself, includes coffee. One thing you will NEVER hear over here: "Can I give you a warmup?" meaning, can the waitress or waiter top off the cup with hot coffee. Over here cups are super small, probably 8 oz or less, and they are most times WARM- not hot. We can complain and find our favorite places, but the fact is, we will probably get a small cup of warmish coffee- but it IS good!!

All in all we take the good with the bad and this lifestyle is not for everyone. What will the next six months teach us? We'll let you know!

Date: 08.26.19/ Final Thoughts on Romania

We stayed in Brasov for less than three weeks. It was an amazing town with wonderful scenery, great people, and the perfect size to keep it interesting, but not too busy. We used Brasov as a launch point to rent a motorcycle and drive the amazing Transfăgărășan Road, all 150 km of it, plus visited four or five castles including the infamous Vlad the Impaler (AKA Dracula) castle in Bran, which was less than impressive. Sorry...During our time there the hospitality of the residents was noteworthy. We became friends with our AirBNB hosts who invited us to their home for an all-day lunch which also included a two hour ride through the hills in a horse and buggy. That was about as close to nature and experiencing the TRUE Romania as we could get!

After Brasov it was time to move towards our next location for a while: Split, Croatia, where we stayed a few months ago. After Brasov we found the lovely town of Sibiu, recommended by some fellow American travelers. This town was about one third the size of Brasov and we got here while they were having a medieval festival, which is always fun. Some of what we saw highlighted differences between things (and attitudes) HERE vs. the US. They play for *real* as they staged sword fights in the center square with real, authentic, sharp swords! There is little concern for lawsuits and litigation and people take responsibility for their own safety and well-being. We have noticed that throughout our travels we saw few barriers to keep visitors safe. Of course they post signs, but anyone can venture out to cliffs or high places and if something were to happen, then it remains the fault of the people. No frivolous lawsuits here.

Another thing cool in Sibiu was the display of medieval equipment and devices which were also REAL, which made sense since those events in history happened right HERE. It brings things into perspective when you realize the names we learned from history walked some of the streets we may have walked on.

From Sibiu it was on to the city of Deva, a three hour bus ride. The public transportation system in Romania is NOT that good, and trains are very, very slow, but local bus companies are inexpensive and one of the best ways to travel from city to city. Some are less than impressive, however, since they are small vans holding anywhere from six to 18 people. Even though we had the (mostly unused) Eurail pass, these local buses made that waste of money less painful.

The bottom line on Romania is that it is much better than expected and certainly a country to return to. Besides, there is yet ANOTHER road which were told about which is even MORE impressive than the Transfăgărășan Highway. It's called the TransAlpina and it is 2145 meters above sea level, about 7000 feet, and it's rare to DRIVE a road with that elevation. Stay tuned!

Date: 09.01.19/ The Importance of Being Flexible

Six plus months ago we started our journey from the US and had the outline of a "plan." We had guidelines to follow, the most significant being visa restrictions that kept us in the European Union for only 90 days within a 180 day period. Last week we started a new journey, exiting Romania and eastern Europe, which included stops in three different countries. After Romania the plan *was* to go to Budapest, until that changed, when Kathleen said, "What do you think about Belgrade (Serbia)?"

Serbia had come up in conversations several times as we explored the many countries we could visit, and since we had already BEEN to Budapest, Kat's suggestion was a good one.

Flexibility. We have found that when we are too rigid or set in our ways it can become complicated. With that in mind we try to let the Universe guide us when we feel inspired or decide that another way may be better.

We did go to Belgrade, spent three days there, and it was much nicer than we thought, and we enjoyed the combination of relaxing after a few very early mornings, walking along the Danube, eating at great restaurants along the river, and of course, exploring yet another castle: The Belgrade Fortress. I've lost count of how many castles and forts we have visited and yet they are all different and mostly worthwhile.

The first night we were there we walked along the river, which is filled with restaurants and nightclubs on barges tied to the bank. These are all **stationary** barges, and they don't move, and some of these restaurants are pretty cool, but as we walked along the bank we saw a hostel on the water, which surprised us both, so Kat went to explore.

We usually avoid hostels because they normally offer single or bunk beds, plus they are a bit noisier than we would like, and maybe a bit too transient for our comfort level. Forty years ago it would have been a different story.

This lobby looked like something out of a Victorian movie, filled with stuffed chairs and lots of charm. Kat went upstairs to check the room, which had a King sized bed (pretty rare), PLUS another single bed, plus our own bathroom- no sharing. The price? Twenty euros each.

We knew we HAD to stay there since the chance to sleep on the Danube on a barge doesn't come around very often. We had already paid for our three nights at our other room, which also had its charm, but was a bit boring. Waking up to the sun rising over the river was pretty cool, and sitting downstairs with coffee while swans came over to feed was a novel experience.

Can you see yourself here??

Later that day, another five hour bus ride to Zagreb, Croatia, and the beginning of our next leg, which also will last about six weeks. Kathleen will return to Split, Croatia, a city we know, since we were there for 60 days already.

Quality versus Quantity

We started our Nomadic Life staying six weeks at each location, but the LAST six weeks have been different as we attempted to "use" our Eurail pass which afforded us 15 days of travel over a 60 day period. We will end up using just four of those travel days and in hindsight, it was a waste of money.

Or was it??

The original "plan" was to travel every two to three days and work our way up to the Scandinavian countries, then back down the south west side of Europe, and we figured we'd hit about eight countries. It didn't work out that way due to a hot spell, a crowded holiday season, and exorbitant prices that accompanied them, so we turned east instead. Rather than a new place every few days, we slowed down and decided that *quality* was more important than *quantity* and checking countries off on a list.

Our journey and our lives have been about choices. We gave up homes, cars, and understanding what people are saying around us, for visiting new lands, and absorbing new cultures and history. We (still) get confused by train and bus stations, and currency conversions, but these are the choices that WE have made. For those that may be inspired by what we do, GOOD! Nothing will expand your mind like visiting unfamiliar places and you will be humbled walking through buildings that were built before Jesus walked the globe. Makes you realize and appreciate that we are here for just a few moments in time. Enjoy them.

Date: 09.07.19/ 14 Cities in 49 days

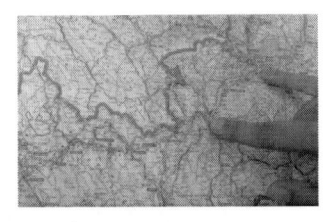

Our typical MO has been to stay in ONE location for about 45 days, which afforded enough time to get a feel for the area, the people, the restaurants, etc... From July 18 until September 4 we hit 14 cities and stayed in 18 different rooms. Exhausting, both physically, mentally, and emotionally as traveling to a new location every 3.5 days can cause stress with traveling partners.

Croatia, Hungary, Austria, Czech Republic, Poland, Slovakia, Romania, Serbia are checked off, and in some we were only there for a few days, while Romania got most of our focus, covering 30 of those 49 days. We came VERY close to getting to Slovenia since it was just on the other side of a river we were traversing, but the rain clouds threatened us on the way from Zagreb to Rijeka on our BMW motorcycle, so we skipped it. We did get rained on; no, wait, we got DUMPED on; the sky opened up, the thunder just above our heads, so we pulled onto the driveway of a small house on the roadside and sought refuge under their patio cover. Almost sounds like a movie!

The elderly owner, Josef, who spoke no English, came out with his umbrella to make sure we weren't there for nefarious purposes, and left us alone. His more compassionate wife took pity on the drowned American rats and invited us in for some coffee and heat, which we gladly accepted. Trying to converse with no Croatian on our end and just a FEW words of German I remembered from high school made conversation one-sided, but the angels offered us just what we needed, and we were on our way after an hour or so. BTW, HUGE props for Kathleen who remained brave through the downpour and prayed our way through it.

We met many other kind people on the journey, both American and foreigners from many lands, and in Sibiu, Romania, we had a cool conversation with a professor of travel from Austria, plus learned many lessons on this fast paced journey, including discovering *us*, individually and collectively. We agreed that slow travel vs. fast travel ie, quality over quantity, works best for both of us. Maybe the Millennials can hit new cities every few days, but for me, I'll pass and take it slow(er).

Many ask us if I plan to return to the US to live and the answer remains "no." Traveling as we are brings more meaning, fun and adventure than anything I could do in America, so we will continue to Travel Younger. Glad you can join us!

Next chapter(s):

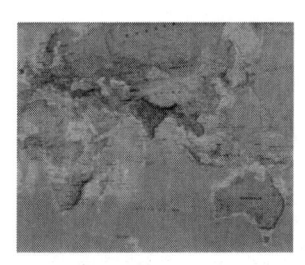

After 6 months on the road we can say that we love the life we've created. No question, some things must be left behind for the sake of adventure and fun.

There is a minimal amount of "nesting," which is something many woman, Kathleen included, like. Not to generalize, but historically the females have been the ones to take care of the cave while the caveman goes a-hunting. Kathleen also misses the "getting dressed up" part of life, too, since we carry a minimal amount of clothing options and combinations with us.

Cooking on the road is not the same as having your own kitchen, where you know where everything is, and you bought most of the things in it. Beds change, as do bathrooms, where you have everything in appointed places. Not having a car is a drag since any time you want to GO anywhere, you must plan ahead.

Realistically we will not do this forever, we decided that we don't need to go **everywhere**, and will be selective based on weather, comfortability, and ease of getting there.

Whether the end includes "settling down" remains to be seen.

END of Part I

Life on the Road: HOW They Do It; WHY They Do It (Excerpts)

After we started our journey in 2019 I started thinking about the WHYS of the new life we were creating. What drove us, and **others like us** to be nomadic and live in different parts of the world?

The "younger generation," AKA, the Millennials, were a big inspiration to me even before we started Traveling Younger. These so called "Digital Nomads," lived anywhere and everywhere they had internet access, and created successful careers all over the world, but I found out that they were NOT all in that age range. There were nomads of all ages who had been "on the road," for as little as a few years, to as long as several decades.

I reached out to them. I wanted to know WHY they did what they did and when I heard their stories, and analyzed MY whys, I came up with SIX basic drivers that motivated me as well as others. That was the genesis of a book idea called, "Life on the Road," etc...and after interviewing two dozen travel writers, bloggers, and various Digital Nomads, COVID hit and stopped us ALL in our tracks, as well as me continuing with the book.

The book idea never went away and I stayed in touch with many of these fellow nomads. Some still live on the road as before, while others have created a more permanent base, maybe in their home country, or maybe somewhere else. I went back and reviewed our conversations and am sharing some of them here as part of this book. Whether I will create another specifically about Life on the Road, remains to be seen.

The Six Tenets of Nomadic Life

Here are some of the reasons that people travel; they may be the reasons that YOU want to travel, or maybe you already do!

1. Seeing history from a whole new perspective: from hundreds to thousands of years old.
2. Eating foods from different countries prepared in entirely new ways.
3. Meeting locals, enjoying their company, learning their cultures.
4. Experiencing new things, traveling in new ways outside your comfort zone.
5. Seeing the beauty of the world.
6. Relaxing for the sake of doing nothing- just because you can

Mary Anne and Ricardo Machado: Querétaro, Mexico

Mary Anne, age, 55, and husband Ricardo, age 56, live in Querétaro, Mexico, a city of 1 M plus population, and they left the US at a most unique time; March of 2020, just as COVID was changing the world. They split Chicago, the Windy City, for a more comfortable life in Mexico, and are still there. Ricardo is from Venezuela and they have been married for 32 years and ready to enjoy this next stage of their lives.

Like many others, Mary Anne graduated from college and shortly afterwards took off to Europe with a friend on her first airplane flight; from then on she caught the travel bug. They met in Ohio where Ricardo was going to school, and have been together ever since.

In Venezuela in the seventies, life was good and the country prospered. Today, and for the past several years, it has been a tumultuous country with unrest and much instability. The middle class, where Ricardo came from, is no more, but forty years ago it was customary and fashionable for young high school graduates to go away for college, to experience the rest of the world. His parents tried to share the travel experience with their kids, so Ricardo had the benefit of parents who took them many places, especially outside Latin America.

After college graduation Ricardo changed career into IT consulting and that afforded the two of them a great opportunity to travel the world in comfort and rack up a lot of frequent flyer miles! They did that for two decades and proved to them that there was a good lifestyle outside the US.

Along their journey while they were in the UK in 1994, and especially when they visited London, Mary Anne had that, "I could live here," experience. That duplicated itself in many other areas and planted the seed that living abroad WAS a real possibility, but still, they rarely stayed more than one week in any one area.

Ricardo officially retired in 2019 and they set their sights on Spain and thought that might be their future home. But since Mary Anne has seven siblings, and a large, connected family, she was turned off to the distance they would be away from them, so they went to plan B, which was Mexico. It offered the benefits of ex-pat living, yet was still close enough to return to their relatives when they needed to. Plus they spoke the language and it was affordable, so the cards all fell into place.

They zeroed in on the region north of Mexico City because it was fairly close from where they were living and they liked the elevation and the weather. Like many, they had fears of "living somewhere, hating it, and getting stuck," said Mary Anne, but when I sent them a note for an update for this book, I was informed that they still remain in Mexico, in the same city, and in the same house! I guess they like it there.

"Back in 2015-16 we had the idea of taking an 18 month sabbatical," Mary Anne shared, and they discussed spending six months in Mexico, Central America, and South America, and renting out their condo in Chicago while they were gone. Around that time Mary Anne started a strict eating regimen and worried that they wouldn't be able to find the right food and have a decent kitchen, so they stepped back from that idea and instead decided to find a place to stay for at least a year. "I couldn't envision going from temporary room to temporary room," she said. "I knew I needed to feel comfortable in order to make this idea work."

Their motivation was not driven by what drives many nomads, but instead they were truly trying to find a new place to make a home. That is by far the biggest reason that people ever leave their home countries; they are looking for alternatives and not necessarily looking to STAY on the road. But others do.

They don't live in an area with a super huge expat community, they said, but they are very happy that they have at least SOME type of community and have developed friendships in their time there. And what makes it interesting is that the foreigners who do live there mostly speak Spanish. That is unusual in many "expat communities," where people fall back on easy language skills and hang out with others of "their kind." The net result is that Mary Anne and Ricardo get the benefit of lower cost of living and fun lifestyle, along with becoming integrating with the culture and history of the area.

In 2020 they were paying $1000 USD monthly rent for a two-bedroom plus a den, with a great view, AND the most important feature: a large and well-equipped kitchen. That is more than some places considering they are not near the water, but they are a few blocks from city center, shopping, and everything they need. The area is considered semi-arid, more desert than jungle, and that keeps the temperature in a comfortable range of low 40 degrees F, and mid-80s on the high side.

For now they have no desire to move elsewhere and have found contentment in creating a new home rather than staying in constant motion.

Everyone has their own comfort level and determination of what makes them happy. For some they like the security and creature comforts, while others prefer the excitement of life on the road.

"The key is to recognize fear and overcome it, and also to be open hearted and curious," they shared when I asked them what advice they could offer. "This is such an adventure in courage, and overcoming humility, especially when it comes to understanding different languages. This is what growth feels like, and when we're older we don't experience that as often as we did when we were young!"

They continued: "there is a wealth of resources out there to help anyone at any level. We've been here three months and just met someone new in town recently. She was asking us for guidance and information—and we had the answers! Facebook has great expat groups and between Trip Advisor, AirBNB, Uber, and other online apps, we all have information at our fingertips."

Something to consider that Mary Anne mentioned is that some people just do not WANT to travel, and that is OK. They may be content right where they are, and they owe no one any excuses or apologies. On the other side are those that DO want to go and they think they need "approval" from others, which is just not so. No one needs permission from anyone else to follow their dreams, to follow their hearts.

UPDATE:

Mary Anne: "I sometimes find myself thinking about the Mary Anne who had all the hopes and made all the plans from 2017-2019, and I'm so grateful to her.

My Spanish has improved significantly, to the point where we're taking a course (for native speakers) called Conociendo Querétaro, where we learn all about the history of this region. Through this class and other opportunities, we've made friends with a number of Mexicans, which has been a real gift. I love my fellow extranjeros but I would hate to be trapped in that bubble.

I can't remember if we were still in the mindset of spending a year in Querétaro and then moving on when we met you. I think that was something we told ourselves so we would not feel trapped if we found ourselves unhappy here. But it turns out we've built such a lovely community and comfortable home that we have no plans to leave for the foreseeable future.

Becky Gillespie: Japan (now)

Becky and I have never met, but we have been online friends since our first conversation in February 2020. She has been a nomad since 2004 and has also been a travel podcaster and interviewed me twice, and I have returned the favor by including her story in my book!

Born in Ohio, when she was young her family took a lot of road trips, especially to Florida, where they were part time snow birds. But that curiosity about travel presented itself in movies and books, and when she was still young, that is how she did it. Virtually. She was dedicated to becoming financially secure, so went to college in Ohio, which allowed her to save money so she could travel internationally, which was her goal. Fortunately her school offered a seven week overseas study trip as she was entering her junior year, and at age 21 she was able to visit five European cities.

And the light was lit.

With 120 fellow students and two professors, they did their studies in the hotel where they stayed, and with a four day (Mon-Thurs), four hour study schedule, she enjoyed her remaining time to explore with her friends. By the end of their three day (Fri-Sun) break, their duty was to be in the next city on the agenda, so that instilled a great sense of independence since she had freedom to go as she pleased. She also recognized that she was not afraid or intimidated by the "unknown," and adapted comfortably to different languages, currency, and customs.

"I was comfortable with uncertainty," she said, "and that made the experience more manageable. All those foreign films I watched help a lot, plus I studied French and Spanish, so that also eased the language barriers."

By the end of those seven weeks, she visited seven countries, ending in the Greek islands on a sailboat for a week, and with this experience behind her, she knew she was hooked. But she realized that *traveling* was more expensive than to MOVE overseas, so that drive for a more "permanent" overseas home was accelerated by a movie: Lost in Translation, with Bill Murray, which was set in Tokyo, Japan. A Japanese recruiter visited her college in her senior year and offered "a year in Japan," and with that, she was on her way. That move was helped by finding out that an old friend was also recruited by the same company, so that would ease the transition to a new country.

As Becky and I compared notes we recognized we both had a wanderlust spirit, that drive to go elsewhere besides where we were born. She had no desire to stay in

Ohio, and I had no need to stay in Pennsylvania, and even though the unknown was risky, it was also fun and adventurous. I have recognized over the years that many people thrive on "the unknown," while others shirk it and stay put. She and I both recognized that there were people we grew up with that never left their birth states.

In Tokyo she was paid with Japanese yen, which was a strong currency, so her financial concerns were minimized, and with her extra income she was able to pay down her school debt. This was in 2004, and she found herself in the company of a budding movement of young, mobile college graduates: the beginning of Digital Nomads. At that time the internet was growing exponentially and internet bandwidth was doing likewise, so the dream of living "anywhere" was becoming a possible reality. Becky stayed there until 2017 and had different jobs in different cities, and carried with her a great memory.

"Japan became my second home," she shared, "and since it was so safe, it was very comfortable. Ironically, I felt safer there than in my hometown of Cincinnati! We were also close to so many interesting areas, and over the years we went to Beijing and other parts of China, along with much of southeast Asia."

After she left her corporate job in 2017, she recognized that she wanted more freedom and did not want to work in an office, so became her own version of a Digital Nomad. She is a permanent resident of Japan which allows her freedom to come and go as she chooses, and also gives her affordable health care, but she usually stays for only 90 days at a time, and in between goes elsewhere.

As she approaches age 40, Becky has come up with a comfortable combination of "life on the road," combined with the security of staying in several places, and she moves effortlessly between Thailand, Japan, and Portugal. She works as an editor and proof reader of scientific journals, and is able to work her own schedule, and we agree that the term "location independent" fits our lifestyles more than the Digital Nomad label.

The term Digital Nomad, in addition to becoming a cliché, has also become a kind of "hippie label," and many times when you see a picture of someone working on the beach with their laptop (hard to do!), and having drum circles or yoga classes by the pool, it almost becomes a caricature.

I asked Becky what HER drivers were, and why she lives as she does. "I love people," she said. "I love hearing their stories and sharing them on my podcast. Everyone travels differently and for different reasons, and I learn so much. I also love finding new and unexpected adventure, especially in nature, and I don't mind spending thousands of dollars to go somewhere where many don't."

She has been to the Mount Everest basecamp and climbed Mount Kilimanjaro, plus visited Nepal and Bhutan, enjoyed safaris, and even now has an extensive Bucket List yet to accomplish. She has also done less exciting things like housesit, which offers stability along with the fun of animal sitting in many cases.

Another driver for her was food, especially since she did not grow up around or appreciating "good food," since it was not part of her family's lifestyle in Ohio. But Tokyo? Tokyo is considered to be one of the food capitals of the world, and Becky loved it!

"I learned good food from average food, and that included many ethnic varieties, not just Asian. I was introduced to food from India and from many other places, so now when I travel, I seek them out. I look at food reviews. I find the 'under the radar' places that are known, but not popular, and I share it with others. I have had many life changing experiences in so many different places! Plus it's a great way to connect with people because, after all, we all have to eat, right?"

I shared with her a conversation I had with a fellow traveler I met at the airport who was eating something unfamiliar to me. He asked me if I wanted to try it, and I did, and it was good. I told him my trepidation of trying some of the street food in Bangkok (where we were staying at the time), and how I should handle it. He gave me some good advice: "I'll try almost anything, especially since it's so cheap, maybe a buck, maybe two. If I don't like it I don't feel obligated to pay for it, I'll just toss it."

His suggestion hit home, and after that I became more adventurous to try new foods. Becky offered me another suggestion.

"When you go someplace new that is known for the cuisine, try to find a food tour. They will take you to quality places and teach you about the food, and you can try and sample so you know what to order on your own." That was a great idea, and I have done that several times.

I caught up with her since I wanted an update for this story, and she was back in Japan, after visits to Thailand and Vietnam. She has pretty much used Lisbon as her base and will return there in summer and is looking to possibly buy a property. She has created a great rotation between several different countries, which is a great solution for those (like us) that like variety and are not necessarily looking for a permanent home.

In Q1, 2023, she and I had a great conversation which you can [see here](https://youtu.be/1ugOz-KnlH8):
https://youtu.be/1ugOz-KnlH8

Tiffany Parks: Rome, Italy

Tiffany is an author, podcaster, and tour guide in Rome, and went on her first international trip with her mother and sister when she was 14 years old. She had a fascination with Italy—and especially with Italian opera—and between that and the romanticism of her age, she was lured in. That trip started in France, then went to Florence, Italy, and she immediately felt "where I belong," in her words. Some people believe (like I do) that we have a calling to do something with our lives, or go certain places, whether it be a career or a dream of visiting a certain city or country. This may be the case here...

Because of that attachment, the language came easy to her and lured her back four years later at age 18, followed by annual summer trips back to Italy. Fortunately, Tiffany lived a comfortable and semi-affluent lifestyle in the Seattle area, and proved to her parents that she was not caught up in some adolescent fantasy, and showed her dedication to Italy by studying music and opera.

She went to college in Boston and toyed with the idea of an overseas college, but decided that it was too complicated. Even so, she was 3000 miles closer to Europe, which made the trek easier.

"I never wanted to be a traveling nomad," she confessed, "though the idea of doing it for a short time did excite me. But my heart was drawn to Italy, so that's where I focused my energy."

Finally in 2005 all the pieces came together as she realized that she had no attachment to any physical location in the US. She had no career at that time, had just finished a relationship with her boyfriend, so all the directions started pointing to Italy.

"I was completely untethered," she said in her own words, "and if I was going to do it, now was the time."

The irony was, some told her that Italy was NOT the place to go to pursue opera, which she found to be true, mostly because of intense competition and difficulty getting started.

Due to naivety and desire to stay, she flaunted many of the rules of the European Union, which only allows Americans (and many others) to remain for 90 days, then they must leave. She did not... She left as often as she could, but fortunately the immigration people were not that strict then, nor as computerized as they are today. They turned a blind eye to her "illegal" comings and goings, and even though she got nervous every time, she only had one close call and almost got threatened with trouble—but with the UK, not with Italy!

Her first year was challenging and she started teaching yoga, then later got unto tourism, primarily because there was not much happening in her opera world. The learning curve was difficult as she had to deal with landlords, lack of friends, and everything else we run into when living in a new country, but soon she got her groove and never looked back.

She met her Italian husband about 2010, and married in 2011, and that allowed her official citizenship. She now has a child and has become part of the Rome landscape. That process of obtaining citizenship is universally bureaucratic and cumbersome almost everywhere in the world, and many of us think that "all it takes" is a marriage license, but in many cases that is just the first step. That legal recognition took four years, and Tiffany shared that, "sometimes I have to pinch myself to be sure I'm not dreaming! From that little four year old child who pretended to be speaking Italian, using hand gestures, and acting silly, and now I am a real citizen of Italy."

I often compare the "Rules of Travel," as a game, and sometimes you have to learn how to play the game, and practice it to perfection. Immigration rules, different languages, different currency—different everything—is part of the fun and lure, but if you do NOT understand—and accept the rules—you will get slammed.

CULTURE was the biggest driver that made travel so enticing for her, and even though her heart was in Italy, there were other places she would have considered making "home."

"A few years after I got to Italy I got acclimated and traveled almost monthly to different places within a few hours flight. Discount airlines were just becoming a 'thing,' and AirBNB was just starting, plus I had friends in lots of different cities. I also did my first and only backpacking trip to India for six weeks; I ruled that out as a place to live!"

"I had no idea what I would do for six weeks, but I started in the south, which is a bit more cultured, and then worked my way up into the more challenging areas. I studied a specific type of yoga several years earlier and they had ashrams throughout the country, which was a magnet for me to connect with people I could relate to. I took a train trip to Mumbai, along the western coast, and loved it much more than I expected to. On the other hand, avoid Delhi like the plague! I foolishly allowed three days there just before I was due to part, and that was 2.5 days too long."

Point taken.

She finished up that trip at the border of the Himalayas and had a hard time leaving. The country appealed to her so much that it startled her, and that in itself is a lesson that I have learned, as have others. Many times we are drawn to a particular location and we MUST go. Sometimes that reality is not what we expected, and sometimes it is. The opposite is also true. Sometimes we don't have a big drive to go somewhere for various reasons, yet when we DO go, it draws us in.

She started a podcast in 2007 called "A Bittersweet Life," which she shares with fellow traveler, and lifelong friend, Katy Sewall, who lives in the US. Katy had a background in Public Radio, and since they both loved travel, the podcast was a logical step. Katy did live in Rome for one year, but decided that Washington state was a better fit for her. Over the years they have recorded almost 500 shows, which is truly impressive in the podcast world, and they have a loyal and always growing audience to hear the world class authors and thinkers they bring to the show.

She shared that she is NOT a foodie, but along with culture, she is drawn in by the history of different areas.

"I love being in motion," she confessed, "being in a train or bus is so interesting to me, and sometimes the journey is truly better than the destination. It teaches us what we are capable of, and if/ when something goes wrong, you have no choice- you have to handle it. We develop confidence and that is so critical with travel. You cannot just collapse into a puddle on the street or you will be run over."

True enough, and words of wisdom.

Dave Hailwood: France

Dave is well known in the expat community and has a podcast/ radio show called Expat Radio. He got an early head start in Manchester, England, and even though he was a shy child, his father, a police detective, bought Dave some audio equipment when he was a teen, and Dave found his gift: his sense of humor. Put him in front of a microphone and he lit up and started DJ'ing at events and parties, but between that, his daytime job selling phones, plus his love of football, he found himself burned out in the early 2000's. He fixed that by dropping it all and moving to a small beach town in France.

I asked Dave if he was an expat or a nomad, and he said he was both.

"Even though I'm in France, I looked at other places, too, including Greece. I was a DJ on the island of Rhodes for many summers, and considered moving there full time," he shared. "Sometimes I feel like I'm a kid in a toy store, and when it comes to travel, I always want more!"

He has been through most of Europe along with much of Asia and Africa and sometimes shakes his head at wonderment when he speaks with others in his new hometown in France.

"When I tell them where I've been they ask, 'Why did you go there?' and many have never been more than 100 miles from where they were born. I can't understand it!" he laughed.

He loves experiencing the food as well as the cultures of the various places he has visited, and recalls how he felt when he first moved to France.

"To hear everyone around me speaking a different language just blew my mind, and even now when I go to new places I am so amazed at how many ways there are to live our lives all over the world."

I can totally relate, and still recall how I felt in Valencia Spain when we first started our journey. We had a coffee shop around the corner, and for the first week or so I felt uncomfortable going in there. Everyone was speaking Spanish, of course, and the TV was in Spanish and I couldn't read a word on the newspapers or magazines that were strewn about. But after a short while I realized that THIS would be my new norm.

The upside of that is that you don't hear the bad news on the TV, or see the latest war updates in the paper, nor do you get caught up in any of the local gossip!

Dave has adapted to the French lifestyle and says that it is very innocent, naïve, almost childlike, when you get outside the large cities. We have found some of that as well, and it's important to go where the real population lives, if possible.

The upside of that is the way the children are raised in many other parts of the world, outside the US. They are taught respect. They are taught manners. They are taught responsibility. And in many cases they are taught other languages.

Nomad(ic) Life for All Ages, Part II

Introduction

Traveling the World Six Weeks at a Time, Vol II

When we started our nomadic world trek in Feb 2019, we had no idea how long we would do it. Our pat answer to that oft asked question of "How long will you do this?," was, "As long as it's fun!" And it **has been, and still is**, but we were stopped in our tracks in March 2020, by travel and visa restrictions and COVID.

After March 2020, the **World Changed**, but we were still able to visit Italy, Tunisia, Greece, Singapore, Thailand, Vietnam, Cambodia, and just barely make it to Mexico. Our travels were halted and instead of the travelogue feature in part I, this part of the story focuses on the challenges of being *forced* to stop, and how our time in Mexico may (or may not) change things in the future.

Date: 09.24.19/ The Bubbles of Comfort Zones

This whole "*traveling the world thing*" really puts a lot of things into perspective. Aside from seeing how the "other half" (or three-quarters) lives, it also allows for reflection from our own/my past lives and histories. After two visits to the US (home), I have a new and amazing clarity on what I term "***bubbles***." These bubbles can be time oriented, but mostly they are locale focused.

Orange County is unlike most of the United States. It is a dichotomy of very wealthy, both old money and new, usually drawn to the beautiful weather and the coast. There is the growing middle class who are squeezed by the gap between upper and lower class, and they find that middle is not as comfortable- or as promising- as it used to be. That was me... And there is also the lower class, which, in this sense, is comprised of those just getting by, living in poverty or semi-poverty, and the growing number of immigrants who have become the majority of parts of California and Orange County. But "lower class" does ***not*** have the connotation that it used to.

This is not a political riff or anything along those lines, but merely shares the observations of the various lifestyles that people live, or have lived, including me. In hindsight, I am 100 percent happy with my decision to leave my bubble and experience the world. You may be frustrated with ***your*** bubble too, and many have said "I wish I could leave, but can't."

I had a trip scheduled to Portland, Oregon on my return visit, and didn't know what to expect. It is an eclectic town that seems to get off on being different; unique. The term *Diversity* is big there and they insinuate that they love, embrace, and accept everyone. Great intentions. Walking by a yogurt shop I saw a poster that said: "All Welcome! All races, religions, sexual orientations, genders, abilities. You are SAFE here." I had to take a picture and wondered, "Are some people ***not*** safe at other yogurt shops?" So that's Portland.

My Orange County visit had me staying with different friends in their own bubbles, including tony Newport Beach, among the rich, and the wanna' be rich, and those that appear to be that way. I also stayed with a friend further inland behind a private gated community in a beautiful house where everyone lives perfect lives with perfectly manicured lawns and perfectly polite children who spend their time at soccer, dance, and a host of other activities. It was perfect, but I felt out of place. Del Mar, California, is a nice beach town where they may make it a *law* than anyone living there must have a dog! They were everywhere, and virtually all restaurants were designed to accommodate the four-footers. Their owners were tanned, in shape, seemingly affluent, and loved their canines.

And then there's the bubbles of places where we lived overseas. They each have their idiosyncrasies and unique footprints, but they all seemed more real and more authentic than lifestyles in the US.

Maybe I'm becoming a cynic, but I don't think there are any bubbles in the US that would entice me back.

Date: 10.16.19/ Travel Angels...

If you have done any significant traveling you have probably met Travel Angels. You need not be religious or even spiritual, but if you keep yourself open to them, they will show up when you need them. We have met many and have even been travel angels ourselves! It takes no training, preparation, or wings; you just need to be there to help someone in need.

Recently Kathleen was in need as she realized she left her phone behind on a bench in Croatia, and when she returned it was gone. She sat at three different locations, searched them all and wondered what to do. The added stress level was heightened since there were some personal items in the phone case, ie, credit cards. That could have opened up an even worse nightmare of identity theft. I'll tell you now the story has a *happy ending*, but here's what happened.

Cool stuff to know...

The first step most people take is to use their "**Find my Phone**" app to track it down. If you don't have that app on your PC or on another phone, ***do it now***. That app allows many things, including the ability to wipe out the phones memory so nothing can be retrieved. When she used the app it appeared that her phone was heading south out of town, but that can be deceiving since it is not always 100 percent accurate or up to date. She fretted over it and stayed calm and tried to set up her other phone, which is always something good to have available. But her travel angel showed up, a fellow traveler from Australia who spends his time between Split and his home country, who found the phone on a bench. He set up a meeting place to return it, she got the phone back, and the man would not accept any reward or money for his troubles. It ended Happily Ever After.

And this gentlemen was not the first Travel Angel we have met! In our eight months as traveling nomads we have lost:

- A credit card at Los Angeles airport the day we were leaving! We left it at the check in counter and never knew until the gate agent paged us to get it.

- And yet another credit card was left in a grocery store terminal in Barcelona. I did not realize it until the next morning, so went to the store and found someone I recognized from the night before. The card was in the manager's office, another happy ending.

- A passport...yes, really. In Sevilla, Spain, it fell from a pocket while fishing for change. We realized it 15 minutes later, returned to the spot, and happened to talk to JUST THE RIGHT PERSON, who brought it back. That could have been trouble...

- At the Lisbon, PT airport we were running late and were in the **wrong line** to board, since we had luggage to check, which is a rarity. An angel saw us in the wrong line and told us we needed to go to another area to check the luggage ***first***. She even took us there herself. Because of her blessings we checked the luggage, got in the right line, and all was good.

- And finally, we had an unknown Guardian Angel as I left a backpack sitting at the BUS STATION in Deva, Romania, which has a notorious reputation for petty crime from gypsies. After our three hour bus trip we took a taxi to our room and when grabbing our bags realized one was missing. We hauled ass back to the station...and there it was. Our Angel was watching over our bag which had lots of items which would have been missed.

All these Angels, known and unknown, were there at the right time and helped turn a stressful disaster into a minor inconvenience- and learning lesson! And there have been those we have helped as well, mostly because of the experience we have learned along the journey. The first time(s) for everything is a challenge, but we ***love*** helping people avoid some of the mistakes we have made and teach them from our experiences.

As wise and generous as they are, sometimes angels can't help...and so far we have lost:

(1) two jackets in Cadiz, Spain (left behind),

(2) another backpack at a train station in Prague with chargers, cords, but nothing valuable,

(3) some towels in Croatia, and

(4) my cell phone, which was lost on a river raft. Truth is, these things can happen anywhere, any time, but since we move so often we have gotten this process down to a science (?)- or so we hope!

UPDATED: 2023

As this is being updated there have been a few more instances of travel angels coming to our rescue!

I left my phone at an airport gate and did not realize it until we were seated on the plane. I contacted the flight attendant, she contacted the gate agent, and in a few minutes my phone was back in my hand. Crisis averted.

I lost my passport at another layover--it apparently fell from my jacket pocket--and I realized it when I got to our departure gate. I went back to find it from where I thought it was, and after a few minutes of looking, there it was under the seat where I was sitting. Our travel angel was not a person, per se, just my Guardian Angel keeping a watchful and protective eye! In both cases these items were not lost, just misplaced.

We lived in Turkey for eight months and found it to be a very safe, very friendly country, even though the perception may be different. Until I got there I was suspect of the country, but any fears I had were dispelled.

We were on our bike trip into Greece and at our last Turkish city we went shopping at a nut store, and when we came outside I looked for my money clip, which was missing. In a moment I realized that I took it out at the cashier when I paid and started back into the store. No sooner did I turn around when a nice young man came out and said, "You left this behind." It was all there, he turned to go back into the store, and Kat followed him to offer him a thank you reward—which he refused. The Muslims take honesty very seriously, and we found them to be very charming and kind people.

Date: 10.19.19/ The Significance and Singularity of *ONLY* Things

Rome has a famous staircase called the **Spanish Steps**. I saw them in pictures before and thought, "*It's only a staircase, no big deal.*"

But it's the **widest** staircase in Europe and is called the Spanish Steps since it was originally built in 1723 to link a French church at the **top** of the stairs with the Spanish square below. Both were officially in two different countries, so the stairs were a bridge between the two. *Who knew?* Not only does it carry great historical significance, but it's also gorgeous and is one of the most famous meeting spots in Rome, attracting the Rich and Beautiful for many years.

I was actually on my way to the **Trevi Fountain** since it's one of the most spectacular and famous **fountains** in the world. Mind you, I have seen some amazing fountains throughout my travels, including the Villa d'Este in Tivoli, with its 300 plus fountains, all gravity fed, but Trevi is in a class by itself. After all, "*it's only a fountain, right?*" By the way, it *is* magnificent, **more** than just a fountain and worth the visit! And BTW, #2, the one at Caesar's Palace in Las Vegas is modeled after this one, not vice versa...

While in Rome I had a few hours to tour, so I made it over to **St. Peter's Basilica**, one of the most famous religious gathering places in the entire world, and over 500 years old. It is believed that St. Peter, one of the Twelve Apostles of Jesus, was buried there, and he had the privilege of being the first Bishop of Rome. But it IS "*only a church*" right?, and I have seen many over the last eight months of travel. But if you'd like to see **THE POPE**, this is probably the most likely place you will find him outside the Vatican. He was busy, though, so we never connected.

As easy as it is to dismiss "***it's only a ...***" the truth is, there are only **one** of **most** amazing things in the world, and as jaded as I have gotten after visiting dozens of castles, forts, and ruins, I must keep sight of the significance of singularity.

There is only one me; only one you. There is only one Mona Lisa painting and one Great Wall of China, neither of which I have seen. But maybe you have.

Rather than trying to see the entire world, which would be tiring, time consuming and arrogant, we have decided to go with quality over quantity. And there are many "***it's only a ...***" singular places on my list to visit!

After all, it's only a big friggin' pyramid, but ***it is*** a pyramid (Great or not), and I have never seen one, ditto a Sphinx, so they are on my "must see" list for Egypt. Also on the list is Israel, which is a must visit place, along with Australia and New Zealand, mate! How long we may choose to stay at any place is unknown. On the other side of the world, South and Central America are also on our radar, since they have the Galapagos Islands and Machu Picchu, which "is only" a significant citadel (what they call it) that is 8,000 feet above sea level with a wealth of mystery and symbolism associated with it. Even Mexico is rife with Mayan history and their own versions of pyramids.

Date: 10.23.19/ Next stop: Waking in a New City- and a New Adventure!

This morning we awoke in a new city: Palermo, Sicily, Italy. If you didn't know (I didn't), Sicily is the island at the very bottom of Italy and is the *toe* part of the boot on the map, which we used to laugh about. We recently left Croatia after being there more than anywhere else, about nine weeks for me, and almost four months for Kathleen. We left with great memories and vowed to return, and the plan is to make it a regular "go to" place.

As we flew to the west, we got a chance to see the Croatian islands- 1185 of them I found out!- from the air, which was magnificent; a boater's paradise. There are more islands in Croatia than you could probably visit in several lifetimes. The flight to Rome, our layover city, was fast, less than an hour, and we spent most of the airtime flying over the interior of Italy. There are amazing mountains here, and it's no wonder this is the land that birthed Ferrari, Maserati, Ducati and all the other exotic and fast machines that end with "i."

The city of Palermo is very noisy and crowded, with lots of trash everywhere, but we are only here for the day so we can pick up a bike for the month, and then head south to Syracuse (not NY), which is a more mellow seaside town, just what we like.

Our future destinations have one requirement: water proximity. We don't always get it, and we don't necessarily swim or go *in* the water, but just being by it is peaceful. We are preparing to be staggered by the geology of Sicily since it is a still active seismically active island.

Date: 10.26.19/ An Island of Contrasts…

We have been on the island of Sicily for a few days and spent most of that time in Palermo, on the northern coast, but we are ready to relocate to Siracusa on the southern coast. Palermo has a lawlessness about it (could be the Mafioso influence, but not going there…), and I felt like a local who would never think twice about being such a scofflaw!

Siracusa was a 3.5 hours trip south via bus, and was a beautiful ride through the center of the island, and what a different feeling here. The prices are pretty amazing, and we could easily stay here for longer than the 30 days planned, and we might end up doing that since we have another 30 days after that before we must exit the EU.

Schengen update: Croatia, which we viewed as a safe harbor **outside** the EU, is now a Schengen country, so under the same guidelines as the EU.

Palermo: busy, chaotic, crowded, trash on the streets vs. Syracuse, which is clean, with a bit of class and a coastline you see on postcards. There are ruins here from thousands of years ago and we have only scratched the surface of things to see. Archimedes, the Father of Mathematics, was born here, and Mt. Etna, the only "active" volcano in Europe, is just 50 miles away. You know damn well we're going there! Aside from Hawaii I've never been to an active volcano, and this one was a huge influence on the entire island.

I have been "back" in Europe for about a week after being in the US for about six weeks and have had time to reflect. The saying **"*you can't go home again*"** may be true here, too. It usually refers to the feeling you get when you visit your hometown or where you grew up. Trees look larger; your old home looks smaller, and the streets may be less familiar than they were when you left. Time marches on no matter **where** you are, and progress seems to continue unabated. I got to visit with friends and a few relatives, and the good news is that no matter what the distance or the time, most relationships (but not all) remain intact.

Date: 11.04.19/ Living Like a Local

We've decided to extend our time in Sicily since we've loved it so much. We have a room across from the ocean, so that's a plus, and the food here is terrific. We are finally doing what we **said** we'd do on our travels: eating like a local. That means the farmer's market every few days, where we can get everything including fish, fruit, nuts and veggies, and the prices are exceptionally good. A few days ago we got some fresh salmon, which was delicious, and some sea bass a few days later, which they filleted for us, making it much easier to prepare. So far we've only gone on one long bike trip (to Taormina last week) and have enjoyed walking everywhere. I found a gym just a 30 minutes' walk, and on the way is a great grocery store which has everything we need. So far the weather has been terrific, but good luck making plans based on rain predictions! There can be zero percent chance of rain and yet, it rains just a few hours later. Maybe it's the island volatility due to winds and coastlines, but planning in advance is iffy.

We recently found out that Kathleen's son is getting married in North Carolina in March (2020), so that changed our travel plans and directions.

- We'll stay in Sicily about 10 extra days and then head to...

- Tunisia, which is a 10-hour ferry ride, and that will allow us to cross Africa off our list of continents visited. We will skip Malta for now, maybe another time.

- Greece. We have to be mindful of our Schengen 90 days restrictions, so can only stay a few weeks, but that time will be spent between Athens and the island of Santorini. We'll be there for Christmas **and** New Year and this will be our first Thanksgiving outside the US and away from friends. Part of the price we pay for being Traveling Normads.

Date: 11.09.19/ WHY Six Weeks?

Some have asked "*Why do you stay at each location for six weeks?*," and there are multiple answers, including one that came to mind over the past few days as we took a side trip to several cities in Sicily. Since we've stayed in different locations as nomadic travelers, side trips have been wonderful breaks from our home bases. In Valencia, Spain, we took side trips to Madrid, Sevilla, and San Sebastian and in Tivoli, Italy we took just one to the Amalfi Coast. Quality over quantity there. In Croatia we hit the coast from the northern city of Zadar to the western Istrian peninsula, down to Dubrovnik and south into Montenegro and Bosnia. These six weeks stints allow us the *time* to feel we aren't rushed, so when we leave our base we can enjoy being away for a few days. As a **TOURIST** we don't have the luxury since we have "X" days to arrive, tour and then depart, but as a **TRAVELER**, we can take time to smell the roses and in many cases, just do nothing.

Sicily is rather small, only 10,000 square miles, and about the size of the State of Maryland. We traveled up the eastern coast to Taormina, which was amazing, and over the past few days went up the southern and western coasts, stopping at cities that were recommended. Our first stop was Noto, which didn't wow us, then Pozzallo, a port town that I wanted to visit in case we *did* want to take another side trip to Malta, since that is their departure port. That didn't rock our world, either, so we didn't stop. Our intention was to stay the night in Ragusa, which we heard good things about, and it WOWED us AND ROCKED our world, too!

It's a very historic city, built on two large hills (quite common), with a big valley between them. There are centuries of stories there, but the rock cliffs that people built their homes into was stunning. How they were able to build cathedrals and castles on such imposing inclines continually confounds me. The following day we went onward to Agrigento and the Valley of the Temples, which was probably the most awe-inspiring historical area we have been to yet. There were about eight temples, in varying conditions, and viewing these massive structures which were built with primitive machines 4,000-6,000 years ago, still boggles my mind. I'll share more about Agrigento later, but back to the "WHY six weeks question."

Aside from having and taking the *time* to enjoy each location, there's the visa issue. In the Schengen area it's 90 days max, as it is in most countries. When we started our journey in February we decided that if we stay in *two* 45-day locations, then we'd have to leave the EU, and that was how it started. Six weeks Spain, six weeks Italy, then depart the EU, so Croatia fit the bill. At the beginning it was easy tracking the ins and outs of Schengen, but it got complicated a few months ago when we bounced back and forth between EU and non-EU countries during the summer.

Date: 11.16.19/ History from a Personal Perspective

Since we've been traveling we've been blessed by some amazing historical places of interest, which always fascinate and intrigue me. When we look back of how long "mankind" has been around, it's been millions of years, and when we look at how many "civilizations" there have been, there haven't been that many.

We are currently in Sicily, Italy and spent some time in Rome, and yes, there is lots of history there, and here, too.

The other day I went to the Paolo Orsi Museum, and for 8 € the price was easily worth the two plus hours I spent there. Orsi was an Italian archaeologist from the late 1800's to early 1900's, and over the course of his 50-year career, he uncovered numerous historic temples, necropolises, walls, palaces, coins, and other sites in Southern Sicily, plus wrote 300 papers in his field. Pretty impressive, as is the museum that bears his name.

I am not usually a museum junkie and have been to my share that do not hold my interest. I've viewed tons of pictures and paintings, but statues and archaeological finds pique my interest more, and this museum had some of the best I've seen. Granted, not Smithsonian or New York Museum of Natural History quality, which are opulent and in a class by themselves, but still impressive. This museum felt very personal and had more pottery and artifacts than I have ever seen in one place. Pottery that was 12,000-15,000 years old which were found in pieces, yet painstakingly pieced together. That takes more patience than I've ever had! In the town square is the Temple of Apollo from 6000 BC, and in the museum they had scale models that showed what it looked like when it was intact. Amazing!

When you think about something simple, like pottery, it's been around longer than farming!

Today we went to the Archaeological Museum which includes two theaters, one called the Greek Theater, and the other Roman. The Greek Theater is in amazing condition considering it was built in the 5th Century BC, rebuilt 200 years later, and has had to deal with centuries of weathering and warfare. Which is another thing that amazes me. Over thousands of years many of the places have been invaded, destroyed, and rebuilt many times. I can only hope that going forward they will not be impacted by more war.

On our journey, nine months as of tomorrow, we have traveled tens of thousands of miles and have visited 15 countries. I'm glad we started with Roman history, which is one of the newer civilizations, and in a few weeks we will head to Greece, which is even older. Egypt will be forthcoming, older still, but not for a while.

Date: 11.23.19/ The Importance of Flexibility

I had a chance to take a side trip to Paris, so for a few days I returned for the second time. But being there in August is a lot different than November, as I woke to 33⁰F temp (1/2⁰C) and that is a number I have not experienced for a very long time. I wish to keep it that way. Anyway, what can you "*do*" in Paris in one day? I set to find out.

Cool stuff to know...

The Notre Dame Cathedral had a fire in April 2019 and I was curious to see the damage as well as the renovation. I was able to walk entirely around it and from the front it looked intact, but the rear and sides were severely damaged. Scaffolding was everywhere, workers hung by wires, and it's an amazing undertaking to piece together a structure that was built starting in 1163. The technology, tools, equipment, and material were all so different and I'm glad that some people know what to do. The President of France optimistically said it would be done in five years (2024), but most scoff at that and think it will be longer. The world is supportive of the efforts and have contributed over $1B in pledges towards the work.

I decided to skip the Louvre since I'm not a museum guy, unless it's really old architectural artifacts. Most paintings and such don't engage me, and I knew it would take more time than I could commit to it. Yea, I know the Mona Lisa is there, but she'll have to live without me.

I had never been to the Palace of Versailles, so I took that 50-minute train ride for something novel to do. The Palace *is* impressive and if you want to know where "bling" started, look no further. There is shiny over the top gold everywhere (actually a replication since the original golden gates were destroyed in the French Revolution), but I did not do the inside tour. The grounds, ie the "Garden of Versailles," are impressive and extend as far as I could see! It is almost 2,000 acres and one of the largest gardens in the world, and just the *land* is worth about $40B and the Palace another $10B.

Being in France I had to rethink what language I should be speaking since I heard so many this year. How someone can *think* in more than one language blows my mind because for me it's an effort. I know JUST ENOUGH Spanish to say "hello, goodbye; yes, no, please and thank you." I can pull it off in Italian, too, since I've been there twice this year. France has some similar words, but others, not so much. I found myself having to concentrate on which language I was thinking in before I blurted it out. Again, kudos to you that can do it.

As for flexibility, that came up as I reserved a room (actually just a bed) at a hostel, my first hostel in many years. The **Generator Hostel** chain Is well known in Europe and it is not just for "youths." This location has more beds than any hotel in Paris, almost 1,000 of them, and most are filled by those under age 25. But there were Boomers there, plus some in suits and there for business, and a number of mother/daughter traveling duos. Staying in a room with five others requires some patience and adjusting, but my fellow roommates were very cool and hailed from Egypt, Australia, Canada, and Japan. At only 35€ per night it was also affordable.

There are many advantages of being a Traveler rather than a Tourist since I did not have to cram a day's worth of visiting into one. Knowing I can come back and visit again takes off some of the pressure. Also, for the first time I *really* felt comfortable using the Metro! The Paris Metro is very efficient, practical, and easy to understand-relatively speaking, and I will do a blog on how to negotiate public transportation for those that are new to it or feel overwhelmed.

Flexibility Part II: On New Year's Eve night/morning we have a NEW plan and will fly from Athens to **Singapore**, which will be a new experience for both of us since it's so different than anywhere we've been. We were able to book a direct, nonstop flight because we **were** flexible enough to fly that night. The plan is 60 days in SE Asia, with most of our time in Thailand. Traveling as we do, I think it's important to take advantage of all opportunities, be open to new experiences, and to remain flexible.

Date: 11.28.19 (Thanksgiving Day)/ American Holidays Outside America

Several holidays have come and gone since we started our travels. Most of them were minor, but Memorial Day, July 4th and Labor Day are All-American holidays, and signify the beginning, middle and end of summer. Since we've been "following the warm weather," **we** have been chasing summer, so the calendar is not our driver; our desires for warmth is. July 4th came and went in Croatia and truthfully, we have seen more fireworks this year than ever since many places celebrate everything with explosions!

We are now starting, the "holiday season," and today is Thanksgiving, followed quickly by Christmas, and the New Year.

No turkey or stuffing in Sicily, but Christmas decorations are popping up on the street. Without the commercialism that you cannot escape in the US, it's been wonderful not hearing incessant ads for Black Friday and holiday shopping. We have no Walmart's, Targets, or similar chain stores, so things here are more moderate and intimate. Christmas Day is less than 30 days away and we will be on the Greek island of Naxos, one of the Cyclades Islands, and known for mountain villages, ancient ruins, and long sandy beaches, which I have missed!

Naxos is only 163 sq miles, about 100,000 acres, so we aren't expecting a big Christmas parade. The entire island has only 15,000 residents and Naxos Town, our destination, about 2,000, about the size of a small housing tract in Southern California. We will embrace the solitude and quiet since the following week we will jump into one of the most congested cities in the world; Singapore, with 5.5 million people crammed in a ridiculously small area. We will hang there for a few days, then on to Bangkok with 9.5 million people over a much larger area, but because of its larger size, it's about half as congested as New York City.

Some closing thoughts on Sicily.

The island is small-ish, plus majestic, and mountainous along with having wonderful historic ruins and ancient sites. Being there in summer would be much different since now is not "beach weather," and we have seen some beautiful ones along the coast. Unfortunately, the roads were not designed for breathtaking views, unlike the Amalfi coast or the coast of Croatia, but still gorgeous. I have great respect for the Italian architects, builders and workers who fit amazing structures on the sides of hills and at the very, very top of tall mountains. The effort and hard work must have been backbreaking.

The food here has not blown our minds, but we had a farmer's market with great fresh fish, produce and fruit, so we've eaten more at home than ever before. Palermo, the capital, is a city of chaos, but yet, it all works! Vehicles, walkers, and scooters move in and out of the city with a hive mindset and work together well.

In Syracuse we stayed at a lovely apartment across from the beach and hearing the ocean has been a blessing. We had some challenges as we lost wifi for a few days from a storm and the house two doors down had a major internal collapse and required outside repairs, which was annoying. That will be covered in another entry called "Rolling with it," since sometimes, that's all you can do!

Date: 12.07.19/ Next stop: The Misconceptions- and Realities- of Tunisia

Our motivation to visit Tunisia was driven by two things. One was the desire to set foot into Africa (a **new continent!**), and the other was because the city of Tunis was proximate, just a 12-hour ferry ride from Sicily, and a whole new adventure.

We had some concerns, along with misconceptions, and even a bit of fear. We had never been to Africa nor to an Arab country. In America, most of what we know about other countries is driven by media, and that is not always accurate or positive. The fear of terrorism is an ongoing concern in America, and unfortunately we sometimes tend to group Muslims with that same ugly label. Truth is, we have home-grown radicals in the US, and there is no guaranteed safe place in the world no matter where you go. Crazy individuals are not limited to one country, one faith, or one race.

Also, the people there had a different interpretation of "personal space," so tended to crowd in much closer than these Americans felt comfortable! We were more wary about dishonest intentions and kept everything close. Plus Kathleen needed a few days to adjust to the glares and stares of the men. They were not rude, but she and I stood out, and they don't see many Americans here. After a few days we both adjusted and smiled, and they smiled in return.

Dealing with the garbed women and men in Tunisia took some getting used to, but we did within just one day. We were seduced by their friendly nature, their willingness to help and also to satiate their curiosity about us, which was no different than what we felt for them. Walking through the Medina marketplace, we stood before a food stand trying to inquire what was in a particular pastry. A lovely young couple came up, asked if we needed help, and we spoke for several minutes as she helped us understand what was offered. Another wonderful surprise at the marketplace was the chill attitude of the shopkeepers and merchants.

They usually engage us with "bonjour," and when we respond in kind they know we're not French, so they try English! They invited us in cordially and let us look, but they didn't get in our way or try to push us into a sale. When we left it was not awkward, and later we had a conversation with a young man who filled in the back story. They are taught that God will bring a buyer when the time is right, so they leave it in God's hands and stay out of His way. Smart! We should all do the same thing.

Back to food...

We were concerned that the food would be "weird" or not to our liking, but that was 100 percent wrong, and what we ate was flavorful and delicious! We enjoyed their native foods, including couscous, but were challenged by coffee; they like it strong, really strong! We adjusted to that, and usually our cappuccinos had to go back for more milk. Coffee here *is* an acquired taste and we're not sure if we'd ever adapt to it.

English speakers are not that common, but more common among the younger generation, who engaged us with curiosity every time we had a conversation. They were hungry to speak English and learn from us. We were also surprised a few times with some people *our* age who spoke well enough to communicate. We did not know that French was almost a second language to their native Arabic, so make a note if you plan to visit. With a decent French vocabulary you'd get by just fine.

This Tunisia experience has been eye-opening. It introduced us to an Arab country, a totally different language and writing, and left us positive and feeling that most people worldwide are basically "good," friendly, and helpful whenever possible.

We can only hope that Americans do the same...

SUPPLEMENTAL about our amazing ferry ride!

people slept everywhere on the ferry!

A 10-hour ferry ride leaving at 2:00 a.m. took us to Africa for the first time, and the third continent we visited. We were due to arrive late afternoon, but were delayed getting out of Palermo, Sicily, so we got to Tunisia just before dusk. We knew we'd be in for a shock since this was our first Arab country, and there were many things different than the Western World we came from.

Our brief taxi ride from the ferry (incredibly inexpensive), took us through the city of Tunis, and when we got to our AirBNB location we knew we were not in Kansas anymore, Dorothy. Streets of dirt, women and men cloaked in long tunics, and livestock (mostly chickens and roosters) wandering the street, caused a bit of concern with Kathleen, since this would be our home for the next 11 days. We found our room in a typical, but primitive neighborhood, and were pleasantly surprised at the unit itself.

When we arrived our host was kind enough to drive us to the market for supplies, and we had little Tunisian money. It was late and we were hungry, so he offered to drive us through the neighborhood and took us to his favorite eatery, where we had a delicious meal for about $4.00 USD each. He insisted on paying for our dinner and our initial concern about Tunisia was quickly dashed by the kindness and friendliness of the people.

And that continued the entire time we were there.

We spent many hours strolling through the Medina, their open outdoors market, where we bought some items, including Tunisian oils and clothing. We left with amazing and pleasant memories. English was fairly common, and many engaged us with a "HELLO!" in the streets to show their friendliness and desire to talk. They were as intrigued by US as we were of them and we learned a valuable lesson: **Stereotypes are bullshit.**

We have been conditioned to be fearful of Muslins and Arabs by media and yes, some history, too. There are bad apples in **every** country, including the US, and we may have more to fear from domestic terrorism than from afar. Ironically, many people we met from different countries consider **AMERICA** dangerous because of gun violence. In Tunisia and many countries, gun ownership is illegal or tightly controlled, so what **they** hear puts fear into them.

Tunisia was a trip. Our ferry ride was super crowded with entire families sleeping on the floor- and outside our cabin! Most of them smiled at us and some offered us food. That is how big their hearts were; offering to share what little they had.

We did not travel too far outside the city since their train system sucks, the roads are horrible, and we enjoyed the area we were in. Even hearing the Muslim chanting from the mosque five times a day (including before dawn!), became normal, along with rosters crowing all day. It's hard to believe that we became accustomed to dirt roads, battered old taxis and domestic fowl in the street, but we did. But the best memory of Tunisia was the Tunisians themselves, some of the loveliest people we have met yet.

Date: 12.14.19/ Trying to "Control" Travel Plans: Sometimes...Shit Happens

That's our front door!

The other day we were "stuck" at the Tunis, Tunisia ferry port for almost seven (7) hours. We never knew the cause, but when one ferry is late, they all lag behind. That got me thinking about how often we try to "control" things. I certainly did that in my career, my marriage and within my role as a stepfather, but in 2013, when my life changed, I changed as well and let go of a lot of control. I learned to live in Faith and allow the Universe to do its thing. Granted, sometimes I balked, but let's talk about travel.

When traveling, we/ you usually have a plan; an agenda. We want things to go a certain way because we usually have a limited time, so don't want the inconvenience of rain, missed trains or things that can (and do), sometimes go wrong. But, shit happens.

Since travel is my/ our lives and we have no home, inevitably things go wrong. Mostly we flow with and let it go, but sometimes BIG things go wrong. For example.

We arrived in Syracuse, Sicily on October 25 and were greeted by mild showers which turned into an amazing lightning, thunder, and rainstorm later that night. We saw the lights outside flicker and go out so knew that our power was out too, and there wasn't anything we could do about it. A huge thunderclap and lightning strike towards morning caused a spark in the kitchen and we had no idea what it was until we discovered our wifi was out. And it stayed out for about four days since our *router* got fried as well as the cable lines into the city block where we were staying. The thick concrete walls blocked mobile and data services, so the only way for us to get wifi or data was to go to a local coffee shop or hotel. An inconvenience, but still, no big deal: shit happens.

A few days later we returned to our unit to find a firetruck in front along with a dozen firefighters, locals, and neighbors. For a few days we had no idea what happened since we couldn't communicate, and were told that an *interior* staircase collapsed in the unit a few doors down. The city put a **DO NOT ENTER** sign on the building and no one could go in or out. No worries. A few days later the city started repairs on the unit and erected six floors of scaffolding *outside our back doors*, followed a week later by the same thing in the *front*; then they started tearing up the street. **Now it's a nuisance**. For several weeks workers walked by our doors, making continual noise and unplanned distractions.

But there was nothing we could do and we were told the day we vacated that they estimated it would take **two years** to finish the work on that building! They should have condemned it, but they rarely do that with a 500-year-old building. And so, shit happened.

Oh, the old lady that lived in the unit was the local cat patron, too, so when **she** left, the cats came 'round and cried continually at our doors, looking for their handouts. Even as a cat lover I reached my wit's end, but again...it happened.

And now we sit, waiting for a ferry that is **way** late (the one to Tunisia). They were "supposed" to offer us water and food, but did not and instead of leaving at 6:30 p.m., we finally left port about 1:30 a.m. the following morning. And there wasn't a damn thing we could do about it.

The moral of the story is that "shit happens" in travel, in life and certainly in business. Sometimes we just have to let go and Let It Be.

And so it is.

Date: 12.21.19/ Next stop: The Realities of Island Living

Who **doesn't** want to live on an island?

I mean, really, we've seen the movies and read the books, and aside from being on an island due to a **SHIPWRECK**, it all seems very idyllic, even romantic.

We have been on the (Greek) island of Naxos for just a few days and I am happy to report that it *is* idyllic, and even romantic! This is one of the Cyclades Islands about four hours off the coast of mainland Greece, and one I never heard of until just a few months ago. When we think about Greek islands, the ones that come to mind are *Santorini*, of the blue and white homes built into the cliffs, and *Mykonos*, known for wild nightlife and trendy atmosphere?? (They refused us admission...) This is the second island that we lived on during our Travel Younger journey, but not the only one I have considered moving to.

My first island experience was Hawaii, probably one of the first for many of you, where I visited in January 1979. Oahu is an island, but Honolulu was like any big city, only with beaches and palm trees nearby. It wasn't until I went to the north shore that I sensed the ***allure*** of islands.

Over the next 30 years I went to Hawaii often and fell in love with Maui, which was a combination of civilization joined with island waters and beaches, peppered with extinct and dormant volcanos which only added to the mystique. I gave serious thought to moving there and even started a business there. I still own a timeshare near Lahaina and visited other Hawaiian Islands, but none compared to Maui.

Jamaica was cool and was my first taste of an island ***country***, with its own language, currency, and road rules, plus its uniqueness due to the reggae and cannabis influence.

When Kathleen and I were "testing the water" about leaving the US, we went to one of the Balearic Islands called *Menorca*, off the coast of Spain, and loved the 10 days we spent there. I called it "the island that time forgot," since it seemed mired in the 1970's with no large hotels, timeshares, or chain eateries. It is about 130 miles east of Spain, just a one-hour flight, and is not as well-known as neighboring Majorca and Ibiza. Those are the party islands, which is why we passed on them. One of the things that struck me was how crisp the air was out there! With few cars, little pollution and daily winds, the air was in constant and invigorating movement.

That was where we concluded that **YES** we *could* make the exit move, and Kathleen still has a spiritual connection to Menorca. We will return.

When we planned our Greece trip we knew we *had* to hit one of the islands, and that is how we got to Naxos. By design. I spoke with the locals and asked what it's like living there, especially in winter, when we arrived, and was pretty quiet. Many restaurants were closed for the season, along with other tourist attractions and car rental outlets. Our lodging was inexpensive in offseason, so that was a plus, but even so, there were still great restaurants open, along with a beautiful coffee shop where I sit as I scribe this.

Neither of us is looking for a "second home," but still considering places we'd like to visit for longer. Our plan was "six weeks at a time" and if we find a place we *really* like, we can extend that to three months. It's a balancing act between getting "rock fever," since we *are* 132 miles or so from Athens, and enjoying the intimacy of a small community. We know this place is nuts in summer, just like *any other* island destination. So was Newport and Laguna Beach, where I lived for decades.

Before we left California we had dinner with a Spanish friend who used to live on Menorca and I expressed concern about being "too isolated" living on an island. I was referring to the limitations of Hawaii, which is 3,000 miles from *anything*. Not so in Menorca, Naxos or virtually any island in this part of the world since civilization is close. From many of these islands you can ferry to the mainland in 12 hours or fly in one, and from there the world is at your doorstep. With that said, an "Island Life" is a very real possibility.

What about you? Have you lived on a small island? Do you want to?

Date: 12.29.19/ Santorini from Top to Bottom

We knew that Santorini (and Greece) would be a magical place since it has such a long history and mythology behind it. After all, we studied Greek history and know Zeus, Neptune, Athena, Apollo, et al, like they were real historical figures. And they might be! Add in the long history of volcanoes and earthquakes in this part of the world, and Santorini now becomes a Shangri-La that dreams are made of. Before we got there I knew little about Santorini other than the reviews and suggestions of other travelers and writers. Many said that you *must* visit here, and others said it's overrated; both may be right.

First, there's the geology of the island, which was created and recreated several times over the millennium. The volcano Santorini has been active throughout history and is on the rim of the African tectonic plate, which is in constant motion. The Santorini volcano **blew** in about 1646 BC according to historians, and many believe it was the second largest explosion in all of recorded history. The net result was five separate islands, with Thera (Santorini), being the largest.

If you review *Roman* history, Mount Vesuvius and Pompei left behind a long legacy when it blew in 79 AD, along with artifacts and skeletons. The Santorini explosion was horrific and was "centered" in what was then the capital city of Akrotiri. Apparently, the residents knew something bad was about to happen since *no bodies* have been discovered, although many artifacts did survive. We did not explore this area as much as I would have liked, so put that on your list.

When we entered the *port* of Santorini via ferry, which IMHO, is **THE** best way to arrive, you can see the geology right in front of you since it is magnificent! The harbor is *inside* what used to be the INSIDE of what blew, and you can see the layers upon layers of rock that have been left behind. Do this instead of flying in, even though the port is chaos!

I made a list of suggestions of what to do/ not do and see in Santorini, so please add any suggestions you have and ask any questions!

Cool stuff to know...

1) **Read** up on the geology of the island beforehand. There are lots of videos and web sites, and they make seeing it in person much more special.
2) If you can, take a **ferry** from Athens or better yet, from Naxos, which is where we stayed for a week. The ride from Naxos to Santorini is about two hours and the experience of entering the harbor is indescribable... BUT, check the weather since ferries can be affected by storms and rough sea.
3) **Rent** a car; taxis are crazy expensive. From the ferry port to the city of Fira (Thira) could be 20€, which is just a few miles. And don't bother with a fancy car- the roads are crappy! We were offered a "newer" car with bells and whistles for 40€/ day, but instead got an older one for 25€. Be sure the tires are good and inflated since some of the rental agencies do not take good care of them. They *do* have a bus from the ferry, but they only operate during certain hours.
4) **VISIT** the town of Oia, which is at the northern tip of the island. It is a "walking" town, no cars, which means you park outside town and walk along the rim of the crater while viewing the amazing architecture and buildings. You know all those iconic pictures you see of Santorini? THIS is where they come from. During winter fewer shops and eateries were open, and it was VERY, very peaceful, which was great. In season being bumper to bumper to people would diminish the beauty.
5) **VISIT** the Monastery of Profitis Ilias (Prophet Elijah), which is at the highest elevation of the island, 1860 ft above sea level. With a 360 degree view you can see the entire island, though the narrow road is not for the faint of heart...
6) **VISIT** Vlichada Beach if you have never seen a black sand beach. The sand pebbles vary from very fine to smaller pebbles and the cliffs behind the beach are made from pumice, which is strewn over the sand, very cool. BUT be mindful that black sand is *hotter* than the normal white sand you may be used to if you go in summer...
7) Santorini is pricey, including food, so staying in the capital city of Thira (Fira) is probably your best option. If you do have a car, eating outside the tourist area saves you money. There are also smaller semi-fast food places which are reasonable. In winter, the island is a popular destination for those from India and Asia, though we did hear some American voices, too.

I wish we had been able to visit the nearby island of **Nea Kameni**, which is totally comprised of volcanic rock and is still smoldering! It is quite small and to the right side of the port as you enter with the ferry. No tours or ferries were offered in winter, but we *do* plan to return in September.

Date: 01.03.20/ Next stop: Singapore: "You will LOVE it!"

Over the past year we have met and spoken with many "new friends" we met on the road, plus the ones we still had at home. When we mentioned we were going to Singapore on New Year's Day we got one overwhelming response: **You will LOVE it!**

And you know what?

We did.

Our initial departure point had challenges as we almost got stranded on the island of Naxos, trying to get to Athens. We were successful leaving Santorini (which we loved!) a few days prior, we got back to Naxos, and then the weather turned. We had a ferry scheduled to Athens the following morning, December 30, but when we checked with the ferry company about an hour before departure, we were told they were **all** canceled for the day and possibly the next, too. We had **no** Plan B since our Singapore flight left from Athens the following morning and we **had** to be on it. But the Gods were smiling as we hauled ass to get to the airport to catch the **only** flight off the island that day, and it was also postponed. We sat in a teeny tiny waiting room for an extra two hours, and the Gods continued to smile as the skies cleared, we left late, and arrived to a very cold (32⁰ F, 0⁰ C) Athens. We had enough time to get to our room, sort through our items, and get ready for the next day's 10 hour, 5,620 mile flight.

We celebrated New Year's Eve 2020 with no champagne, no balloons and certainly no fireworks, but we did it at 36,000 feet with about 300 of our closest strangers! The interior lights came on at midnight somewhere over some ocean, everyone took pictures as the flight crew wished us all the best, the lights went out again, and it was business as usual until we landed at 0300 to a very quiet and peaceful Singapore airport, which was gorgeous! All the stories we heard about how strict they were evaporated since we were the first in line at customs and walked out the gate five minutes later. Since the Metro didn't start till 0600, we wandered around and chilled until it geared up.

It was a weird way to begin a NEW YEAR in **so** many ways, since Southeast Asia was a first for Kathleen and me, and we had no idea what to expect. It was also odd since I had never been this close (70 miles, one degree) to the equator and finding almost

90⁰ F/ 32⁰ C temps on the first day of the year. Even those warm New Year's Days in Orange County didn't compare and here it was, just two weeks after the beginning of (their) SUMMER! To say that this worldwide voyage blows my mind and senses is all too true.

What we found was the strongest English language presence of any place we had been in the last year. Everyone was kind and helpful, the same as we found most everywhere else. We took the metro to our room, which I will not go into (!), and had breakfast of chicken, eggs, and green rice on the street from a "hawker," which is what they call the street food courts. And what a cool and shocking experience!

Interesting foods, some familiar, some not, and ridiculously cheap prices (like $3.00 USD for breakfast), plus we found very pleasant people working there. We were exhausted and able to drop off our luggage at the hostel at 0900, but not take our bed until 2:00 p.m. That meant that we were free birds, so off we went, exploring the belly of Singapore. The "centerpiece" in my mind, was the **Marina Bay Sands** hotel and complex, with 2,500 rooms worth of luxury and, to top it off- literally and realistically- the hotel has a large "ship" connecting the three towers. Here's a 35-minute video created by someone with much greater skills than me!

The view from the top was indescribable, along with the enclosed shopping mall with every imaginable high-end luxury retailer in the world represented. It was worth the money to get to the 57th floor to intake that view of the very crowded harbor and the forest of large skyscrapers. When I use the words "amazing and spectacular" they only convey a portion of what it was really like.

Aside from the towers, the city itself was impressive, with spotless subway stations that were well marked and **orderly**, with everyone politely toeing the entry lines. Some have said that Singapore is a bit too Big Brother-like, too militant, but the cleanliness of the city and how well everything was maintained was a refreshing change from some of our prior locations. It was also fascinating to see the integration of so many cultures and ethnicities, since this is called one of the most diverse cities in the world. We are staying in "Little India" which is interesting, and I was not aware of the variety of different countries represented here.

Singapore factoids:

(1) the Singaporean natives (yes, their titles), speak English like a Brit since they are taught the Queen's English rather than American English. That makes sense since they were a British Colony for many years.

And (2) even with 82% humidity and 80⁰ F. temps, I've not seen or felt any mosquitoes! Which is awesome.

They said we would love it here, and I think than anyone who visits, **will** love it here. But we also heard the same thing about Thailand, Cambodia and especially, Vietnam.

I'll let you know, since Bangkok will be our base for the next 30-60 days and be used as a jump point to visit Angkor Wat in Cambodia, places to be named in Vietnam, plus islands and other cool places in Thailand. It's a little weird thinking about visiting Vietnam since many fellow Boomers have a much different memory of that country. When I was 18 I came within one year of visiting that country under different circumstances...I'm glad that the country recovered and has prospered after too many years of horrors.

Date: 01.12.20/ 30 Days in Bangkok (about 27 days too long…)

That was the plan: 30 days. We had a fun trip to Southeast Asia on New Year's Day after catching a great flight from Athens, GR to Singapore. Singapore had a rep for being expensive (it was), so we decided to stay for just a few days, then head to Bangkok for 30 days and use that as a "base" for other treks. We will be returning to the US for a bit come March 4, so we had about 63 days to explore this part of the world and get a sense of whether we liked it enough to return.

Speaking of return, Thai immigration rules are pretty strict, so they would **not** allow us to board our Singapore> Bangkok flight without a return ticket OUT! Staying for 30 days was not an issue, and can be extended very cheaply , but regardless, they make sure you do not overstay their welcome. We bought a return ticket on the spot to complete the transaction. Whatever! Immigration rules are specific to each country and some are easier than others.

After we arrived in very hot, very humid, and busy Bangkok, we weren't quite sure how long we **wanted** to stay! We had an amazing condo, 36 floors up, in a newer high rise with a gym, lounge, and infinity pool, so this was not roughing it at all! This unit also required us to stay for 30 days, but it was less than $400 USD per month. One of our options was to stay **there** and extend another 30 days, which we did, and our initial plans continued, including side trips to Chiang Mai, then Ha Long, Vietnam (immediately after), then two more jaunts to Angkor Wat in Cambodia and Phuket here in Thailand. BTW, the distances to anywhere are close and the costs to fly **and** to stay are inexpensive compared to most places in the world. Our room in Ha Long Bay, Vietnam, with a water view, is about $25 USD a night.

Back to Bangkok.

This is a busy city and the most visited one in the *world* (22.7M annually) per Forbes, easily surpassing Paris, London, etc… Add in 9.5 million residents and an infrastructure that is outdated, and you get an overwhelming, incredible, and different experience from the "Western" world.

It is a city of contradictions with beautiful spiritual temples and monuments combined with horrible living conditions; modern technology, malls and restaurants strung with electrical wiring hanging like a spider web on poles and buildings. Yes, their diet is very different, including bugs and interesting types of seafood, but some of these unfamiliar tastes are quite good! Prices are low, from restaurants and food court eateries, to housing and taxis.

In our almost 11 months of travel, this is as different as anything we had experienced and Kathleen was a trooper here- and patient- while I had to work through some uncomfortable surroundings for a few days. But now, one week in, we're venturing out, exploring further, and enjoying the night, which is **loud** and very colorful.

Travel Younger was started to encourage and teach non-Millennials how to travel *like* a Millennial. To get the 50 and 60-year old's out of their comfort zones and realize that you **can** explore and live like a **Traveler** (vs a **Tourist**), and travel with less stress and less money. But I must give the Millennials the props they deserve! We meet many and by comparison they are <u>MUCH</u> better at dealing with some of the "*discomforts*" of life on the road, like hostel beds, long uncomfortable bus and train rides, and eating food that I, personally, have a hard time with! I respect the "younger generation" and remember when I also had that same laisse faire attitude.

Age changes us and there *is* a comfort level for everyone. But, you do **not** need to abandon everything in the US (or wherever you live), to live like permanent Normads. This was **our** personal choice, but now that 2020 is here, I hope that you evaluate what is important to you at whatever stage of life you are in. There will come a time when we put on less miles and find more places to settle for longer periods. My stats for 2019 include 18 countries, 197 cities and 88,415 km (about 55,000 miles), so we'll see if we can maintain that pace in 2020.

As to whether we will return to this part of the world, the answer is YES. Kathleen and I have concluded that we like *Mediterranean* climate more than *Tropical* or any other, so that will be our focus.

Date: 01.18.20/ Lessons Learned: Time Lost, Money Wasted, Health Jeopardized; New Experiences to Share

Traveling Younger *is* an ongoing education, and even with research and advance planning, sometimes, well, shit happens. Over the last few days we have been tested by things, some within our control and some not.

We went to Chiang Mai, Thailand for three days and loved it. The small town was a nice change from Bangkok, but one thing we did not escape was *poor air quality*. When we got to Bangkok two weeks ago we saw about one out of five persons wearing face masks. I always thought that people wore them here due to crowds and preventing illness, but it seems they do double duty since the pollution is that bad. Almost from day one we said that we should get and wear masks over here, but never did. I had a raspy throat for a few days which I think I've adjusted to, but in Chiang Mai we also found bad air. We discovered that Thailand has a "burning season" and this one knocked Kathleen out for several days. It required a hospital emergency room visit at midnight and various meds to open up her clogged sinuses and lungs. The burning can release lots of pollen and allergens and if you *do* have an allergy it will only be compounded by the burning process. I am sure our two hour hike earlier that day (to an 8,400 feet elevation) didn't help, either.

Cool stuff to know...

Lesson learned: ***don't mess with your health***. Better to look dorky and breathe better than to suffer the dangers of bad air.

Supplemental health lesson #2: traveling in different countries involves exposing yourself to their water and their food. Be careful, but not paranoid. Bottled water is cheap, but brushing your teeth with tap water is ***probably*** OK. Street food is always a risk, and look for stands that are clean as possible.

We were supposed to travel from Chiang Mai to Vietnam the night Kat got ill. We spent several hours in the ER and fortunately her vitals were good, so she was discharged with half a dozen meds to help her out. We stayed up the rest of the night and got to the airport for a 0800 flight, stood in a too long line, then were denied entry. We knew that Vietnam required a visa to enter and offered what is called a "visa on arrival." When you arrive you pay a fee and are allowed a 30-day visitor's pass. But even with our research and speaking with people, we were not aware that we also needed **advance** permission from Vietnam to enter. They offer an online e-visa which usually takes a few days, but can be rushed if you want to pay the premium. It didn't matter since there was **no way** to catch a flight that day, so we had just two options.

Stay in Chiang Mai, deal with Kat not feeling well, find another room and try to rush a visa through. Or, return to our home in Bangkok, apply for the permit from **there**, and let Kat recover in a place where she was more comfortable. So that is what we did. We ended up losing the entire trip cost to Vietnam, but we learned...

Lesson learned: even if we **think** we know the rules, double and triple check everything. Bureaucracy lives here just as much as in the US. These mistakes cost us money plus time since now we have to reschedule our return.

Lesson #3, but this one is harder to predict.

We always planned to visit Chiang Mai, but didn't know we would like it so much, and 2.5 days was **not** enough. In hindsight, we should (and could have) stayed for a week, it was that cool. Unfortunately, side trips can be affected by things like liking or not liking a certain town **and** the weather. Our planned trip to Halong Bay in Vietnam would have found weather that was **not** good: cold and rainy. That would not have been good for Kat's recovery, so who knows, maybe this all worked out the right way?

Supplemental:

When we were initially in Thailand, and specifically Chiang Mai, we had never heard of the coronavirus or COVID 19. Of course, that virus changed our plans along with the rest of the world.

After we got Kathleen back to Bangkok, she was ill for several days and in hindsight had all the symptoms of the virus. At the hospital, the doctor was **very specific** about his paperwork and diagnosis, and instead of reporting what HE observed, he wrote, "patient reports no fever, no chills, no cough, etc..." which was not true. As the news of the virus unfolded and more information was revealed, we found out a few weeks later that Chiang Mai was one of the first areas in Thailand to have the virus outbreak. It never became a pandemic there, but their numbers initially were extremely high. Their burning season was a factor, but not why she got sick. Our conclusion is that they were trying to downplay her symptoms and not reporting accurate information to the health officials.

Back in Bangkok Kat had no appetite for several days, was bone tired with no energy, and generally felt horribly. Again, in hindsight, we were and are thankful that her illness was not worse.

Date: 01.27.20/ A NEW View of Thailand!

After three weeks in Bangkok dealing with the smog and crowds, we finally found the **other** side of Thailand that people love: the beaches, the water, the islands. There were many options to choose from, including Phuket and Krabi, which seem to be the top beach destinations for South Thailand. Instead we found a place that we had never heard of: the Chumphon region.

It was an hour's flight, about $100 USD round trip, and we found an amazing resort called the Tanisa. About a 40-minute drive from the airport through roads that totally cried **ALOHA** (Hawaii)! If I didn't know we were on a mainland I would have thought we were on an island. Palm trees, birds singing, and fluffy clouds greeted us at a very, very small airport, and it was a great way to begin the rejuvenation and recovery from The City.

When you book a room you never know what you'll get, but when we pulled up and saw that it **looked** very Hawaiiana-like-- sweet! Our room was large with concrete floors and a huge shower. The small pool was nice plus they had a café with a menu that could compare to Cheesecake Factory! (For those that don't know, it's big). Plus, the room was $20 USD per night, a fraction of what you would pay in the States or most other areas. It was not near the water, but a scooter for $8 per day was perfect for getting us there, and just a 20-minute ride.

I had never seen a tropical beach like that. Wide open spaces and palm trees resonated, but seeing small islands and rocks protruding from the water, well, that **was** unique to me. I didn't know the water temp, but it was like a slightly warm bath, but not hot, and quite pleasant. We walked the beach which was composed of the finest grains of sand I had seen, and it was strewn with shells and the artistic diggings of sand crabs.

The "reality" of nomadic life is that it is full of uncertainty and unknown. It can be intimidating and scary while at the same time fresh and exciting.

As I reflected upon our decision to commit to 60 days in our Bangkok Ivory Tower, in hindsight I wish we had not done it. We were swayed by the cheap price and the beautiful facilities, but the energy of the town and the people wasn't working. So now we will use our $13 per night room (the average) to store our stationary luggage, while we make side trips, relatively untethered by excess clothing and such. Considering we've stayed at five "long term" rentals and up till now, loved them all, the Far East has been a true learning experience and we hope to impart those lessons to you. Visas are critical over here, which means that exits out of a country are as important as when and how you enter. Food is different, spoken English is a luxury and not to be expected, and pollution, both air and water, seems to be a reality in this part of the world. I have gotten feedback from many who say that they could not stay for long in parts of China due to brown air, so that diminishes our motivation to go.

When we started our Travel Younger journey almost a year ago, we decided that we would do it "as long as it's fun." When it comes to visiting places that are questionable, for now I will take them off the table if they are **not** fun, and certainly if they are unhealthy.

Of the 241 countries in the world, per the United Nations, the majority I have no interest to visit. The US recognizes less than 200 of them and as I reviewed the world list, I have about 50 more on my radar. Last year we hit 18, so the rest may be attainable.

Date: 02.02.20/ Next stop: Vietnam: A Whole New World

We had issues in Thailand almost from the beginning, primarily from poor air quality, too many people, and feeling uncomfortable with the food and language. We resolved some of those challenges by leaving Bangkok and visiting smaller towns, like Chiang Mai and Chumphon. They both went a *long* way to making us more comfortable and we liked Chumphon so much that we went back for 10 days more. We found a small hotel cabin right on the sand for less than $20 USD per night, so we used that time to focus on writing and other obligations, plus getting into that warm water several times a day.

After our debacle getting our Vietnam visa- and losing a $300 flight in the process- our second attempt was more successful. We reviewed the rules over and over and applied for an i-visa (or e-visa) which cost us $90, and sweated it out until we received it via e-mail the day before we were due to leave. A printed hard copy was required and at the airport we still had some uncertainty since the visa and flight tickets did not match our passports; some included **middle names**, and others did not. Luckily, the gate agent approved us, and in about 90 minutes we landed in Vietnam, country #31 for me and our 13th in less than one year.

We went to Ha Long Bay primarily for one reason: the beauty of the pinnacle rocks just off the coastline.

With about 150,000 people, Ha Long is not one of the largest cities, but sneaks into the Top 20 per the census. The local area known as Cat Ba (where we stayed) is certainly in the top 10 Most Beautiful Cities and is known for their national parks and island rocks; the city of Ha Long is considered the number three most beautiful place in Vietnam.

The island rocks are called **Karst Pinnacles** and comprised of limestone and seashells from millions of years ago which have been compressed and eroding ever since. They are like icebergs in that most of the structure is beneath the surface and the rock is typically very porous and prominent with caves. The rock's erosion turns the surrounding waters green and is diluted by the blue colored sea water. When we awoke our first morning, we went up to the third floor outside balcony and there they were before us. And they were spectacular!

Even though they were the highlight of our short (six days) stay here, there were others. This smallish town is a nice size, with wide streets that were large for the small amount of traffic on them. Everything was clean, everyone smiled when we passed, and the best news? The food was amazing! On our first night we walked to a local restaurant, read the English language menu (!) and after dismissing sandworm, false dog, and bullfrog, we settled on yummy noodle dishes, one with seafood and the other beef. The quantity was impressive and **one** meal was easily enough for two, and for both meals, plus two beers, it was less than $10 USD.

Their local currency, the Vietnamese Dong, is considered one of the weakest world currencies and to put that into perspective ONE US dollar is equal to 23,000 Dong. When we cashed in just $30 USD we got over 500,000 Dong, all in paper bills, so the conversion took some time to get used to. The bills are plastic coated and there are no *coins*, which is nice. The sensation of being a "Dong Millionaire" is quite a thrill, but just a coffee can set you back 60,000 Dong in a few minutes!

When I stop and realize **where** I am, I succumb to a bit of soul searching mixed with nostalgia.

When I was a teen the Vietnam War was in full swing and was a fixture on the daily news. Back then there were only three prime TV stations and few other outlets. The war, one of the most controversial in US history, took almost 58,000 US lives. Most of the soldiers went with great reluctance and experienced some of the most modern and deadly warfare of that time. I knew many that went and died, and I was fortunate in missing it since the mandatory draft ended just one year before I turned 18. In the prior year, my enlistment number was very low.

Call it luck, call it timing, but for those that weren't lucky or were born at the wrong time, my heart could feel their presence, which was quite surreal. And for those that **went** and did return, thank you for that. The fact that I could experience the glory of this amazing country was such a blessing and one taken with daily gratitude. We were staying in the former North Vietnam, the top one third of the country, which was all Communist ruled.

I hope you get to visit Vietnam and I give it high praise. We didn't get to Ho Chi Minh City, Hanoi, or Da Nang, but we will likely return. But **not** in winter since our timing *was* off here with temps in the 60's- and no long pants! Live and learn.

Date: 02.11.20/ A Tale of Three Cities: Chaotic, Busy and Normal…

Thanks to Google Maps and their amazing Timeline feature, we are able to track every location we have visited since we began our journey almost one year ago. In 2019 I visited 18 countries and 197 cities, plus in January (2020), three more countries and nine more cities. Of the 200 plus cities, some were just a drive through, long enough to get "pinged" on Maps or maybe just a spot to gas up or grab a bite. We probably "stayed" in 40 of them. I identify them several ways, but also include their "busy" factor, like Bangkok, Palermo, and Rome…

Cool stuff to know…

Rome is quite busy, and a city I would ***not*** want to drive in! I never have, but the cliché about Italian drivers and Rome taxis is not an exaggeration! I put Rome into the "chaotic" category along with a few others.

Palermo, Sicily, was our first TRUE example of crazy drivers and traffic and having to drive there. We rented a bike and it felt like "every man for themselves," and it brought out the rebel in me! Passing on the wrong side? No problem. Driving down one way streets the wrong way? Yup, did that, too! Lane splitting? A necessity in Italy and in many countries. Palermo was crazy and noisy and had an ultra-high energy vibe that was exhilarating! But not a town I would want to stay in for long.

Bangkok took all that crazy and chaotic to the extreme.

They drive on the left side, and traffic and noise is constant. Crossing the street is risky and most major streets have elevated pedestrian crossings. We did not rent bikes in Bangkok, but did in other areas, which was fine. Bangkok is a city of contradictions, with some great Zen areas with temples and monasteries and just outside- bedlam!

In Vietnam we only stayed in Ha Long Bay area, so it would be unfair to paint the entire country by one city. They drive on the right side and they drive like ***snails***, but the ***scooters***, like frenzied bees! And yes, the pictures you see of scooters carrying rooms full of furniture are not exaggerated! On the way back from the airport the taxi driver constantly was on his horn and driving like an octogenarian. We thought it was only him, but it seems that they ***all*** honk constantly! "Watch out, I'm heading your way," they command, and even bikes are always on their horns. Their buses and trucks even have what sounds like sirens and are warning everyone that they are coming. It got humorous after a while. No, I take that back; it was always irritating as hell!

Of the "busy" cities we stayed in, our first leg of our journey, Valencia, Spain, fit that category, and was not quite chaos. It's a city of 800,000 people, but they're spread out and have a very efficient mass transit system. "Busy" is good and one I can manage much better than chaos! Athens was busy, but not chaotic and also had a good rail system. Split, Croatia, busy, but well within reason, and crossing the street was not a life-threatening undertaking. We rented bikes several times in Split and always felt comfortable.

And then there's "normal," however we define it.

I find that cities of 250,000 or less are my sweet spot. Large enough to have cool stuff to do, but small enough to learn your way around. They typically have metros or trains and finding a train station to take you *out* of town is usually easy.

And then there's the fourth category of city: the small ones. The chill ones. THAT is where you/I find your/my quiet place, and we have stayed at many.

Tivoli, Italy, about 20 km east of Rome, was our first. A "medieval town" where most buildings are hundreds of years old and no metro system aside from a local bus. We walked everywhere on very hilly streets. Brasov, Romania was also a small city and easy to navigate on foot. Naxos is a small city on the island of Naxos, so again, very chill, and easy to love.

We are now at the most chill place of all; a small cabin on the beach in a town called Chum Kho, about 10 minutes from Chumphon airport and a million miles away from Bangkok. Within five miles there are probably just a few hundred people and we are isolated without being "without." There are several restaurants within a few minutes and the always available and iconic 7-11 store is a 10-minute drive. There is minimal traffic and the only sound we hear is the ocean, just a few yards away. With a strong throwing arm I could hit the surf with a baseball.

And the price? Less than $20 USD per night.

When people read about our "Travel Younger" journey and say, "*I can't afford to travel*," I suggest you take another look. You can stay at expensive hotels and eat at high end restaurants, but that lifestyle is hard to maintain for long periods. If the experience of the experience is worth living a less lavish lifestyle for short periods, then you, too, CAN Travel Younger. Being a TRAVELER is much more rewarding than being a TOURIST.

02.17.20/ One Year After Leaving the US: The Top 10 Memories and Experiences

As we approach our one year anniversary of leaving the US last February 17, I asked Kathleen to share her best memories and experiences. To keep this fair (and brief), she came up with her top FIVE and I did the same. They are in no particular order and most of them have been addressed in greater detail in my Travel Younger blog.

Cool stuff to know...

1. Climbing down the hill at Cabo da Roca, Portugal (August 2018)

While Kathleen and I were still in our, "can we do this?" research mode, we spent six weeks exploring Spain and Portugal. Just north of Lisbon is Cabo da Roca, which is the furthest west point in Portugal as well as the continent of Europe AND of the Eurasian land mass. It was a beautiful location with a huge lighthouse and great view. From the top of the hill you could see down to the beach below, which appeared to be quite the climb, as the people at the bottom looked the size of ants. Like a couple of crazy people, we decided to hike down the next day, and it was breathtaking. However, the hike was more treacherous than expected and we forgot to take extra water. Kathleen was dealing with some dehydration and a lovely couple from Poland offered us a bottle of theirs as we headed up. The hill was quite steep, and Kathleen froze with fear. She was literally holding on to the roots of plants on the side of a small mountain and could not move up or down. I guided her moves one step at a time, she practiced her breathing and eventually we got to a safe place where we could stand upright and feel safety. Kathleen admits it was one of the scariest moments in her life, but she proved her strength in getting back to the top, but will probably never do it again!

2. A two-hour massage in Budapest- for $20 USD (August 2019)

Not all experiences are life threatening or momentous. Sometimes they are smaller things, the finer things of life. Kathleen tried to get massages at many of our stops since traveling can be hard on the body, plus they are so much cheaper than in the US. You win some, you lose some, but when she left her two-hour massage with a grin from ear to ear and only spent $20, it was a moment she relished for a long time.

3. Santorini Island, Greece (date: 12.29.19)

You've seen pictures of Santorini and we took lots of them, but the beauty of Santorini is impossible to collect. The former volcano has a caldera that is hard to take in, with incredible colors. Combine that with structures built almost vertical into the hill and you have the picture of Magic. Add to that the pristine December day we were there, which was unseasonably warm, and Santorini, after only two days, left an indelible mark.

4. The Transfagarasan Highway, Romania (date: 08.15.19)

We rented several scooters and small cycles during our travels, but Romania, with majestic hills and spectacular roads with hairpin turns, required a bigger bike. We rented a BMW 750, which was larger than normal, but on the Transfagarasan Highway it was a blessing. Of the hundreds of amazing roads I have ridden on a bike, this beat them all. Miles and miles of twisty turns, panoramic views, and little traffic, made for a fantastic day, and we even got a hotel room on the fly and played more the following day. This was a special day for both of us.

5. The Acropolis, Athens (date: December 2019)

We heard mixed reviews about Athens and were not expecting to like it as much as we did. Kathleen loved all of it...from the unique little shops, great pastries, and amazing history throughout the city, to the Acropolis, where the Parthenon sits and is breathtaking. But for her it was much more; she also fell in love with the colorful graffiti artwork that covered the city. The hike up the Acropolis was reasonable, and the monuments and temples were in amazing condition, undergoing constant renovations since 1975. Considering the stone and pillars are over 2,000 years old, they look wonderful. We were all taught Roman and Greek mythology in school and have probably seen many movies, so it's not hard to fire up the imagination and see Zeus and Athena and Apollo and Aphrodite playing up there!

Norm's list:

1. Las Fallas, Valencia, Spain (date: 03.10.19)

Valencia was our very first leg of this one-year old journey, and it started out with a bang! We were rattled awake at 0800 on the first Sunday morning after our arrival by the sound of what appeared to be bombing! It turned out to be fireworks and the beginning of an annual event in Valencia called **Las Fallas**- the Fires. It celebrates their patron, St. Joseph, and the end of winter, and is one month long and filled with noise! Daily fireworks downtown at 3:00, plus kids of all ages throwing firecrackers in the street make for an auditory overload. But that was overcome by the Ninotes, which are enormous (up to 70' high) statues and artwork with caricatures of people, animals, musical instruments, and you name it! The creativity of the ninotes is a competition with over 300 of them on every street corner, which culminates on the last night by burning them. Yup, in the street with people everywhere, they are ignited with firecrackers, then erupt into flame which the fire department keeps under control. We had no idea of this event, but over one million people come into town during the month, so as noisy and irritating as it was, it left an indelible mark.

2. The rainstorm in Croatia

In Zagreb, Croatia, we rented another BMW and headed west to the coast, about 3.5 hours away. The day started nice, got overcast by hour one, then on hour two the clouds blew in, the thunder erupted, the lightning flashed, and the heavens poured upon us! Again, **so good** to have a big, stable bike! As soon as the rain began we passed a farmhouse with a carport, so pulled into their drive, hunkered under that roof, and waited. It was August, but cold, and it took a long time before the rain let up. The lovely older couple that lived there kindly invited us in for coffee to warm us, but they spoke no English and I had a meager memory of German, so that was our half-assed attempt at communicating. Again, Kathleen was amazing, kept her cool in the rain, and we made it to the coast, which was worth the trouble.

3. Romania: roads, food, and people

We didn't intend to visit Romania, but changed direction towards eastern Europe to avoid the holiday crowds and expenses. We stayed in Brasov for about three weeks, had a nice BMW for about 10 of those days, and enjoyed the hell out of the twisty roads and the joy of passing traffic that was sitting still. Add in the food, which was amazing every time we enjoyed it, and polish it off with the people who were genuinely friendly, kind, and hospitable. We became friends with our AirBNB hosts who invited us to their home for a BBQ and a two-hour horse and buggy ride through the hills. It felt like a movie and we both left Brasov (along with three or four other Romanian locations) with great memories.

4. The Palermo, Sicily ferry to Tunis, Tunisia (date: 12.07.19)

As we arrived at the Palermo port on foot, cars were driving in and loading on the ferry, and boy, were they loaded! Many Tunisians come to Italy and bring back everything they can't get back home, including some kitchen sinks! The ferry ride was packed with people and families sleeping everywhere-- including outside our room. The traveling Muslims held their group prayers throughout the day and the entire ride was beautiful. When we finally disembarked, late, it was our first time in

Africa and an Arab country, and this was a total shock to both of us. Again, the people there were wonderful, curious about us as we were about them, and making efforts to communicate. No doubt, that ferry ride was a "never forget" experience.

I don't get excited by too many things, nor let things get me down very often, but the experiences above sometimes brought out the child in me. This past year has been one of adventure, change and pushing ourselves outside our comfort zones. The world is vast and so different everywhere, yet people are mostly the same. Can't wait for more of the same and more different and to share it with all of you.

Meanwhile, here's my #5

5. Marina Bay Sands hotel, Singapore (date: 01.03.20)

I remember seeing this hotel profiled in a video and was blown away. The Marina Bay Sands is iconic since the roof is shaped like a ship and connects three individual towers. The roof has an infinity pool on floor 55 with an impressive observation deck. The entire structure and complex houses shopping areas plus a convention center, and amongst all the other beautiful buildings in Singapore, I think this is the coolest. Taking the elevator to the top floor was combined with wonder and curiosity of what it would look like and it did not disappoint! The view of the harbor was surreal, and we got a bird's eye overview of all the other amazing buildings in Singapore. And to have this happen on New Year's Day, 2020, made it even more special.

With 21 countries and 93,150 km (58,800 miles for you Westerners!) behind us, those are our collective Top 10 memories and experiences of 2019; hope you enjoyed reliving them with us.

Date: 02.25.20/ Thailand: Land of Many "Firsts"

We have been in Thailand for almost two months and in a few more days will be heading back to the US. Thailand has been a country of contradictions and extremes. From the high-tech, high energy vibe of Bangkok, to the quiet, tranquil rural communities where Thai citizens live in shanties with few amenities. No question, Southeast Asia has been more challenging than any place I have ever visited and has nge of emotions and concerns. From the chaos, crowds, and pollution in Bangkok, to the mellow beaches of Chumphon and other rural areas, it has made me appreciate the beauty of the world as well as be thankful for the life I have lived and continue to live.

Cool stuff to know...

Meanwhile, here are some firsts in Thailand:

- Driving on the left side of the street: it's one thing sitting in the back seat of a cab, but different when you are *in* the fray on a tiny bike! The first night we rented a bike in Chiang Mai I was nervous and uncomfortable driving on the left side, but after 24 hours it was easier. A few weeks later we rented another bike in Chumphon and it soon became as natural to drive on the left as on the right. By the way, the whole experience of **renting** was a bit surreal! When I brought the bike back later than planned it was no big deal and they had little worry over miles ridden or the cleanliness of the bike when returned. Thailand is as chill as *any* place I have ever rented!
- My first jungle: I have been in heavily wooded areas, but never in a true, dense, sticky jungle! Driving through the rural areas I always kept a look out for wild animals- especially monkeys- and we were lucky enough to come across them several times.
- Speaking of wild animals, we saw thousands of wild, untethered dogs, in the rural areas of Thailand. They are called "wild", but they were not aggressive, but instead, seemed timid and unaccustomed to human interference. In some places the locals put food out for them, which we thought was great, but our hearts were broken to see how tough life was for them. Skin and bones, flea infested and seeing them not happy, was tough for both of us.
- Elephants! These wild animals were more fun since we got to feed and bathe them. We chose not to ride them since some say that is "inhumane," but I'm not

so sure. The weight of a human is paltry compared to the strength they have, and as long as they are treated humanely, I think riding them is fine. We missed our chance but hope to have another.
- Being destroyed by sand fleas at the beach. We spent 10 days at a remote beach cottage with few amenities (we did have A/C) and as nice as the beach was, it was still infested with bugs. It seems that some beaches are sprayed, but not where we were. I'm pretty lucky that most bugs, except mosquitoes, leave me alone, but I admit that I was so bit up that scratching almost brought on fits of ecstasy!
- Street food took some getting used to and after 60 days we were much more comfortable eating it. Our criteria was the cleanliness of the cooking area, getting a sense of how fresh the food was, and how long it may have been sitting out. Some come to Thailand, and specifically Bangkok, *for* the street food, but that is not enough of a draw to bring me back.
- Beach living: Thailand is a mecca for ex-pats and digital nomads who brag about sitting on the beach working on their phones and laptops and living an idyllic life. It seemed a bit of a fantasy, but our 10 days at the beach came close to a dream come true. The price of living in such an isolated spot and still being able to function, work and be accessible, was a treat and that one I **would** return to.

Our Travel Younger life is now 12 months and counting. During these 365 days, that included 21 countries, over 300 cities, almost 100,000 kilometers and thousands of new experiences involving food, places, and people. We have been asked: "*How long will you do this?*" and the answer remains the same: "*As long as it's fun.*" Kathleen and I have been very blessed in that we have had no significant challenges that gave us pause. We did have two medical emergencies that required a hospital visit, but they were both minor and treatable and lasted just a short while. Meanwhile, just as we are ready to leave this part of the world, there is another threat that we have chosen to be wary and cautious of, but not paranoid about, and that is the Coronavirus, the COVID-19, that has taken the world by storm.

Many have asked if we are worried or afraid and the answer is "no." We **are** careful and aware, but our biggest concern has been potential travel interruptions and cancelled flights. I will share more about our experiences on that in another entry.

Date: 03.02.20/ Next stop(s): Leaving Cambodia, Thailand, etc…

With just three more flights to go, it looks like we will be able to leave Southeast Asia and return to the US. **We were never worried, but we were worried…** Not about getting sick, but about flight cancellations and increasing levels of threat protection in different countries from the growing Coronavirus Pandemic. I'll get to that in a moment, meanwhile there's Cambodia and Angkor Wat!

Angkor Wat was not what we expected, but it was not disappointing. Just the opposite. It is the largest religious structure on Earth, and just one of the temples encompasses almost 500 acres. Initially we thought it was just one temple, but found out that there are over 70 different ones of various sizes.

We had a room just outside of the downtown Siem Reap area, and it was a bit of an oasis among chaos. We had a nice room, with bath, swimming pool and a well-equipped cafe. But as soon as we left the front door, there was crazy traffic, vendors, and tuk-tuk drivers waiting at our beck and call. Not chaos traffic like Bangkok, since this is much, much smaller, but with hundreds of small scooters flittering around everywhere, many carrying little pre-school age children sitting, standing, or held in the driver's arms. I never quite got used to that!

We met some Americans who had been there for a few days and they taught us what shortcuts to take. They suggested hiring a driver for the day and frugal me initially balked at that, but I realized that there was great value in saving time, inconvenience, and not walking around aimlessly. Make a note of that folks! Due to low currency valuation, it was still cheap.

Cambodia is an impoverished country. We saw that the people struggle to get by, and without Angkor Wat, Siem Reap would be in the middle of nowhere with no reason to visit. Like most of Cambodia. But the people are genuinely kind, friendly and try to communicate in English. American dollars or Euros go a long, long way and they deal in US dollars *more than their native currency*. For what we paid for our lodging and food we could stay there for a month on about $800 USD.

I will be doing a recap on our entire Southeast Asia trip, but considering that we stayed in Singapore, Thailand, Vietnam, and Cambodia over a 2-month period, my overall impression is positive. Aside from Bangkok being too smoggy and too crowded, most of this area is really quite lovely. The heat can be oppressive and the bugs and mosquitoes can be a nuisance, but overall, I give it a big thumbs up.

As for the Coronavirus, that has made traveling unpredictable. It is precarious and if we had a flight home via Rome (Italy has been quarantined…), a common transfer, who knows what might have happened? Some airlines are cancelling up to 80% of their flights and I **think** our flight to Singapore tomorrow morning might be one of them.

We cannot get any information online so will get to the Bangkok airport tomorrow five hours early in case we need to book another flight. The good news is that our original $70 flight is now under $40 due to less demand.

Travel Younger will continue and this new paradigm (which **will** pass) will teach you how to make lemonade from this lemon.

Date: 04.11.20/ Places We ALMOST Visited!

Since we can now only travel virtually on TV, watching movies, in our imaginations or from past experiences, I thought I'd dig into the memory banks and look back at places that we had intentions (or opportunities) to visit, but it didn't work out.

Morocco was the first country that we almost made it to, but ran out of time. We were in Spain and Portugal and took a bus from the west coast of Portugal (Lagos) through Sevilla, Spain, and then to Gibraltar, where we spent the day taking the cable car to the top of the rock. We were just a breath away from Morocco, 36 miles via ferry, and we actually wish we spent more time in Gibraltar itself and added a trip to Africa. This leg was part of our initial six-week trek in Aug-Sept 2018, before we started Traveling Younger, but it opened our eyes to places to return to. (We did get to Africa earlier this year, visiting Tunisia)

Our train from Vienna, Austria to **Warsaw**, Poland involved separate rails, and this was when we learned that our Eurail tickets could not be reserved in advance, but only validated in person. We got to the train station early for a 10:30 train, but even so, it was sold out. Plan B was a detour to Krakow, then switch trains and head to Warsaw from there. Instead of taking the a.m. train, this new ride didn't leave until late afternoon which would put us into Warsaw too late to check in. Plus, we had another unexpected delay as the train stopped to switch engines along the way and we sat there for several hours until we resumed. There were few passengers, but we struck up conversations about Plan C, since we now missed the *new* train from Krakow, too. Instead, we all took a bus, got into Krakow late, and found a lovely room which we rented for three days. Since Auschwitz is Krakow proximate, the visit I wasn't sure I could make seemed like an obvious alternative.

We cancelled Warsaw, which was not a loss to me since I had been there, (but cost us about $300), and instead stayed in Krakow and loved it. The people and the food were amazing, and this was one more example of the Universe creating a better plan than the original.

Slovenia, which is sandwiched between Croatia, Italy, and Austria, was just a few miles away while on a motorcycle trip from Zagreb, Croatia to Rijeka, on the west coast. The three-hour ride was spectacular and as we traversed the Slovenia/Croatia border we saw signs that showed how close it was, just 15 km. But the weather was not our friend that day! Along the way we got hit by a torrential "the sky is falling" rainstorm, and we had to hide out under a carport while it passed. Meanwhile, we were drenched and chilled even though it was August, and concerned about more rain and pending nightfall. We wanted to get to Rijeka before dark since it makes finding our way around a strange town much easier, so Slovenia got bypassed.

Of course the next day the weather cleared, and it was beautiful, so we stayed an extra day in town and then took the highway (rather than the back way), back to Zagreb since we had to return the bike. Slovenia still beckons and we will return.

Turkey, twice. Once just in conversation, that almost got serious, but the second time we had real flight tickets from Krakow, Poland to Turkey. It involved two flights, two countries, and two different carriers, and the second leg had us flying through Kharkiv Airport in Kiev onward to Istanbul. Neither of us had done any research about Russia or Kiev, but when Kathleen started reading US Embassy warnings about Russia and the Ukraine, she got uncomfortable.

We've seen Embassy warnings before and they can be intimidating and scary, so when we read that *"The US will not help you if you get into trouble..."* that gave us pause.

Mind you, our spying days are behind us, but it made us feel uncomfortable and canceled our flight, so we never made it to Turkey. I heard good things about it and find that warnings from those who have **never** been there, ring hollow, and the opinions of those who *live there* or *have visited* carry more weight.

When we arrived in Singapore on New Year's Day of 2020 we knew we'd only be there for three days since we had a flight to Thailand after that. **Malaysia** was only 21 km to the border, but would require a bus or train and with tight timetables we usually don't have much play for play time. We heard great things about Malaysia (again) and much of SE Asia is still appealing, but will have to wait till who knows when.

Date: 04.18.20/ To Cook or Not to Cook

I thought I'd explore the question of "Do we (or can we) cook, or shall we eat out?" That question specifically pertains to our traveling days, on hold for now...

| Cool stuff to know... |

Imagine having to ask yourself that question 37 times over a 14-month period, since that is how many different places we stayed from Feb 17, 2019, until our current hangout in Puerto Morelos, Mexico. At some locations, including hotels, eating in was not an option since they offered none, and some had small kitchens, but they were impractical for anything beyond reheating or pulling something easy from the fridge.

Our first stop was Valencia, Spain for six weeks, which had an awesome kitchen. Normally it was breakfast at home, maybe an afternoon snack, and dinner out most of the time. The kitchen had plenty of room to cook and counter space to boot. Our next stop, Tivoli, Italy, had a tiny, tiny kitchen and our entire place was really only one large room, which we called "The Cave." We did a surprisingly good job cooking pastas followed by some wine, which we were able to appreciate for about $2.00 a bottle. Croatia was stop #3, with an even smaller kitchen and an electromagnetic stove that I **hated** and always caused me fits. Access to a few great restaurants and coffee shops within five minutes' walk made cooking at home less appealing. It also did take us long to realize that eating out was sometimes cheaper or cheaper than eating in.

Fast forward through a series of quickie stops and usually a small kitchen we didn't use, if they had one at all. By this time we were in Eastern Europe, including Romania, Serbia, and Poland, where the restaurant food was unbelievably reasonable.

Sicily was our next six weeks long term stop and we were able to appreciate a great kitchen in our oceanfront unit in Siracusa, plus a farmer's market with fresh food- and fish- within a 10-minute walk. Again, wine was cheap, so we enjoyed that along with fresh salmon, pasta, and veggies. From there it was two more short trips to Tunisia and Greece, and it wasn't until Bangkok that we stayed somewhere long enough to consider cooking. But this lovely unit on the 36th floor of a luxury high-rise was **not** set up for gourmands! The kitchen could fit into a bathroom and consisted of a hot plate, fridge, and microwave. It really didn't matter since the ease of street food made that the best and most practical option for dinner. A Pad Thai dinner just a 10-minute walk away cost 60 Baht, about $1.84 USD. The picture you see here is our miniscule kitchen.

Along the way we bought *some* items to make eating/ drinking more enjoyable, including a high-end Nespresso milk frother (for coffee), which we carted around for a while until it was time to leave it behind. Along the way we had to leave a fair amount of food behind, but that's just the way it is.

But now we're in Puerto Morelos, Mexico, more or less "stuck" here, but it's actually a good place to be stuck. We have an awesome kitchen and since we **are** here for the long-ish haul, we bought a toaster oven, crockpot, coffee maker and other kitchen doodads to make life more comfortable and cooking easier. Kathleen has gotten into serious cooking mode since she has found a "nest" for the first time in a while and I get to be the beneficiary of her skills!

Date: 05.09.20/ Next stop: Why I Got SOLD on Mexico!

My 40 years of living in Southern California did not tempt me into living in Mexico, but I knew that the border towns of Tijuana and Rosarito were not truly representative of what the country was like. A few trips to Cabo San Lucas decades ago, along with Puerta Vallarta once, did not sway me either, even though I knew there was a **huge** draw for Americans to live there. Since we were not looking to "live" anywhere, we stayed on the European and Asian side of the world and liked it just fine. I have Eastern European roots and my Mother was born there, so I felt comfortably uncomfortable. Affordable, nice weather, great people and access to water hit all my needs.

Then COVID.

Were it not for a wedding in Ohio in March we would now probably be in Europe somewhere, but since we were coming to the States, followed by a business trip to Florida, the plan was to move along quickly. Kathleen had friends in Puerto Morelos, about 30 minutes south of Cancun, and we were due to hang out here for two weeks. Now two weeks is six, and six weeks will surely turn into six **months**, maybe longer. I am getting to like Mexico, and maybe even more. Here's why.

- The Water (Ocean). Aside from the beach being **closed**, which is only temporary, it's still just a 20-minute bike ride away or a $1.25 taxi ride. The water here is the most radiant turquoise I have ever seen, and I have seen many beaches over the past few years. The water temp has *just* enough cool to make it fun, but it will get warmer as we get into summer. I am told *no* jellyfish and no sea urchins, so that's a big plus! We're pretty far south and the water temperature doesn't fluctuate more than a few degrees all year, ditto the length of days. Sunrise happens between 6:11 and 7:27 (approx.) all year, and sunset fluctuates about an hour on both sides of 7:00 p.m. They do not "spring forward" so we are permanently on Eastern time, but it's really Central time.
- The Cost of Living. We stayed in Thailand, Cambodia, Vietnam, Serbia, Poland, and a few other very affordable places in the world, but this is actually better than all of them. Grocery food (and alcohol) is very affordable, along with utilities and rent. We were aware of the drinking water issue, so we get a 20 liter bottle every 10 days or so, which is less than a buck, with tip. And we don't worry about using tap water for cooking, coffee, or bathing. I had to get front

- and rear brakes on a bike I bought for $40 USD and that cost me about $6.50, which would have been many times that in the states.
- The People and Language. Let's face it, these are trying times, but I sense no bad juju from any of the locals. They are quick to smile, and many have a basic understanding of English, which helps a lot. Forty years in So Cal gives **me** a rudimentary Spanish vocabulary and I waiver back and forth on taking my Duolingo lessons. Truth is, I really don't have the passion or desire to LEARN, even though I have the desire to SPEAK. We'll see which one wins that battle. But since we can't go **out** to eat we have a list of delivery places who communicate well on WhatsApp, the worldwide phone and text app of choice, so that's a plus. Every meal we've had has been great including an amazing Sweet & Sour Chinese food dish that I got three meals out of. The price? Cheaper than a Starbucks coffee, which thank goodness they do not have here.

Along with that, there are lots of Canadians and Americans, too. We haven't been able to socialize with many yet, but we will.

- The Weather. It's hot, even warm, and humid, about 70%, so that's an adjustment. But we dealt with the same thing in the Far East. Here we are blessed to have a decent breeze most of the days and just a few insect issues. They seem to find Kathleen tastier than me, so I guess they don't want Kosher! We see monkeys playing in the trees several times a week, including from our bedroom window, which is cool, and iguanas rule here, too, though I've only seen a few. There is a morning chorus of birds just before sunrise and that is a great melody to wake up to.
- Getting in Shape. It's not *Mexico* that is giving me time, but since we are warned to **stay home**, we do, although I do a bike ride several days a week, and at 0630 the temp is still good. We have a second bedroom which is now a gym, so I do daily workouts along with daily meditation, so staying Zen. My blood pressure has been an issue for several years and I was on meds, but my BP is down 30 points, so take them less often. Sweet!
- History at our back door. This is the land of the Mayans, Aztecs, and Incas, who created amazing civilizations and buildings many centuries ago. Their culture can compare to Egypt, Rome, and Greece, with temples and buildings completed without modern tools and technology. Mind blowing. Plus there are dozens of "cenotes" just a few miles from us, which are underground caves filled with water for swimming and snorkeling.

Life is what happens when you're busy making other plans, so I guess that's what's happening here. Our "plans" got sidetracked, but opened up Central and South America sooner, and we're close enough to the US to have friends visit, so it's all good, plus just eight hours from Europe and five hours from California, both great options.

Date: 05.23.20/ Cenotes: So Much Fun

e experienced one of the more unique attractions of the Yucatan Peninsula—cenotes.

Many believe that the giant meteor that wiped out the dinosaurs 66 million years ago generated so much heat and debris that it formed a huge underground cave and water system in this area. BTW, that meteor hit just a few hundred miles from here, so I figure we're safe because, hey, what are the odds??

The soft limestone bed in this area is very water soluble (it used to be underwater, so much of it is dead coral), and forms underground caves and sinkholes of various sizes and closeness to the surface. These are not limited to Mexico, but they say there are more than 6000 on the Peninsula, and we have dozens within 50 miles of us. Some of these underground systems go for hundreds of miles, though not all are accessible and then only with scuba tanks, but those will have to wait. With some digging I learned that two of the longest underground aquifers in the world are here in Mexico, one 353 km long and the other 270 km long. These waterways were huge contributors to the growth of Mayan civilizations during the past 13,000 years.

I had never been to one, though Kathleen had, and I was taken back by the beautiful underground cavern filled with cool/ cold water that was probably 66⁰ F. or so, just a bit chilly. Fern and lichen grow around the perimeter of the holes down to the water, and the one we visited, Cenote Oja de Agua, had four different entry points, including some that were "jump only" access! (27 feet or so they **say**...)

I wasn't quite ready for that, so instead entered in through one of the others. The water color is hard to describe and varied between aquamarine and greenish depending upon how the sunlight struck it. The grounds were lovely, with cabanas strewn around to hang out, chairs to lie in and changing rooms, showers, and bathrooms. The jungle was everywhere and as "modern" as it was, it was still a very rustic, wild setting.

This was a family owned, private cenote and not open to the public during the "off season," which will last until next fall. We met a fabulous local tour guide, Martin, who knows all the best spots. He shared this one and we have more journeys planned so we can catch up on our Adventure Shortage. BTW, these cenotes are magical to the Mayan culture, and many believed they were access points to their "underworld," where their Gods lived, and spirits went after death.

Outside media: (published stories)

Supplemental #1: 07.22.19, Total Croatia News- <u>A Digital Nomad Reflects on 63 Glorious Days in Croatia</u>

I guess I had to face the truth: I WAS a Digital Nomad, just like the kids!

Supplemental #2: 06.02.20, Perceptive Travel article: <u>*Beating a Hasty Retreat from the USA in a Private 737 Airliner*</u>

I feel proud that Perceptive Travel, one of the leading travel web sites, has chosen my article to include in their June issue. They get submissions worldwide and pick only three per month, so that humbles me.

It shares our journey as we were "chased" by the COVID-19 virus throughout Southeast Asia, and stayed just one step ahead of border closings! That continued even in the US as we had concerns about getting to Mexico (we did) as solo passengers on our own Boeing 737 aircraft.

Supplemental #3: 6.17.20, Newport Beach Independent article: **<u>A Newport Nomad in the Pandemic Age</u>**

I lived in Newport Beach, California for several years before we left on our Travel Younger journey. As the pandemic changed our plans, along with everyone else's, I was able to share with my old hometown readers.

Date: 07.18.20/ Is it Time to Consider Leaving your Country?

We're called expats or ex-pats or expatriates, but they all mean the same thing; we are people who have specifically chosen to leave the country where we lived. Sometimes it is the country where we were born, sometimes we were there because of family or business circumstances, or a host of miscellaneous reasons. But the reality is, unless you live in a communist country, and forced to remain (which is pretty rare), most people are not *obligated* to stay where they are. We do not live in a prison (usually), but live in a very flat world. Covid-19 notwithstanding, travel is so easy compared to what it was decades ago, and people have been leaving their countries for many years.

If you go back to caveman days, many of them were wanderers, usually for more food or better temperatures. Over the centuries explorers of well-renown (and not) wandered for glory and riches or for a better life. That's how the Pilgrims got to America 400 years ago. In the United States, people were told to, "Go west, young man!" and many did, and in the 1950's Jack Kerouac wrote "On the Road" which espoused the adventure of life on the road.

The truth is you don't need to *live* "on the road," and you can live in many other countries.

This conversation came up due to an email I got from a friend in Las Vegas who said that friends were asking about *where* in the world that she would recommend moving if you were a "spoiled American." And unfortunately, many of them/us, are... So she asked me that question and I have *lots* of ideas!

Important Traveling Info

Kathleen and I "think" that *scores* of "Angry Americans" will consider or are considering bailing out of the US and here's why. Without getting political, that *is* a big incentive. America is *not* what I grew up with 40-50 years ago, and there is too much BS for this Baby Boomer to deal with. I also sense an underlying anger and resentment going on and I believe that arrogance is prevalent.

Economics is another reason since we can (and do), live in many places for a fraction of what it costs in the US, and especially, Southern California. Yes, we may be *"spoiled,"* but you need not give up the creature comforts! I told her that I didn't think her inquiring friends were "nuts" and may be more sane than those that remain!

When I reflect about where in the world to go, here's some points to consider on what **kinds** of country to consider:

- First world countries, like Italy, Spain, Portugal, etc... We have been to all and started the visa process for Spain, which did not work out. These are top notch countries and except for language and currency might feel like "home" -with a lot more history.
- Second world countries, like some of the former Eastern Bloc nations. Some examples: Croatia (LOVE, loved it!), Romania, very cool, etc... These countries offer most of what the civilized world requires, but sometimes mindsets are old-fashioned, mass transit may be questionable, and access to some things may be more difficult. Even so, these places are cheaper than the US by as much as 50%. Much of South and Central America fits in here, and food has been exceptional in these places!
- Developing nations. This one is more difficult to put a finger on, but Mexico, where we are currently, is more this than Second World. We have very civilized places, like larger cities, and we have small villages with nothing. Thailand and Cambodia reminded me of this and I'm not sure which category they "officially" belong in. Living expenses there can be 75% cheaper than the US...

Our town of Puerto Morelos is a major draw for Americans and especially, Canadians. We can afford to rent a 2 br apartment and stay at the beach 2 days a week for a fraction of my Orange County (CA) rent.

This may be one of the more controversial blogs I have written, but know that I am and always will be an American, born and raised. But quality of life and determining my own fate and direction is my decision alone. Yours is your decision alone.

Date: 08.11.20/ Top Ten (10) Most *AMAZING* Places We have Been; 10 Most *MEMORABLE* Places We have Been

Kathleen and I were reminiscing about some of the amazing and memorable EXPERIENCES we have had since we met and started traveling in January 2018, even before we began the *real* journey 13 months later in February 2019. That triggered a conversation about the difference between a place that is/was AMAZING vs. one that was MEMORABLE. Some places are BOTH, but there were only a few experiences that either choked me up, brought a tear or had me staring in wonder—those are AMAZING—and they are infrequent.

We agreed that some experiences hit **both** marks, some just one, so we listed the ones that fit in either category. Since NO ONE (including us), is currently traveling, it's fun reflecting, reminiscing, and living vicariously through our own memories and of others.

While we watch the world carry on and virus numbers go up and down, see airplane flights offered, then canceled, and wonder, "WHEN will the madness end?" please enjoy! (To keep this brief, some of the experiences from both of us have been combined)

Cool stuff to know…

Norm's Amazing List:

1. Transfagarasan Highway, Romania: 90 km (56 miles) of the most jaw dropping scenery I have ever seen. It reaches an elevation of 6700 ft (2042 meters), then enters a **very** dark 2900 foot long tunnel with barely enough light to see. The scope and panorama I will never forget.
2. La Sagrada Familia (Anton Gaudi cathedral, Barcelona): This was man-made, but surely God inspired, as Anton Gaudi started construction in 1882 and it's **almost** done! Imagine spirals and colors and staircases from an MC Escher

picture, and that is what you see. Add gargoyles, Biblical figurines, and mind blowing stained glass and you have **maybe** a hint of this place.
3. Marina Bay Sands Hotel, Singapore: We landed at 0300 New Year's Day (2020) and wandered the streets of high rise buildings and architecture that took my breath away. The city was pristine, almost deserted, and felt personal. The hotel (the one with the "ship" on top), was magnificent in its' opulence, and from the roof, the boats in the harbor looked like toys.
4. Ponta da Piedade cliffs in Lagos, Portugal: We hit Spain and Portugal in Aug-Sept 2018 when we were questioning if we **could** make the move overseas. The cliffs were spectacular, and knowing we could visit them any time made that possibility all pretty enticing. The town itself was (and is) a contender for places we might want to **live** for a spell, too.
5. Monaco, very man-made, very artificial, but jaw dropping. On a motorbike, mid-January, the town was eerily quiet, like a vacant movie set. The streets, buildings, everything, was **pristine** and felt SOOO fake. The Land of Royalty, Grand Prix street races, casinos visited by multi-gazillionaires--and James Bond-- **had** to be surreal—and amazing, and it was.
6. Las Fallas event, Valencia, Spain: The beginning of spring in this city and the noisiest 30 days I ever experienced! Daily fireworks and constant turmoil. You can read more about it in blog #10 from March 2019.
7. Sicily, Italy: Our second stay in Italy, in a beautiful place with the waves crashing across the street. Add in the farmer's market with fresh salmon several days a week, fantastic and cheap wine every night, and a very walkable town with restaurants and coffee shops galore. Plus the visited cities of Ragusa, Taormina, and Agrigento and even the crazy driving town of Palermo; yup, all amazing.
8. Getting **back** from Southeast Asia via Cambodia, Bangkok, Singapore, Taipei to Los Angeles. Five major flights over four days, with each one in jeopardy of being cancelled! We **could** have been stranded in Bangkok or Singapore, but made it back to the US, then MEXICO, as the **only** passengers on a Delta flight from Ohio to Cancun, Mexico. Scary **and** amazing!
9. The Amalfi Coast, Italy: We were back seat passengers while someone drove, so I could focus on the views instead of the road. We spent two days in Positano and Sorrento and were awed by **how** those buildings were constructed on the vertical cliff faces. It wasn't beach weather, but the water was incredible, and also amazing all the way!
10. Hungary was Amazing since my Mother was born there and during her whole life she wanted me to join her to visit her hometown and Budapest. Hearing Hungarian spoken around me our first morning brought tears—and regrets—for not accepting her invite. Even so, the town, the buildings, and the bridges were spectacular.

Kat's Amazing List:

1. Santorini, Greece

2. The Amalfi Coast, Italy

3. Angkor Wat, Cambodia

4. KRKA Falls, Croatia: An experience that immerses you in water as you wander along walkways, over streams and eventually come into open areas with a vista of waterfalls. A nature's paradise that we were lucky enough to swim in, which has since been banned.

5. The Acropolis, Greece: From the bottom looking up to the top looking down, everything within eyesight takes your breath away. The history, beauty, and magnificence of the size of the columns and statues are must see.

6. Tivoli, Italy gardens

7. Lagos, PT, cliffs

8. Sicily towns on the hillside

9. Valley of the Temples, Sicily

10. Cave Bar, Menorca: Imagine a bar where you enter into a cave, walk downstairs, and exit within the cliff hundreds of feet above the rampaging ocean. THAT is the Cave Bar, an iconic location that made Menorca even more amazing.

Norm's Memorable List:

1. The island of Menorca, Spain, was memorable in several places, including coves with crystal water, rock faces and clothing optional beaches. We stayed there 10 days in Sept 2018, and concluded we **could** make the move overseas.
2. Sintra Castle, Portugal, north of Lisbon. We loved all of Portugal and this castle, pulled from a Disney "land," was trippy. Very colorful, lots of history and we were able to get there on a scooter, bypassing all the traffic sitting in long lines. Sweet. That helped us visualize how amazing it would be to *live* over there!
3. Santorini Island, Greece. Take a look at blog #69 to understand why…
4. Villas Gregoriana, d'Este and Adriana, Tivoli, Italy. I wrote an article on Tivoli called "The Land of Three Villas" and each of these was unique, very historic, and beautiful beyond words.
5. Getting caught in torrential downpour on a BMW 750 in Croatia on our way to Rijeka, and waiting it out under the carport of an old Romanian couple's home. Not cool, but very cool!

6. Monkeys in Angkor Wat, Cambodia, which just added to the experience of the history that was before us to be climbed upon. This was our last major visit before returning to the US, barely staying ahead of COVID.
7. Auschwitz Concentration Camp, Poland. Memorable because my Mom spent three years there, and to walk the grounds and see the torture in person was emotionally shattering.
8. Belgrade, Serbia was a quick visit and even though the city seems a bit mired in the past, it was very cool as we walked along the Danube river, stayed in a houseboat AirBNB, wandered over to (another) amazing castle, and had food which made my mouth water!
9. We wanted to add Africa as another continent to our list and the Palermo (IT) ferry to Tunisia did the trick. It was an overnight, surreal Twilight Zone experience with people sleeping everywhere, including outside our hotel room! The trip was memorable, as was our 10 days in Tunis, which we loved in so many ways.
10. Besalu Castle, Spain. I had a surreal and spiritual experience as I *felt* pain and suffering of those who lived—and died—there, and sat in the street and cried for five minutes without understanding why. The city, just outside of Barcelona, was the first castle/ city I ever visited and it was uber cool.

Kat's Memorable List:

1. Amazing two hour Thai massage for only $20: From the moment I walked in, the serenity, the people, the aroma all drew me in and I learned to love affordable massages taught by those offering these services for decades and more! All for a fraction of the cost in America.

2. Opening the shutters and viewing the La Sagrada Familia in Barcelona (our AirBNB room)

3. Motorcycle ride on the French Rivera. Imagine being in a movie set from the fifties, just cruising along the French Riviera on a bike, looking at islands and the water below you. Memorable? Hell yes!

4. The Ferry Ride experience from Sicily to Africa

5. Cabo de Roca (PT), climb down the mountain. This is the western most point of Portugal and Europe and the cliff went down to an inviting beach we just had to get to. But, danger encroached as the steepness was more than we expected and we had to crawl up the side of the hill grasping roots, plus we did not have enough water and the exhaustion took its toll. But it did have a happy ending and was a memorable experience.

6. Cambodia fish pedicure. We've always wanted to try this, but never had the chance, and were not prepared to be tickled to laughter by tiny fish nibbling on our feet! After we adjusted to the sensation we were happy for the experience that cost us all of $4 apiece.

7. Deserted beach in Thailand. Everyone needs to spend 14 days at an almost vacant beach bungalow and even though it was **not** an island, it was like our own private paradise with pano views, amazing seashells, jellyfish, and we will never forget, the most aggressive sand fleas ever!

8. Transfagarasan highway, Romania

9. The infinity pool and gym overlooking Bangkok. How often do you stand over the city of Bangkok from the top of a 42-story building watching the city lights and traffic below you? All while standing in an infinity pool. And the price was $394 USD per month, not per night!

10. Auschwitz

What will the next 10 experiences bring?? Within Central and South America and Mexico itself, lots of new adventures call. Who knows when they can begin? We hope sooner than later.

Date: 08.15.20/ When Something Bad Happens in a Foreign Country

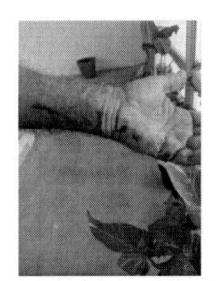

One of the most common questions we get asked about being nomadic travelers concerns healthcare. What happens if you get sick or have an accident? It is a question that we have asked ourselves, and Medicare takes some of that responsibility away from us, but not all.

I recently required healthcare when I got clipped by a passing car who took off as I tumbled off of my bicycle. What could have been a tragic event was instead a few hours of pain and inconvenience followed by a police report and a hospital visit. I'll not go into all the details, but I can say that it has a happy ending!

In this small town of Puerto Morelos, Mexico, there is no PUBLIC hospital, but there is a private one. Due to the virus, a clinic I used to pass by was closed, so after the accident I returned home, showered off my blood and abrasions and laid down to collect myself. I later decided to file a police report so **they** knew of the event in case they cared and kept track. Normally we would ride our bikes to wherever we wanted to go, but instead called upon Omar, an English-speaking taxi driver who was both my interpreter and my angel.

The cumbersome police report would have been complicated even in America, but was compounded by the language barrier **plus** found out that this was not a "local" police matter, but a regional one. Like local vs. State Police in the US. It was a frustrating learning experience and reminded me how much I hate paperwork and bureaucracy! With that behind us, Omar took us to a private "more expensive" hospital, but I was not dissuaded.

After a 30 minute consult, checking for anything broken, I paid the bill, which was 250 pesos, $12 USD. In the US, just going to an urgent care for an initial visit and checking of vital signs would have been $250 USD or more. A US medical office would have suggested every possible test, burden us with paperwork, and do everything to cover themselves from liability or lawsuit. Plus to jack up their bill. Other countries don't react that way. There was no paperwork and I left with just a receipt for the money I paid.

Omar was with us for almost two hours between the initial pickup, first one police department, then another, a ride to the hospital and then back home. His time and expertise were worth whatever he asked, but I was shocked when quoted 150 pesos: less than $7 USD. Insane, but I doubled it because he was worth even more.

Lessons learned: Healthcare outside the US is generally better than good and sometimes better, so don't be afraid to use them. Mind you, some Podunk towns might not be, but most larger ones are OK. This is one reason why legal residency in your country of choice is a big plus since it usually provides access to their health care system, but truly, it's almost easier paying for most things out of pocket. Look into travel insurance, there are many options, and see if they make sense for your peace of mind.

If there is a crime, report it, for nothing more than proper response and recordkeeping.

My wounds are healing, we now have another friend in Omar and knowledge of how things work. The chances of finding the hit and run driver of the car is probably small, so I will let the Universe dole out any punishment, since this too shall pass.

Date: 08.30.20/ Do These Things When You Can; You May Not Have Another Chance

There were some things we **should** have done when we had the chance, but didn't, and I realized that there are things you should not hesitate on when you travel; it's possible you may never get a second chance.

Our travels to Europe have been delayed and it's possible we may never get back to the Far East. We may decide that we don't want to. Being in one location for almost six months has been surprisingly comfortable, and between the ocean proximity, beautiful weather, awesome people, plus great affordability, Mexico may be a longer stay than we expected. Regardless, I made a list of some things that you should do if and when you travel, whether you are a novice or an experienced nomad.

1) If you get a chance to go somewhere, *go*, as long as it's reasonably convenient and practical. The "convenient, reasonable and practical" terms are subjective, of course, and what works for one person may not work for another. We never made it to Slovenia, even though we were just 15 km away.

Kathleen and I were on a full size BMW 750 bike traveling from Zagreb to Rijeka (both Croatia) on some amazing roads and almost running parallel to the Croatia-Slovenia border. We ran into a torrential downpour (an experience in itself!) and the ride took longer than planned. As we traveled on a series of back roads, a sign showed "Slovenia 15 km." We were tempted, really tempted, but darkness was close, and we were in new territory heading to the Istrian Peninsula. In hindsight I wish we had more time.

We also never made it to Turkey, even after having tickets, but that didn't work out either. The "fear" I have is that we may never pass that way again, and that would be sad.

2) Take advantage of different cultures, including food, festivities, and events. Our first stay was Valencia, Spain and during our time there we experienced the month-long Las Fallas Festival, which was incredible. We told ourselves that we would seek out local events whenever possible, but didn't always do that. We chose to not attend a pre-wedding party just outside our doors in Tivoli, Italy, because we were,

"too tired"... I regretted that, but we **did** get to watch the post-wedding procession out of the church, which was cool.

3) Know the travel rules with 100% certainty **before** you depart for somewhere. We got skunked and lost $300 USD on our flight from Thailand to Vietnam because I **thought** we had the right visa. It seems we needed a PRE-visa before we could leave in addition to a Visa on Arrival. We did resolve that mistake, but it was a tough lesson to learn.

4) Try to learn at least a little bit of the language, like hellos, goodbyes, and thank yous. I'm going to be hypocritical here because languages are **not** my thing and I am having a hard time with Spanish. Thank you Google Translate, and even the few words I **can** remember makes things more personal wherever you are.

5) Don't be afraid to step outside your comfort zone: that's where the magic happens! LOL, this happened several times over the years, but a young man I met at one of the airports shared his theory on street food or things that gave me pause. He LOVED Bangkok, especially for the street scene, which Kathleen and I found a bit scary. He said, "you will rarely get sick, but sometimes you might not like it. So throw it away, it's ridiculously cheap." That brief conversation made me more committed to "trying" new things, which we did with sandworm and bullfrog in Vietnam.

END of Part II

Life on the Road: HOW They Do It; WHY They Do It (part II)

Austyn Smith: Amsterdam, Netherlands (and back to the USA)

"I don't think I've been intimidated by any place we've been," said Austyn, "except for China. THAT was a tough one!"

That was how our conversation started out, and from there she went on to share what makes her tick: goals.

"I've always been goal driven," she confessed. "Take on a part time job: check. Have another kid: check. I love self-achievement and growth, and the more uncomfortable, the better!"

She loves the feeling of doing something scary, so travel was a bold frontier that she was anxious to conquer. She also strives to be authentic, and to be different.

She moved to Portland, Oregon, from New York several years ago, and found contentment, along with their fourth child, until dissatisfaction creeped in. They realized that living the "same life' day after day was boring and unsettling, and knew they needed to change. When she tried to explain that to the other Soccer Moms they were perplexed, and asked, "What do you mean?" They just didn't get it.

She and her husband talked about living abroad, and though Austyn was a novice, her husband previously lived in Thailand, and spoke the language. When they spoke about and dreamt about moving outside the US, they always assumed it would be Asia.

Not so.

When her husband came home from work one day in 2017 and asked, "What do you think about moving to Amsterdam? We have an interesting opportunity if we want to take it."

Even though she was seven months pregnant with her fourth child, she had no reservation and was excited about the possibilities. She knew good things would happen and it would work out. Her oldest child was eight at that time and a bit nervous about a move like that, but as it turned out, he made the transition easier than Austyn did.

Their original plan was to stay for two years, which is a common agenda for many people making such radical moves. Her husband had an eight year work visa, and worked for Nike, about 20 minutes outside Amsterdam. Austyn got the same visa benefit as her spouse, which took care of one of the biggest challenges when it comes to "moving overseas."

With Amsterdam being centrally located to so many other countries, the family took advantage of every school break and went somewhere different.

We talked about her drivers, i.e., what makes her want to go somewhere else, and she said, "Ironically, my husband and I differ in what draws us. He wants to go towards exciting, big and new cities, but I want to not stress, since travel can be stressful in itself. Maybe a spa or hike or something peaceful!"

Many times we do things because we "should," and that can be a dangerous trap. Her family has been to Paris, London, Rome, and all the other major cities. Why? Because they believe they should, and I go along with that. Unless the "should" is so foreign or uncomfortable or dangerous, sometimes we only get one chance, so we "should" embrace it.

She and her husband also travel separately at times, which is the healthiest thing to do for most couples who live a nomadic lifestyle—or not. We all have our own interests, and they do not always synchronize with our loved ones, but that doesn't mean we shouldn't do them. Since they generally take their kids with them, they try to change those destinations as well. They went to Tuscany and stayed in a villa, and took side trips to Venice and Florence, using their home base as what it was.

I asked Austyn if she could ever see themselves moving back to the US, and she said, "The only time I even think about things like that is if someone is sick, and I would love to just drive to Target or Wal-Mart and get some medicine." We have had the same conversation in our household!

Aside from that nice perk of the US, she did not envision ever going back to America. On their first trip back after living in Amsterdam for two years she shared what happened: "We couldn't get out of there fast enough," she said. "It was so weird after living in Europe."

Since Austyn liked getting into new things, she launched a podcast called The Expat Hour, and has interviewed nomads all over the world. Including me.

Like many Europeans, she spent a lot of time in cafes, and since she knew other expats in the city, she asked about their stories since they were all learning lessons. That was a totally new experience for her, and every story was different, unique, and fun to learn. She had the time since her new baby was young, so with that, she launched her show. As I write this in 2023 things changed...and she is back in the US. The future is uncertain for now, but she is still busy being a Mom and wife, which she loves.

About Amsterdam, she shared, "No question, the Dutch are so different than Americans. When they work, they work very hard, but when they don't work they take advantage of every vacation day they can. They are very English proficient, and even though we look lessons to learn the language, we found it unnecessary. The bottom line is that we felt we had the best of both worlds.

And THAT is the best we can hope for.

Sundae Bean: Switzerland

Sundae is a Super Star in the nomadic world. When we first met, she had been living in South Africa since 2016 and not only lives the life of a nomad, but she shares it via a worldwide podcast and also coaches people on how to make the most of a globally nomadic life, but to transition into whatever stage of their life they are looking for.

When we had our original conversation in 2019 the world was a different place. There was no COVID. People were able to travel as they wanted almost without restrictions, aside from the normal passport and visa dealings.

Her family had lived in West Africa from 2013-2016, and everyone loved it there. The weather is good, the kids love school, her husband has a good job, and Sundae has good high speed internet, so all is good. And she is a world away from North Dakota where she was born and raised in a typical Americana household, with a father who was a farmer, and mother a housewife. It was mostly white, but had a number of Native Americans in her community.

And she was anxious to see the world.

The growing world of satellite and travel networks fueled her drive when she was as young as eight years old, and seeing Europe, Central America, East Asia, West Africa and other far away territories made her hungry to view it with her own eyes. She didn't do much about that until college at the University of North Dakota, which was more of the same, so she transferred to Minnesota to a large school with more variation. Like many, she took a semester overseas in Spain as a communication major. School in Toledo was "overwhelming and nourishing," she said, and she wanted more, more, more!

"We were housed in the heart of Toledo, and our rooms were in a converted monastery! It was beautiful beyond belief," she cried, "and I realized that THIS is what living was all about. I was hooked."

Being close to so many countries was inviting, and Sundae went wherever and whenever she could, including to north Africa, to Morocco. She was captivated by the way women were viewed differently in other cultures, so she got intrigued with that and made it a focal point of future travels.

"Sitting on the coast of Northern Africa and looking towards the US, I KNEW, I mean, I KNEW that this was where I had to be. It wasn't a want, it was a need. I saw all these lands in documentaries and travelogues, and I committed to finding out for myself."

Sundae's story was similar to others we have met over the years. Some people are just born resonating with other places or cultures, and we can view it as another life, or reincarnation, or something less exotic, but it is what it is.

A few days after that moment on the coach of Northern Africa she met a woman in Italy who spoke with her about Bangkok, and Sundae also had a pull towards that city as well. "The embarrassing thing is," she confessed, "I didn't even know it was in Thailand! During that phase of my life, I only knew it from the pop song."

Her parents back in North Dakota wondered about their daughter, and how she got so adventurous. They freaked out when she traveled throughout Thailand and said she was making a side trip to Vietnam since they only knew Vietnam from the war. Ironically, she felt safer there than she did in Minneapolis, which is NOT an uncommon sentiment I have heard from MANY who live and travel outside the US. The facts support it since crime of all types, along with random and mass shootings, are a very American phenomenon.

She felt liberated being in places where NO ONE knew her. She could be who and what she wanted to be, as opposed to being back home where her family knew every other family in the area for generations.

Finally, love struck when she met a Swiss man in Vietnam, they spent two weeks together, and something clicked. He said he wanted to see her again but she was working a corporate job and was committed to returning to the US at the time. So he came to visit her a few days later.

They spent time back and forth between the US and Switzerland, but two months later they married and have been together 20 plus years.

During the early days of their marriage they traveled all the time since they each worked in Europe and had the typical four to six weeks annual vacations, and they went "everywhere." Asia, and Central and South America, were their primary destinations, and Africa was not really in their view. Yet. They moved to West Africa when their children were one and five, and they continue to travel with their children.

"My views of culture have evolved over the years," she confessed, "and when I started I was just a naïve farmer's daughter, but now my profession is inter-cultural communication, so now it's more than a like or a hobby—it's my career and my life. I used to embrace all the various ways that cultures do things differently, and in their own way, but now that I understand the fundamental differences of where we all come from, my goal is to understand and teach people how to get along and even think like someone else. It's pretty heavy."

Norm: One of the lessons I have learned over the years is that as different as we all are, or can be, underneath, we are really all the same. We still have the same wants, we all complain about the weather or the politicians, we all crave to live in a safe place, and to enjoy a healthy and happy quality of life.

Sundae is a teacher and student of expat life and she cautions people about what is called "expat fatigue," which can happen at any time in your journey.

"Imagine you get robbed in Portugal. Well, in many cases, the victim now equates the entire country with that negative event, and it becomes an "us," against "them" situation," she said. "So it's important that expats stay grounded and don't get overly tired of any particular situation."

On a personal level we experienced something like that in Thailand and Asia, which was totally foreign to anything we had ever done. The language, the food, the customs, the crowds were overwhelming to me, and Bangkok weirded me out, to put it in non-scientific jargon. We ended up going to smaller places in Thailand to escape Bangkok, and over an eight week period it was very revealing.

In 2012 Sundae's life radically changed when her husband, who worked for the Foreign Service, took a job in Burkina Faso, a landlocked West African country. She had a "job for life" at the second largest company in Switzerland, but recognized as an interculturalist, her learning had plateaued. She was already an "experienced expat" since she had been traveling half her life, so it was time to push the envelope and develop new skills.

After the move she started her own consulting company and had to deal with political upheaval, terrorism, proximity to the Ebola crisis, and many challenges you face living in a developing African country. There was enough concern that she took the kids back to Switzerland until her husband finished his 18 month commitment and then was offered a job in the country of South Africa. They were there from 2016-2022.

She accentuated her expat blog with a podcast, The Expat Happy Hour, and has interviewed fellow travelers and expats worldwide. She viewed it as a way to get personal with potential clients so they could hear her voice and her stories and engage with her on a more personal level. The show is now called IN TRANSIT with Sundae Bean and she has done over 300 shows.

Catching up with Sundae as I was updating our 2019 interview was refreshing and showed the power and possibilities that we experienced travelers can offer to those that are fearful and learning. She left South Africa in 2022 and is now planted back in Switzerland. She works for a global company and still has her side gig helping people living globally mobile lives.

Jens Hoffmann: Germany, and elsewhere

Jens is one of my "newer" fellow nomads who I met when we moved to Saranda, Albania in November, 2022, and one of the few profiled here who I truly consider to be a friend, and one I actually met in person! I heard about him before our initial meeting, and he had the distinction of being "that crazy 54 year old guy who rode his bicycle from Germany to Saranda!" THAT caught my attention, and in addition to being an avid bicycle rider he is also a great hiking leader, and led the group that I joined while in Saranda. He was either blessed or cursed with being at the right place at the right time, OR being in the wrong place, since he was born in East Berlin, and spent his first 18 years under the Communist regime, which restricted all travel to the "west."

"It was an arbitrary line," he said, "and we could go to the seven eastern countries without a problem, but that invisible curtain was off limits until 1989, when the Berlin Wall was torn down and the Soviet Union was dismantled. He traveled extensively with his parents when he was younger and candidly admitted that they got along better on the road, than they did at home, but finally, at age 21, he was able to live in the newly opened free world.

"It was like an explosion," he said, of this new untapped horizon. "The best gift I could have gotten at that age!"

The now accessible West Germany was his first stop, since it was close, as well as mysterious as to what all the fuss was about. Italy came next and he loved seeing all the palm trees, since they were new to him. But his lack of language skills took away some of the enjoyment, so decided to change that.

"There was no sense taking English classes when I was young since there was no place to really use it, but within five months of the wall coming down I was enrolled in University in the western part of the city, and I took English classes. That was difficult and I told a friend who was in class with me, 'we need to go to England,' and that is what I did. He fought me on it since he was tired of school, which had only finished two years earlier for him, but I knew that speaking the language would help me in my travels."

Jens spent three months in England, stayed with a host family, and then focused on taking jobs that either allowed him to travel, or permitted the long breaks that are typical in Europe. He went north to the Nordic countries, and his training in graphic design opened up opportunities to work. After a year of freely traveling he went back to Germany and got a job at a newspaper doing layouts and design.

"I was never on the corporate track," he confessed, "and I only took the job since I effectively worked nine months a year and that allowed me to travel quite a bit. Many I worked with were more career oriented, but not me. And growing up in an unfriendly household turned me off to family and relationships too, so that was not as important as traveling."

As I chatted with Jens I told him how foreign this idea was for an American, where getting three months off to vacation is virtually unheard of, unless you are a business owner or a highly placed employee with that kind of power.

He didn't start out looking for other places to live, but as he ventured out further and more frequently, he found some places more enjoyable than others. He knew he didn't like the German winters, so always took his breaks over that period, and the first country he flipped over was Brazil. He stayed for three months whenever possible, and learned that to truly learn a culture it took even longer.

He never had aspirations of getting a gold watch at the end of a forty year career, so continued to live this traveling one fourth of the year routine for quite some time. Actually for the next twenty years, and in his words, "It didn't get boring, but just the opposite; it got more exciting. And I got more and more opened minded, which I see in many but not all experienced travelers."

I agreed with him on that open-mindedness, since I have learned that when we see and experience other cultures and other ways of doing things, it makes us aware that we don't always do things the best or right ways. What seems foreign to us may really be a better way. In Jen's case, every time he went somewhere else he got energized, and that made it easier to accept new challenges.

He is not financially independent, but goes back to Germany every summer to work at campgrounds. Those several months he works gives him a bankroll to carry him through the year, but he confessed that as he is getting older, and closer to retirement, however we define it, he is thinking ahead and looking for ways to make money and generate income.

As much as he loved Brazil and the Nordic countries, they are out of his price range now, and he focuses his travel time on the more affordable places in the world.

Which is how and why we met in Albania!

"I don't worry about retirement, or even death," he said, "but I believe we must fill our lives with excitement; with joy, and with fun. I recognized that even in my twenties, and as I looked down the road, I knew that at some point I needed to take the steps to live comfortably. Ironically, one of the few things that was good about the former East Germany was that all the citizens were taken care of. We all worked, and even the older retired people were taken care of. No one ever lost a job back then, and there was security in that, but no freedom of life."

Jen's early life and reality of that time was very unique, since most people live in a "free society," as opposed to a repressed one.

Somewhere on the road he did fall in love and lived with his girlfriend for 16 years, and fathered a son, who is now in Sweden. Even with a young child they traveled extensively, and Jens advises parents with kids that they should travel as well.

I totally agree, and have had similar conversations with dozens all over the world. I believe that nothing broadens a child's mind better than travel experiences. Learning a second language is also significantly easier when we are young—and I speak from personal experience on that!

Jens is a unique animal since he has made travel the focal point of his life above all else. Owning a home or business or reaching some of the more familiar goals that we sometimes set for ourselves was not important. Things and material possessions did not appeal to him: fun and adventure did. Jens said he thinks that passion is important in life, no matter how or where that presents itself. He has not watched a TV in two decades.

We both recognized some realities of life, and aside from aging we spoke about COVID and how that changed the world.

In 2020 he rode his bike over five months from Germany to Albania, and he took it slowly since COVID limited his choices. He said that same trip could have been done in two months, though not by me...

When he started, the plan was to visit a friend about 200 km south of Berlin, and he had no design on Albania at all. He did that first leg in just a few days, then thought, "Where are my next set of friends?" so he went off to Cologne. Then Luxembourg, a place he already visited and loved before.

By then he had more confidence and conditioning, so decided to take on the passes of the Alps, the highest and most extensive mountain chain in Europe, which covers 1,200 km (750 mi) through seven Alpine countries. By the time he got to Italy he had to decide if he wanted to ferry over to Malta or Croatia. He continuously ran into border issues since countries were locking down indiscriminately, and he took more COVID tests than he can remember. As he was entering new countries, many residents were leaving, so it became a unique experience every time. Eventually campsites started to reopen and he could travel more freely. He rode south from

Croatia and kept going until he got to Albania, and decided to stay for a bit. Now his future plans have changed and he actually has a long term strategy.

I asked Jens if he would undertake a long bike trip like that again and he said he would. He and I spoke about not just what we want out of life, but also what we do NOT want. That includes places that he has no interest in returning to, and we both have our, "been there, done that, never going back" places, too.

We all have different vehicles to travel. He likes his bike and I love my motorcycle. We have friends who have been traipsing around Europe for two years in a motorhome. Another travels with his wife and two dogs in an SUV, and others travel by boat. It doesn't matter how you do it, as long as we do do it!

Nora Dunn: Toronto, Canada

"I was a traveler pretty much right out of the womb," is how Nora and my conversation started, and it only got better!

"From as young as I could remember," she said, "my parents and I would take the train from our home in Toronto, Canada, to my grandparents, who lived about four hours away near Albany, New York, and I would spend my summers there in the country. We would also take the trains down to the coast, so that was the beginning of my love of train travel, which resulted in many crazy stories decades later!"

At age nine she became obsessed with the question of, "How do children play outside the United States?" which was germinated from watching documentaries in school and at home of all the ways that people lived in Europe. That later transformed into more questions about how do people eat, shop, travel, and what do they talk about at dinner?, "over there," wherever that might be at the time.

That finally went global when Nora was 16 and toured China with her ballet company that she was part of. That trip had challenges, but opened her eyes to how differently people lived in different parts of the world.

Over the following years she took trips to different places, but never was able to stay long enough to really get immersed in the way people lived there. Finally she took a month off from her successful financial planning business and went to South Africa- which freaked everyone out.

"How can you do that? was the pushback I got from everyone, since the idea of taking four weeks off was insane," she confessed.

When she got there she realized that taking a month off—even longer—was not as crazy as everyone made it seem, and people were doing that all the time, and for even longer. Her "aha" moment was seeing that short vacations were a North American habit, and a bad one at that. She decided that she needed to change her life at age 30 when a series of events pushed her to make that change as she worked herself into exhaustion. The ultimate overachiever hit the wall.

She wanted to retire, but not in the conventional sense. She wanted to climb mountains all over the world, to break bread with new friends overseas, and to enjoy the beauty of the planet. And that is what she did.

For 12 years.

She didn't burn any bridges in Toronto, just in case it didn't work out, but she found her way and traveled wherever she wanted. She initially did that with a male friend, which gave her a sense of security in the sometimes dangerous world, but he "became more of a liability than an asset," she said. "He really didn't want to travel full time like I did, and he was not as financially secure, so that became a problem."

Three years later she went solo in Australia, and her self-confidence and experience carried her forward for many years. Nora let her destinations choose her, rather than vice versa, and she was a feather in the wind, and loving the ride. She did a lot of volunteer work, along with house sitting and living on boats, and that enabled her to travel for less money. She sometime stayed as long as two years and used that destination as a launch point for other visits, and sometimes she stayed just a few weeks. She learned to play the chess game of bouncing in and out of countries and extending her visas anew. In 2010 she stayed at most places less than three weeks, so covered a lot of ground, but finally burned out and stayed six months at her next stop.

She recognized that as much as she liked volunteering, it became a job in itself. Between the work and the socialization, plus running her own online business, she knew she had to change that scene, which she did.

We spoke about her motivation for doing this for a dozen more years and she said it was for the experience of traveling and to delve into the different cultures. As much as Nora loves being a Traveler, she still respects the Tourist mindset.

"Hey, not everyone can handle or is cut out for the nomadic life," she said. "If people can only take a week or two at a time, I think that is great." And I agree. She has also found that sometimes taking a tour of places she stays is an accelerated way to learn things she might not have learned at all.

"When are you going to settle down?" has been a common question, along with the children factor, since she was nearing forty, but Nora said that children were never in her picture and has not been an issue. "But I do believe that nomadic travel does have a finite life," she said. "I think you need a contextual baseline so you can truly understand where you are and where you've been. Getting burned out, especially as a solo traveler, is a real thing, and I've done it a few times already."

Over the years she returned to Toronto and stayed for up to six weeks with family and friends. She also recognized her reverse culture shock after seeing so many places that were much less "civilized," and she also saw her need for assimilation with a culture that spoke the same language and had similar backgrounds. Her aging father was also part of that picture since he reminded her that he was not going to be around forever.

In 2020 she got an apartment in Toronto, and that has made her life much easier since she can still travel outward from there, yet has a familiar place to return to. At age 45 she has found that balance, that best of both worlds. She'd been there, she did that; now she's trying something else. And that is the nature of life, to keep on trying, to see what works—for now—and change it if it doesn't.

In 2006 she started her journey as a Professional Hobo, which is her brand, and has been to over 60 countries. She augmented her journey with her income from her financial planning practice combined with free stays in a multitude of places. Now she is at peace, in Toronto, where she writes and speaks and still travels where and when she wants, which is about half the year. That, to me, is a well lived life.

Nomad(ic) Life for All Ages

Dedication

If you've gotten this far then you must be serious about learning about Life on the Road!

This is the start of my third "volume" of my Travel Younger blog, and begins in October, 2020. That seems like a lifetime ago as I am compiling these three volumes, but it also seems like just a few months.

For too long a time the world was a chaotic, confusing mess due to COVID. Millions died, billions of dollars were lost, and the "when" it would ever end was an unknown. It was not until mid-2021 that some degree of normal returned. Masks became less frequent, as well as the need for COVID testing and more vaccine boosters.

Kathleen and I had our bouts with the disease and we were never officially diagnosed, but we believe she got it twice, as did I. Neither was deadly, but they were inconvenient and passed with minimal damage.

To date we have visited 28 countries since Feb 17, 2019 and we are spending time in Albania, which has become a very, very desirable location. I will share the reasons for that as you continue to read...

Over the years we have developed friendships with other nomads, some online only, but others real and in person. We have found many that live like we do, and we are proud that we have inspired many to take the plunge. As we are getting older (shocker!), we still ask ourselves, "How long will we do it?" and truth is, it's still fun and we really do not want to stop.

BUT, the writing is on the wall as we both pass 70 years of age and realize that we will have to "settle down" somewhere.

Date: 10.10.20/ What I Miss About California: Earthquakes!

As a California resident for forty years I always said that I would prefer an earthquake over any other type of natural disaster, and the uncertainty of WHEN (or IF), they might happen is better than knowing a tornado or hurricane is heading your way. That opinion was borne out as we just experienced our first hurricane in Mexico, herein called, Hurricane Delta.

The good news was that the projected category IV (wind speeds of 130~156 MPH) never quite hit that and the rain was minimal. But the damage to trees and power poles was substantial.

The night before, my Lovely said, "*This storm about to hit is now rated a category IV*" which caused me to say something like "*don't overreact,*" which did not go over very well. Granted, I have a tendency to not worry about hardly anything and put myself in the hands of the Universe to take care of us, but her concerns were justified after a very excited conversation about said hurricane. The next morning, the day it was expected, we had a list of items to get at the grocery store since you should be prepared with (1) water, (2) canned goods, lots of candles and food, and (3) portable power for a few days. Alcohol should be on that list, too. All great suggestions and we found out that half the town read the same recommendations and met us at the grocery store about 0900.

I have never stood in a grocery checkout line for 90 minutes, and thought that horrible until we exited the store about 10:30 and saw the line to get IN was about three times that size, extending out to the street. Kudos to the staff as they dealt with what must have been a very stressful day.

Riding our bikes home from the store we saw another line, this one of cars, as they were all heading somewhere. Did they know something we didn't? Truth is, we live on the second floor of a three story building made of concrete. I felt safe where we were, but still put tape on the windows in case of broken glass, since we had no boards, moved furniture away from the windows in case a 120 MPH projectile decided to come through, and stayed busy until 7:00 p.m., which is when power was due to be cut off. I was skeptical of that time since the storm was not expected until early the next morning, and my intuition was right as power stayed on, candles were lit just in case, and at 0245 the winds started, but with little rain, and it stayed that way until 0400 when the power finally did cut off.

Oh, one more thing. Kathleen did not feel safe in our normal bedroom, but wanted to sleep in what they say is the safest room in the house: your bathroom. And we did...with mattress pad draped over the shower basin and on to the floor, and I was amazed how soundly I DID sleep!

For the next hour we were up and down, with torrential winds accompanying bangs, noises and whistles coming from who knows where. It began as a tropical breeze through the window, minimal rain, and lightning bursting behind the clouds, but was very scary for much too long, though magical in its own threatening way.

Then...silence. For about 45 minutes, stillness, and what must have been the storm's eye passing over. Then, the trailing side, with more wind than before. Or so I'm told since I slept through most of it. Finally about 0630, daybreak, and clouds blowing by overhead faster than I have ever seen them move, immersed in a pink hued sky. From our window we viewed the damage, which was severe, with downed trees and limbs, but not catastrophic, which is what was predicted. After a breakfast of cereal since we had no power (or refrigerator), we took a walk through our 500 or so unit complex. It looked worse close up, but compared to pictures I have seen of other hurricanes, this was minimal.

The warm wind was blowing, but still no rain, nor did we have any the entire day. Thank goodness for that because workers, neighbors, and friends all hit the streets and parking lots and went to work on the fallen trees.

I started off by saying why I miss California earthquakes, but that's not really true. Over my four decades in So. Cal. I felt dozens of them, including a few that DID cause me to worry, but none that severely impacted my life. Earthquakes offer no warning. There are no CNN announcements. There are no runs on the stores or for gasoline, at least until it has passed. Their geographical impact is fairly small, though not always, and earthquakes do not MOVE. They hit, they do their damage, and they're gone, likes thieves in the night.

The precursor to natural disasters can be as harrowing as the event itself: paranoia, fear, and panic, all contributing to the damage, even if its psychological. Sometimes those warnings are worse. This hurricane, which I hope and pray will be a one-time experience, offered warnings and suggestions and caused a fair amount of fear before it ever arrived. It is what it is. Hundreds of years ago, before media, no one knew anything about impending trouble until they read the sky and acted. I guess the lesson I share here is, in the unfortunate event of being in the line of fire, learn as we did. Listen, don't panic, take precautions, be prepared, and wait for it to pass. OH, and pray...

Some notes: Delta's wind speed tripled in the span of about 30 hours, growing from a tropical depression with winds of 35 mph the day before, to a predicted Category IV, faster than any this year. As it turned out, it was downgraded to a Cat II and wind speeds hit right at triple digits. One of the worse damages we saw was a side street that got hit with a triple whammy, as two large trees on one side crossed over with a fallen tree on the other. It caused some structural damage, but the aftermath of this storm showed zero deaths or injuries here in Puerto Morelos.

What it DID show was the amazing sense of community and outpouring of support as work crews were out very early, helped by citizens with chain saws, and kids of all ages doing what they could.

Date: 11.21.20/ The Good Old Days of Traveling!

Once upon a Time you took a flight and your odds were probably pretty good that you would get to your intended destination on time, with the majority of airlines being prompt 95% of the time. On time, by the way, is defined as being within 15 minutes of the intended arrival.

The official stats say that most airlines over the last 10 years (up to 2018), had an "on time rating" of somewhere between 70-90 percent. Today there is nothing you can depend on.

I recently took a business trip to San Antonio, Texas, with the first leg taking me to Houston, Texas. My Cancun, Mexico departure was an early one, 7:30, and I thought that surely it would leave on time, since many delays are caused by the ones coming in. Generally, getting an early morning flight gives you the greatest guarantee of staying on schedule.

But not this time....

It's hard to imagine a major airline like United would have a flight delayed over four hours, yes, that's right, four hours, because of a needed emergency landing beacon, but that was the culprit. And unfortunately, since Covid, airlines have all been working at less than peak efficiency, which includes inventorying of parts.

This I found out since I stayed with a friend in Houston who was an FAA flight controller. As I shared my story, he told me that airlines are working with the absolute fewest number of people they can, and whereas they used to keep three or four of the same items in stock, now they maybe have one. So in my instance, the Cancun airport did not have the necessary landing light, and it had to come in on another flight.

Just one of the trials and tribulations of flying during these challenging times.

I spent two days in Houston and then moved on to San Antonio and hoped that this next flight would leave on time.

Nope, did not happen. But at least it was not four hours late, just one, not a tragedy or noteworthy complaint.

A few days later my return trip to Cancun began. Intending to leave from San Antonio back to Houston about 1:30 in the afternoon also did not happen as planned, and the big problem was, even if everything unfolded as scheduled, I had about 75 minutes gap to catch my connector flight to Cancun. Time was not on my side!

As I nervously shuffled at the departing gate and watched the clock tick minute by minute, first they announced 20 minutes late, then 30 minutes late, and it finally took off about 45 minutes late. The good news is that we made good time back to Houston only to find that there was no available gate! We sat on the runway for first a few minutes, then too many, as I saw my window shrinking to catch my last leg home.

We finally got to the terminal and my departing gate as people stood in line for the last of my four flights. I had visions of sleeping at the airport or getting a room in Houston for the night and leaving the next day, since this was the last flight back to Cancun. My last flight WAS delayed, but only by a handful of minutes, so I was able to get back into Cancun at 11:40 p.m.

Normally I am not prone to anxiety or worry, but this tested me more than I wanted to be tested!

Four trips, four delays. What used to be the exception to the rule now seems to BE the rule!

Add to that the problem of returning on one of the last arriving Cancun flights of the day and finding a shortage of options for shuttles and taxis back to Puerto Morales.

Oh, how we all long for the good old days! Most of California has now returned to their most strict confinement, called purple level. Meanwhile, here in Cancun, we are blessed with very lenient standards and Mexico, right now, is one of the few places that Americans visit.

The Caribbean and most of the islands are closed, and many places that people vacation for winter are not an option this year.

No question, Travel Younger's hands have been tied, and both of us are getting itchy feet, wanting to move on, at least for a while. To where, we are not sure, but Central America seems to be the most obvious direction, plus South America, and then hopefully back across the ocean to Europe.

Like all of you we live day by day, week by week, and sadly, month by month. Let's hope that 2021 gets us back on the road to recovery.

Date: 12.19.20/ Exploring Mexico One Island at a Time

Cool stuff to know...

I found out that there are almost 100 islands off the coast of Mexico, so it is highly unlikely I will get to all of them. Of that large number, most are either protected or uninhabited, so that makes the goal of hitting some of the best ones more manageable. Fortunately, many of the top destinations are where we live, in the Yucatan, and so far, Isla Mujeres is way at the top of my list. But that list IS quite small since the only other one we have even been to is Holbox, which we recently returned from. I'll get to that one in a moment.

The biggie, Cozumel, has mixed reviews and is definitely on our radar, if for no other reason than to say we made it. It has been Mexico's largest cruise port, but that ship is not sailing right now, so there is an ideal window of opportunity. Still, it's a top tourist destination and yes, it is supposed to be beautiful (but pricey), and the diving and snorkeling are supposed to be magnificent. That in itself is a good reason to visit. So that's coming.

Island number four I never heard of until a few weeks ago: Isla Contoy. It is just 15 miles north of Mujeres, and seems to be a naturalists and hikers paradise since it is mostly uninhabited and they only allow 200 visitors per day, and they can only be delivered by companies certified by the Mexican government. Kudos to whoever set that up. Like Cozumel and Mujeres, Contoy fronts the amazing Mesoamerican Reef System, running 175 miles just north of Cancun, all the way to the Honduras. I feel blessed that my current home, Puerto Morelos, gets to share that reef as well, which is considered the second best reef system in the world, after the Great Barrier in Australia.

After visiting Holbox I got a greater appreciation for Isla Mujeres, since the only way to really rate "best of" is to compare them to each other. Over the past few years, we have lived on several islands in Europe.

We loved Sicily, which was the largest island we lived on, exactly one year ago. It's at the very southern tip of Italy, the "toe" portion of the famous boot comparison when looking at a map of Italy. It's only eight miles from the mainland, but there is no bridge for easy access, so transport back and forth is via ferry and plane. We were there for six weeks and enjoyed an apartment directly across from the rocks of the Ionian Sea. The island has a surplus of history, with many landmarks and temples going back 8,000 years, plus geography and hills to blow your mind.

We also lived on Menorca, a Balearic Island off the coast of Spain, and number three was our smallest port of call, the island of Naxos, one of the many Greek islands. Each of these islands had their own vibe and history and were fairly easy to access via ferry or plane.

While here in the Yucatan, Isla Mujeres has given us the closest experience to some of our European adventures. Mujeres is remarkably easy to get to, just a 20 minute high speed ferry from Cancun, and even though you can SEE Cancun from the coast, it still feels a million miles away. Their North beach remains our favorite beach so far, and the small village feel of downtown has a surplus of charm. The eastern side has an awesome walkway to explore some terrific shoreline. We have not been down to the southern tip to catch the sunrise, which they say is magnificent. And lastly, Mujeres is very affordable considering it DOES feel like a true getaway.

When we arrived at Holbox, not an easy place to GET to, by the way, we had to feel our way around to decide how it compared to our past experiences. The dirt roads were a muddy challenge due to rain a few days earlier, with flooded sections and potholes galore. What IS nice, is that there are NO gasoline driven vehicles there, except for some commercial trucks and police. All public transport is via ATV, golf cart, motorcycle, or bicycle. The ocean was not as beautiful as I expected it to be compared to the Cancun coast side. The beach had some of the finest sand I have ever walked on and was almost mud-like in consistency, which was the same consistency as the streets themselves. That plus murky greenish water, and I had a hard time deciding if this was a place worth returning to.

Afterwards we found out we had missed out on some things, including the nighttime bioluminescent experiences in the water, but that peaks in summer. Ditto the annual whale sharks are supposed to be amazing from the island as well, but that season runs June to September, plus we found out that pink flamingoes are abundant there, but we didn't know at the time.

The one thing we DID partake of, and something the island is famous for, is lobster pizza. Actually, we opted for seafood pizza instead, with shrimp and calamari. Even so, it was spectacular, the best pizza (and dough) that we have found in Mexico.

Will we return? As I finish this review, the answer is a strong "YES."

Date: 01.02.21/ The New Year is Here; Embrace it!

Whether you are 25 or 65, many of you will agree that this past year of 2020 was probably the most challenging of our lives. Though we may have lived through recessions and wars, we have never had a health crisis like this; certainly not on a global scale. And it is not over yet... Will we have another pandemic when this is "over?" Unfortunately, that may be more likely than not...

With that the case, I believe this is a great time to take advantage of the freedom that may be opening up before us this year. Yes, travel is still a crap shoot, borders are still restricted, and flights will be uncertain throughout the year, but since so many of us have been sequestered and hidden away in closed rooms and dark corners, this year may be a good time to start exploring again, whether in your neighborhood, within your region, your home country, or throughout the world.

And before I raise the ire of those who cry, "stay at home," "don't travel" and such, my suggestions are to BEGIN preparing your journey(s), but use your own common sense and insight before you begin.

Travel prices are insanely low, though still highly volatile. Next month it will be 2 years since we left the United States on our worldwide travels and our efforts to stay at different locations for six weeks at a time. We also got chased by COVID last February and escaped to Mexico, which is where we have been ever since. Seriously, not a bad place to hunker down!

Puerto Morelos has terrific weather (aside from the two hurricanes!!), and wonderful people. There are many English speakers here in this small fishing village which is highly affordable, with beaches and water that cannot be beat,

BUT, we have both been getting itchy feet, and long to hit the road, especially back to Europe. Not because we don't like it here, but because we like it there better. We both agree that the Mediterranean climate is much more comfortable than the tropics and resonates more with our personalities. And cold weather?? BZZZZZ, not an option!! The goal that we started with when we left in 2019 was finding that "50 degrees (or above) Sweet Spot," and that has not changed.

We spent most of our time overseas in southern Europe; Spain, Italy, Croatia, Romania, plus hit some Eastern European countries for shorter periods of time. Aside from the two months that we spent in Thailand and such, most of our time was in that region.

So, we are STARTING to look forward to making that happen again. The WHEN is unknown, but sometimes the anticipation and planning of adventures is almost as fun as the adventure itself, right?? Until COVID, booking an airline ticket was a solid commitment, and getting refunds or making changes was a nuisance and costly. Most airlines now have lenient cancelation fees, and should most of this year. If you DO need to cancel (we have several times), you will probably get a CREDIT, though, and not cash back. Yes, it's inconvenient, but allows you to tap into great prices. Case in point. We looked for prices from Cancun to Rome, and can catch a one-way ride for less than $300. Check out this crazy pricing graph: CUN> Rome chart

I throw these ideas out there to get you to open your mind to WHAT IF and real possibilities. When we left California and the US—permanently—we knew that this was our ONE SHOT to do it before it was too late. Starting in your sixties is still time enough, and I knew that if I looked back in ten years after chickening out, it would be my biggest regret on my deathbed. If you are blessed with youth or are under 60, more power to you and I encourage you to GO FOR IT!

Supplemental #1 (published story): <u>Airplane Travel In The Third Decade of the 21st Century</u>

01.08.21 Manopause article

Manopause is an online magazine that caters to "older dudes," so I'm writing for them about our travel experiences from This Olde Dudes perspective.

This piece shares the different generations, ie, versions of travel that we have lived through over the past 60 years. Version one, the fifties and sixties, were the beginning of "mass airline travel," airplanes (jets) got faster, they carried more people, prices got lower, and the "everyman" was able to enjoy it. Version two (recently) ended, and was our heyday, when online airline access and cheap prices to EVERYWHERE made travel fun! Not so much anymore.

What will version III look like over the next few years? That's what I share, so I hope you enjoy it.

Date: 02.17.21/ Two Years Later...and Counting

Two years ago today Kathleen and I left Los Angeles airport, heading to Valencia, Spain and beyond. Our goal to "travel the world six weeks at a time" generated two books with that title, took us to 23 countries, over 400 cities, and four continents. So much has happened since then, and of course, the world changed at the beginning of 2020 and has still not returned to anything resembling normal. I don't think the world "normal" applies anymore since normal is a state of mind or being at any given time, and that previous "normal" is passed and will never return.

I recently took a trip to the US, San Diego area, and the attitude about COVID is so different there, than what we have lived through in Mexico. In the US, COVID IS a thing, and everyone had their stories and experiences. Many I spoke with had it and recovered, with various degrees of severity and inconvenience. A good friend of mine, Felicia, age 88, contracted the virus just recently and spent about 10 days in the hospital in severe distress, but is now healthy. Meanwhile, the 49 year old owner of a trade magazine I work with, Roger, contracted the disease and went from condition "good" to his demise in just a few days. This illness has no rhyme, reason or predictability, so it's wise we all take precautions.

California, and many other places, SEEM to be on the mend, with the number of illnesses dropping as people either get vaccinations or develop immunity. California removed the "stay at home" order, and outdoors eating is returning, along with the promise of indoor eating due soon, based on the numbers dropping further. According to a good friend in Orange County, CA, who works for the county health department, the numbers are definitely dropping, so that's not anecdotal, but real life statistics.

I think the hope and prayers are positive, but traveling is just not as much fun right now. One morning I walked down the street to get a coffee and a bagel. I couldn't sit inside, and by the time I got my coffee and my food, one or the other was cold. There was no sense of intimacy or relaxation, and everyone was going through the motions to get things done, but some of the fun was definitely gone.

I reflected back on some simple things and how they vary in different countries. Like street food.

In Asia, street food is a major foodie draw and the selection is mind blowing. In Mexico I don't have to go more than a few hundred yards and I can find street tacos and more on any and every street in town. Not so much in the US! Regulations and competition keep street vendors in check, except in the larger cities, where they are on every street corner. But in outlying areas, not so much.

Today is 24 months since we became permanent expats, and in another 30 days it will be one year since we arrived in Mexico. And as much as it IS very nice, Kathleen and I have been anxious to move on. Europe calls us and baring any changes, we will be leaving for Croatia on September 3, followed by Greece and then Albania.

Date: 03.17.21/ The LAST Year-and This New One

The LAST Year (of NOT Traveling Younger...) and This One

The recent buzz has been about the one year "anniversary" of when our lives radically changed, as the coronavirus, AKA COVID-19, upended our formerly normal routines. Anniversaries are usually celebratory, but this is far from a celebration, yet does warrant us taking note. Of how much our individual lives have changed, along with many others who have been more severely impacted, in addition to the worlds of medicine, travel, hospitality and many others. Instead of confining themselves in cubicles and physical offices, many have learned to work remotely, and man, what a shift THAT has been!

Kathleen and I have been location independent for the past two years, and, as many others found that they do NOT need to live in the city where they worked—or even the same country!—the real estate market has changed radically.

Along with the many negative events over the past year, including us not being able to Travel Younger, the good news is that the world "may" be emerging from this mess. I say "may" because there are still many unanswered questions, and even though vaccines are available to more people, COVID is not gone.

Our town here in Mexico still requires masks in many places and we are not even close to living "normally." I have had several trips back to the US and normal is even further away THERE, even though some states are discontinuing the mask requirement, and others are trying to operate business as usual.

For us, the world has opened up, as we recently took road trips to the cities of Bacalar and Chetumal, here in the Yucatan peninsula. Bacalar, one of the "Magical Cities," is about four hours south and even though the normally vibrant blue waters were not as beautiful as usual, it was still a nice getaway. We went to an attraction called "El Rapido," which is a strong current of water flowing from one lagoon to another, which acts almost like a river running downstream. The water HERE was a vibrant blue-green and the perfect temp, as we hiked upstream, got into the temperate waters, and flowed several hundred yards until the movement slowed enough to exit.

The city of Chetumal, just a few miles from the Belize border, is a big city, but even so, had lots of charm. We had a lovely meal on the ocean front with our friends who used to live there, and even though we were just minutes from the border, we could not cross. The virus is still rampant in Belize and whereas many expats used to make a "border run" to renew their six month visa, we were unable to do so. The days of easy border crossings for a few hours, and then returning to start the clock anew, may be gone with the computerization of immigration and border crossings.

Meanwhile, we have several other side trips planned as we FINALLY count the months until it's time to move on.

We had a flight booked in September from Cancun to Rome, then onward to Croatia, and recently discovered that flight was cancelled, with nary a word from TAP Airlines. That changed our plans and now we are looking at other options south of us as we hope and see progress in other countries. Here at the end of the first quarter of 2021, things are still tight, but what will the world look like in six months? It will not be normal as we knew it, but many tourism driven countries lost their entire summer seasons last year and many are loath to face more economic loss. On our possibility list are Ecuador, Brazil, Argentina, Chile and Peru in South America, and Panama and Costa Rico a bit closer.

Date: 04.05.21/ Is It Time to Start Traveling Again?

Welcome to the second quarter of the (still) challenging travel year of 2021. One year ago, when COVID really took hold, we had no idea that 12 months later we'd still be dealing with it. But...here we are.

We are still living in Mexico and itching to move on and will, as soon as we are able. Which brings up the question: **Is It Time to Start Traveling Again?**

That question is a personal one, but here's some factors that you may want to consider. Some of these tidbits are statistical, some are anecdotal or personal, so conclude at your own safe speed!

I looked at three major factors:

- The airline industry and how THEY see things progressing, and their actions/reactions to that progress
- The attitude and perceptions of the PUBLIC, the hoping and hopeful traveling public. The idle and those that do not like to or don't want to travel could care less. Just like a non-sports lover doesn't care about Sunday's game.
- The government, mostly US, since most of my followers are Americans, but not all.

American Airlines, the dominant airline at Reagan National airport in Washington, DC, has increased the number of its peak-day departures from 88 to 141, as of the end of March, and many of the Big Airlines, are seeing demand almost up to 2019 levels: that's TWO years ago.

At a recent U.S. Chamber of Commerce Aviation Summit, United Airlines CEO Scott Kirby said that demand for domestic leisure travel was back at pre-pandemic levels, and has almost entirely recovered. He said that United would see cashflow positive levels for the month of March, which is impressive! As to business and international travel, he said: "Business demand is still down over 80%, and of course international borders, particularly long-haul, are still closed."

So, one out of three sectors for United is at "normal" levels, while two sectors are off considerably.

Other airlines say the same thing, including Alaska Airline's CEO Ben Minicucci, who said "they would also be cash positive for the month of March." They get 30 percent of their business from pure business travelers, and THAT sector MAY be gone for a long time, or permanently.

Airlines are adding new routes and enhancing existing ones to take advantage of the summer demand and United is flying more than 100% of its 2019 capacity to Mexico, the Caribbean and Central and South America, where some countries have reopened to Americans.

Meanwhile, there is a lot of lost ground to recover since the US industry alone lost $35 billion last year, per the Airlines for America, an industry group that represents United Airlines, American, Delta, Southwest and other major carriers, and are still burning through $150M per DAY. American furloughed 13,000 employees as recently as February, but are hiring many back, along with thousands of aircraft that are being brought back from storage and could be back on the tarmac by May.

Will other airlines follow suit? The answer is probably yes.

MY conclusion on that aspect is that the INDUSTRY and the PUBLIC wants to leisurely travel, and that includes international, which is at the whim of any and every countries quirks. Business travelers are not in such a hurry and have learned to work remotely.

To follow that trend, the US State department says passport applications and renewals are way up. Granted, there has been a backlog from the shutdown from last year, when applications sat idle for three months, but there is no question, people want to be ready. Until I researched this information I had no idea that passports have been issued since 1789, and currently they are processing about 1.5M applications per month, almost up to pre-COVID pace. Right now it takes 12 weeks, but can expedite in 4-6 weeks (I've heard faster), and they can issue one in as little as 72 hours in an emergency.

"And the survey says... ," to echo the Family Feud TV show, the consensus of the public is that people are ready to travel. They/ we are tired of being restricted and being confined. Overall 40 percent of US consumers are consistently optimistic, while just under 15 percent remain pessimistic, and more than 50 percent of US consumers expect to spend extra by splurging or treating themselves, with higher-income millennials intending to spend the most. Half of those want to travel, but are still fearful.

Date: 05.14.21/ An Insider's Guide to Learning Inside Secrets

After traveling through 23 countries and staying in most of them, I found an inside secret I wish I had learned *much* sooner!

Important Traveling Info

Picture this: You get to a new town, and the one thing you have more than anything, is **QUESTIONS**! Instead of guessing or wondering, I learned how to get answers: ask the locals. Ask fellow expats. Ask those who previously had the *same* questions, and may have found answers the hard way.

I learned this when I recently went to Acapulco, Mexico, for the first time. One of my initial questions was, "How much should we pay to get from the airport to our hotel?" Since we have dealt with hundreds of taxi drivers over the years, I know that many are not honest, and the range of prices to the same location can vary. So I asked the locals.

They told me that the taxis were federally regulated **AT** the airport, so getting rides **FROM** the airport had little negotiation, but the return trip **BACK** was wide open. This I found out when we paid $450 pesos FROM and $300 pesos TO the airport. Granted, the ride FROM was in a pretty nice car, and the one back was, well, it was a piece of shit! No working speedometer, noisy muffler, rough ride, but a kind, sweet driver who pulled to the side of the road to allow us to take pictures and got us there in one piece. That's a winner. BTW, he offered $300 to start, which I knew was very fair, so he got a nice tip for his honesty.

I also asked about places to eat (got *lots* of suggestions on that one), and since we wanted to see the world famous cliff divers, I had questions on that, too, which got answered. One of the locals warned me that the beaches downtown where we stayed were yucky (true) and recommended one a few miles away called Playa Bonfil. What a find, and a beach we never would have known about. We rented a motorcycle for a day ($20 USD) so took the ride out to Bonfil and found a really nice beach with rows of restaurants offering covered palapas, lounge chairs to lay on, and the cost of this? Just eat there, which we did. For all of about $10 we had several meals and a place to hang for half the day. And another bene was the variety of beach vendors offering lots of cool stuff, like quail's eggs (ate 'em), oysters and clams (passed), and some of the tastiest mango ever, which was probably hanging from a tree a few hours earlier.

In a few months I'll be going to Oaxaca for a few weeks, so I found an expat group for the city and now I monitor their daily feed. Many of the questions that **others** ask I may not have thought of, but they are good questions! As I get closer I will throw my own questions out there and receive more personalized intel. So, if you are planning to go somewhere, do your homework and ask the locals. Here's how:

- In Facebook (probably best) type in "city you wish to visit, expats" in the "group" search, and you may find several. I look for the ones with the most members. They may require you to join, so do that.
- Observe for a few days to see what the chatter is all about. YOUR question(s) may come up, if not, ask them yourself.

And that's it. Mind you this is more suited if you are staying somewhere for a few days or need specific information. If you just want the Top 10 things to do, or something pretty mundane, just Google that yourself.

Date: 05.21.21/ Acapulco Report: Worth it or Not?

Since we were only going to be in Mexico for a short while more, we made a list of places we wanted to go before we left. We had some credit card travel perks, so decided that Acapulco was it, and we spent three days there.

Once upon a time...Acapulco was IT, the **Bomb**, haven and destination of Hollywood glitterati, but those days were replaced by high crime and over building and in the last few years Acapulco was the place to **not** go. These reports came from those that live here in Mexico, or other expats, and we did find the town crowded, noisy and very busy, but manageable. Fortunately we did not encounter any crime issues beyond a dress, of all things, that was removed from our hotel room. In all my travels, THAT was a first. The front desk offered no help and we sadly concluded that it was gone for good.

Before getting there I looked up the Top XX places to go/ things to do, and the cliff divers were in the top three of all the lists. Aside from that, all the others paled by comparison, so, thanks to a very affordable $20 USD day motorcycle, we spent half of day one visiting the over rated Pie de la Questa, which was a nice enough beach, but not worth the time, IMHO. But it was early enough in the day when we were through, so on our way to La Quebrada, the cliff diving spot, we grabbed a quick (and delicious) Mexican meal at a taqueria, and made it to the cliffs about 6:45, just in time for the 7:30 show.

And the cliff divers **are** worth the effort since they are as iconic as any Mexico experience you can see. The video shows it all, and we were right **there**, actually in the way of the divers as they entered the water.

The following morning we were free until we left later in the day, had a few more hours with the bike, so we did find a cool beach which was recommended by a local from their Facebook site. Playa Bonfil was a very nice experience, which I wrote about in a prior blog (An Insider's Guide to Learning Inside Secrets).

This was our first domestic Mexican flight, vs international, and the Cancun airport was MUCH more crowded than we expected, so if you fly domestic, be sure to allow enough time. All along the way we were shocked how **little** was translated into English, so we had to guess at a lot of things. Ditto on the flight. I guess they didn't expect too many Americans.

Some random observations:

- I have never seen so many people SHOP and eat at restaurants bare chested! Don't get excited, it was just the men. In all our time in Mexico I never saw anyone in a grocery store without a shirt, but saw it here twice, and once at a restaurant. Weird!
- The airport there was extraordinarily security conscious and adamant about COVID distancing. Going through their security lines, which was much less busy, was made more difficult since the power mad guards kept stopping the lines and required more spacing. I found it ironic, since we all used the same bins to put luggage on, and they never got cleaned, but just kept churning over and over. Part of the (lack of) common sense in this COVID warry pandemic world.

Is Acapulco worth the time?

Except for the cliff diving, probably not. The cliffs of La Quebrada aside, there WERE other cool ones in the area that may be worth exploring. As far as this traveler, time to move on...

Here's the direct video of the divers if you wish to share:
https://www.youtube.com/watch?v=4zh-PoP--uY

Date: 06.26.21/ You Can't Take It With You?

They say you can't take it with you, but I think you can. You just have to take the things that matter, and that, to me, is very little. The bells, the whistles, the doodads, the gadgets; in the end, they all mean nada. What matters is what you wear, what you need to live, and what you eat.

Important Traveling Info

Since leaving the US in Feb 2019 I have purged several times. When I initially left, all my contents were strewn out on the bed, and I had to determine if they could fit in a 48L backpack; they could not. An additional suitcase was bought and filled, and after leg #1, in Valencia, Spain, those two containers were consolidated into one. The one factor that really makes a difference, is the temperatures of where you are going. Heavy jackets, sweaters, and clothing take a lot of room, whereas if your destination is more temperate, you can get by with a lot less.

Over the course of the last two years plus, old items were discarded and new ones were bought. I have purchased several pairs of shoes, not because of wear, but because of limited ROOM for them to be packed. For clothing, anything that wrinkles is a no-no, and since clothes are cheap outside the US, buying for a "season" is reasonable. In Mexico I got by with one pair of sandals (Keane's), and have bought and eliminated half a dozen tank tops. As a minimalist, I take clothing to the extreme, and spend 80 percent of my waking hours in shorts and that's about it. The umbrella, always nice—and important—to have, has been used a handful of times.

Now I am moving on. After 15 months in Puerto Morelos, I am off to Oaxaca, just south of Mexico City. It is 5000 plus feet above sea level, so colder weather attire IS a must, which I have. The good news is, if I need something more, prices are reasonable. My stay there will be about three weeks, then after a short trip to Las Vegas, it's back, this time to Mexico City, where I plan to stay for a few days because, well, I've never been there. Copper Canyon (look it up!), in Mexico, has been very high on my "must go" list, and I will try to fit that in before departing the country.

The ultimate plan is the South American countries of Ecuador and Peru. Chile was on my list, but since I have only a five-week window and as of right NOW, Chili is off limits without a quarantine, that has been removed. Maybe another time. That period between August 1-Sept 15 (approx.) is totally open to changes, and that is one of the nice things about being a nomad: flexibility. It also is a downside if you like security and familiarity...

I am in discussion with a vape convention that wants me to speak in a place I have never been, but I'm keeping that under wraps until it's finalized. All I can say is that it is an exotic location with some of the world's most spectacular architecture.

This picture here is my backpack and what goes inside. I'll let you know if it does, or if I need to purge again!

Date: 07.04.21/ Travel(ing) Younger is BACK!

Independence Day is a great time to celebrate the new freedom we are just starting to experience—with travel.

After almost 18 months of travel confusion, the view is more clear domestically, as travel is back up to almost 2019 levels! TSA recently screened the most people on that given day than they did two years ago, so that's a positive sign. Meanwhile, international travel is still a checkerboard of different rules and regulations. A COVID test, at least an antigen test, is a given, and the vaccine (which one?) may or may not get you into certain countries and possibly avoid a COVID test prior to arrival. Some countries are still off limits, at least to Americans, and others are only accessible to citizens or those with a legit reason to go.

And the question I asked myself many times over the last year was, "What good is having a travel blog (and guidebooks) on TRAVEL, if we are not able to travel?"

That question perplexed me for 15 months while I whiled away the time in the beautiful seaside village of Puerto Morelos, Mexico, just south of Cancun. When Kathleen and I arrived there the third week of March 2020, we had been chased by COVID from Southeast Asia, landed in Ohio for a wedding, and then quickly left the US for Mexico for a (supposed) two week stay.

I felt like a Gilligan's Island refugee for those that know the show. They left for a three-hour tour, got stranded on an unmarked island, and were there for three years, ie, seasons. Thank God the Professor knew how to make a still so they could get drunk.

But now, the next stages are being laid out, and summer is a huge catalyst for countries to be more lenient since, if they miss THIS summer, that would be devastating to their economy. What happens when summer is over and another cold winter returns? Who knows?

As I write this in July 2021, Kathleen is back in Ohio for the summer to spend time with her new baby grandson and her new step-grandkids, and am in Oaxaca (pronounced Wahacka), south of Mexico City. I have no ocean, which is always a bummer, but the town is amazing in its own way. It has lots of charm and so far, some AMAZING food!! At 5000+ ft elevation the weather is more chilly than I have been used to, and the air is thin. Daytime temps are about 10 degrees cooler, and nighttime temps almost 20 degrees colder, BUT, it's rainy season and that it does— every day! Sometimes torrentially, and it can stop as quickly as it starts.

While here I am taking a six-hour bus ride to the coast, a town called Puerto Escondido, to compare from Puerto Morelos, and today I am booking my first "big" trip in a while-Ecuador- on August 6. My six-week window until mid-September will be between there and Peru, the next stop. Chile is still off limits to Americans. Both countries at high altitudes, and I must be prepared for that, since altitude sickness IS a real thing, and Quito, the capital of Ecuador, is 9350 feet above sea level, which will be an all-time high (no pun...) for me. I have never had any altitude issues, but time, years, and everything DOES take their tolls, so I will be careful.

The past 18 months has been such a mixture of emotions for the entire world. Bad, good, stress, frustration, even sickness and sometimes, death, have been a part of everyone's life. I wish I could believe that it is ALL over, but I think it will be a while yet.

Airlines are bringing planes out of storage and bringing people back from furlough. This SUMMER will be interesting as people get on the ROAD (they already are) and back on trains and planes.

I met wonderful people in Puerto Morelos, mostly expats from the US and Canada. I truly believe that as the world gets more "complicated" and frustrating in those two countries, people will continue to bail in record numbers. Between cost of living, quality of life, and government restrictions and interference, it's no wonder.

Life is about independence- YOUR independence- to live the life you want to live. Enjoy it while you/ we can; it ain't going to last forever! Happy holiday!

Date: 07.09.21/ The Bohemian Lifestyle, Part I

Whether you do it for a day, a weekend, the week, or longer, the Bohemian lifestyle may appeal to you. It is not for everyone since there are some things that you will do without. Screens, sometimes missing. Wi-Fi? Iffy at best. Clothing: optional...

Cool stuff to know...

Yes, Zipolite is the only clothing optional beach in Mexico, so has something for someone who is looking for a totally laid-back atmosphere. The beach itself is only a little over a mile long and except for some lodgings along the sand there's really not much to it. It is a long bus ride from Oaxaca, took me almost 10 hours with several stops along the way. The bus was comfortable, however, fully air conditioned, and reclining seats. There was a stop along the way for lunch since I took the early morning bus, and we finally rode into our destination, Pochutla bus terminal, about 7:00. I lost count of how many mezcal fields we passed, but it must have been in the hundreds, which makes sense since this state is the world capital of the fine agave plant.

Pochutla does not seem to have much going forward except it is the transit hub for the coast cities. My "plan" was Puerto Escondido, with a side trip to Zipolite and Mazunte, but it turned out the side trips took priority over the main destination.

My little beach bungalow was not much to speak of, just a few rooms and a restaurant out on the sand. The room was on the top floor, which included some treacherous stairs, but the view from the balcony was breathtaking. My room had hardwood floors, probably a smart idea since the roof was nothing more than thatch. The mosquito netting was there not just for show and for the first time ever in my life I slept under it.

I was woken up a little after 2:00 a.m. by lightning which was starting over the ocean. I got up and sat outside for 20 minutes trying to take video which required some heavy editing. The expression "capturing lightning in a bottle" seemed to fit, but I was able to piece together half a dozen shots to get 30 seconds worth. I went back in and tried to go to sleep but was restless, and just before 4:00 a.m. my door was literally blown in from the strength of the wind. The lightning was even m prominent, so I took that as a sign to go back outside and take some more vi'

They say that you can always sleep when you're dead, and this was a night where being awake was maybe more fun than the sleep that I missed! Listening to the waves crashing just a hundred feet from my room is not something we experience every day. The humidity was so thick that, to coin a cliche, you could cut it with a knife.

And 0430 the night went a whole new direction as the storm cell finally brought thunder. The lightning increased, the thunder rolled in, and it was very biblical. The rain really never started, but the lightning and thunder put on a wonderful audio/video show.

The next night I had a room reserved in Mazunte, so went the 10 minutes down the road to stay there, but came back to Zipolite for my last night. Puerto Escondido will have to wait. After all, I've seen many large size cities; I'd rather enjoy the uniqueness of the beach here.

As I mentioned at the beginning, this is the only fully nude beach in Mexico, and people take advantage of it. The beach goers feel very comfortable in their skin, regardless of their bodies, and that is freeing in its own way. I know it is for me! One thing that was treacherous there were the rip tides, probably the worst I have ever been in. From one second to the other I was getting pulled out, in, left and right, and if I lost my footing it could be bad. The evening I got there I witnessed this first hand as I saw two young men literally being pulled out to the ocean as though they were on a conveyor belt. It was a blink of an eye. Fortunately, there were two lifeguards who hauled ass, grabbed the two guys, and brought them back to shore. Initially I thought they were kids, but they were strapping teenagers, so what does that say for a less strong person in that water?

I also found out afterwards that "Zipolite" means "beach of the dead," and have drownings year-round.

Date: 07.16.21/ The Bohemian Lifestyle, Part II (PLUS Bonus Feature on Nude Beaches 101)

When last we left our intrepid explorer, he was dodging rip tides and naked bodies in the Mexico beach communities of Mazunte and Zipolite. Today we learn more about the two towns PLUS a special bonus feature on the joys of nude beaches...

Day II:

It's amazing how two beach towns that are only 10 minutes away from each other can be so different. But while the city of Zipolite seems to cater to the laid-back hippie and older demographic, Mazunte is definitely for the kids. In this case kids means anyone under the age of say 30, since that was the most dominant age group that I saw. They seem to live with varying degrees of comfort, ie, some of them look like they don't have two pennies to rub together, and others look like they're very comfortable. The feeling I had was very nostalgic, like I was looking at me and my fellow baby boomers from the late 60s before we had any cares in the world and thought we had all the answers. At one time I also thought that walking barefoot in the streets was cool!

The town itself has a very cool vibe, with lots of restaurant choices. The beach is quite beautiful with many restaurants out on the sand, which is a Mexican coast staple. My room was a great improvement from what I had night one since it had a screen! and great Wi-Fi. As much as I can handle doing without, doing with can be good too!

The following morning, I got up at sunrise and walked out to what they call **Punta Cometa**, the "kite tip." It was about a 20-minute hike up to the top of the cliff where you could see up one side of the coast and down the other with amazing waves crashing on the rocks. The water, of course, was a deep vibrant blue, and was gorgeous as is most of the waters that I have seen in Mexico. I had a light breakfast, took advantage of the Wi-Fi, and got some work done and returned to Zipolite in a pickup truck with a shell and seats in the back! They call them collectivos and that is how most people get around, especially within the towns. You flag down the driver, jump in the back, as long as there is room, then tap on his window when you want to get off. This particular ride was all of 15 minutes and cost $10 (pesos), which is about

50 cents USD. Again, this is not the most comfortable way to travel, and it's not for everyone!! If you are concerned about motion sickness, or feel uncomfortable riding in the back of a truck with strangers who look nothing like you, then this is definitely outside your comfort zone...

My third night was supposed to be in Puerto Escondido, but after talking to several people down there and hearing them say the same thing, which is, "it's just another regular town, but with a beach," I decided to go back to Zipolite. I did not go back to the same hotel room however but was recommended to a place further down on the beach, and still got my sand view for $20 for the night. The room was an upgrade from what I had the first night, but still, no Ritz Carlton. Or even Holiday Inn!

Since I had to vacate my room by noon and my bus didn't leave until 10:00 p.m., so I had lots of time to kill, and did what anyone would do: hung out in a hammock, had two meals there, and chilled. In between I also visited the surf, still as knarly as ever. I took the night bus so didn't need a room that night but got little sleep. At 0800 the next morning I was back in Oaxaca and have wonderful memories and pictures to look back on.

If you do have a chance to visit Oaxaca, I encourage you to take a few extra days and hit the beach and find your inner Bohemian!

BONUS: The ABCs of Getting Naked in Public

Let's face it, getting naked in public for the first time can be an experience, and there is a process, and it is NOT for the faint of heart!

When you visit a "clothing optional beach," oh darn it, let's call it what it is: it's a naked beach for crying out loud, ie, no bathing suits. You can use politically correct terms, but it is about as raw and basic as you can get since the only thing you're wearing is what you were born with.

I was in Zipolite, which is the only naked beach in Mexico, and look how big this country is and how much coastline it has! So, I decided to give you a primer, a by the step process if you ever choose to be so bold.

Step number one is all psychological: it's all in your head. You must be comfortable removing your bathing suit knowing that other eyes may be watching, but truth is, few if any of them are. We all feel self-conscious about our bodies even in clothing, and bearing it to strangers can be even more challenging. But the good news? They ARE strangers, and you will never see them again. For the most part they are NOT judging you, and it's best to not judge them, either. Most of the people that you see at a nude beach are not exactly Sports Illustrated model candidates nor hunks of the month for the GQ magazine.

Number two, make sure that you have something stable to hold on to because taking off your bathing suit while standing on sand, can be difficult to balance. It's one thing getting undressed, it's another falling over with your bathing suit wrapped around your feet. Now THAT will garner some attention!

Number three, now that you are naked in all your glory, what are you going to do? Are you going into the surf? Are you going to lay out on a blanket or lounge? The answer is, it really doesn't matter, just do what you would do even if you had a bathing suit on. If a beach has businesses, like restaurants and hotels, like we have down here, it's usually considered respectful to not enter the premises unclosed. Out in the sun, and on a chair, it's a free-for-all, but if you enter an establishment, probably not a good idea.

Number four is the fun part. Now that you are naked, enjoy it; embrace it! It is not something you do every day unless you happen to live in that space. The feeling of freedom, once we get over our self-consciousness, is quite nice. Going into the water and having the waves splash your entire body, getting into every corner; it's very primal.

And step number five, now that you have done the deed; own it. Brag about it, your friends will be envious! They may even want to join you next time you visit one. And once you have done it one time, the second time will probably be easier, but not always. As is everything, the more you do something the easier it is to do it.

So welcome to the "In the Buff Club."

Date: 07.28.21/ How Your Life Can Change over Five Years

Five years ago...

Can your life completely change in 5 years? I can tell you based on my experience the answer is a big YES!

Important Traveling Info

Five years ago today (July 28, 2016), I left the US on a 3-week trip to Europe, in essence, for the very first time. I landed in Amsterdam and was there for a few days and over the next 19 days visited six countries. I was amazed at how people moved so fluidly from one country to the next, especially the younger generation. Differences in language, currency, and background did not matter at all, and the most noteworthy thing was that people actually do take vacations, which they call holidays. They do not, did not, live to work; they lived to live. That inspired me and made me want to visit more often.

The idea of moving overseas or being a permanent traveling nomad was not even close to being on my radar! But here it is, 5 years later, and I have been on the move ever since.

If you ever wonder if your life can totally turn around in 5 years, I can give you my answer, and in my case, it did not even take 3 years, it took much less. You just have to focus on what you want, and execute. And I have found over the course of my life that execution is the most difficult part of anything and everything.

Dream big, don't let anything stop it from happening.

Date: 07.31.21/ Parting Thoughts of Mexico: Time to Move on (Mar 2020- July 2021) 496 days

I spent a collective 17 months or so (actually 496 days more or less with some of those days back in the US) in Mexico, a long way from what was intended to be a two-week visit. Overall, I liked it more than I would have expected; the people were generally outstanding, very nice and accommodating, and even with no Espanola, I got by. There are things that I will miss and some things I look forward to.

Cool stuff to know...

> Pastry in Mexico is just not the same as any other parts of the world that I have visited. They are good, but there's very few things that I've found that had justified me taking in those carbs and those calories into my body.

>I will not miss the mosquitoes! Whether I was a sea level in Puerto Morelos or 5,000 ft in Oaxaca, it seems that the mosquitoes are part of the culture. The humidity at the coast, of course, was oppressive, especially in the summer, but the air quality in Oaxaca was wonderful. With that said, I spent the last 2 weeks in Mexico City at 7,000 FT elevation and, what do you know?, no mosquitoes!

>The ocean water was never close to being cold, maybe a bit cool, but that's about it. But some of the waves that I saw down in the Puerto Escondido area where some of the most challenging I've ever seen.

>Very affordable food. It's all relative, of course, but still, a fraction of US prices. Overall, it was all good. I had one incident of food poisoning towards the end--it wasn't even a street stand-- and that can happen anywhere, even in the US.

>Even though they lack a (usable) railroad system, the bus systems seems to be pretty good. It can cover many hundreds of miles, but their Greyhound style buses are very comfortable. I took three long distance bus trips, all around 8 or 9 hours, and I was amazed how quickly the time went and how beautiful the scenery was; it's a wonderful way to see the country.

When Kathleen and I started planning our journeys several years ago, Mexico was not on the list and Central/ South America were at the end. This part of the world never drew me in or engaged me, but that does not mean it wasn't beautiful and rewarding in its own way.

Will I ever return to Mexico? It's too hard to predict anything with 100% accuracy, but probably not.

During my last weeks in Mexico, I was fortunate to stay with a friend in Mexico City. She invited me into her home as a guest and friend and we took side trips down to Pueblo and San Miguel de Allende. As a native Mexican she also educated me on many things that I did not know and it made me aware of opportunities that I let fall between my fingers while we were in the Yucatan. I guess sometimes you just can't do it all.

While I was in Oaxaca, I wanted to visit the petrified waterfall called Hierve el Agua, one of only two in the world, but it was closed due to controversy between the indigenous people and the tourists. The Copper Canyon train ride had been on my list for long before I even got to Mexico, and I had it set for the last few days while I was there in the country. Then I found out that the train route had been flooded and they were offline for several weeks, including my short window of time while I was there! Sigh... my friend said this is the risk you take when you travel around the world, and he is correct.

Now it's on to South America (I'm actually there now...) and continent # 5. Just Australia and Antarctica left, and they are iffy. So little time...Life goes by in an instant, but it usually takes decades to recognize that and to do anything about it. Not that there is anything specific to DO about it, but just appreciate it.

Date: 08.03.21/ New "Firsts": Continent, Country, Hemisphere, Living at 9,000 ft Elevation!

Oh yes, there are a lot of firsts going on here!

Ecuador is country number 35, and I'm going to throw Panama in there as number 34 even though I never got out of the airport! I figure, hey, if I'm landing on foreign soil then I'm in that country, but in the short while that I was at the airport it felt very Americanized.

Cool stuff to know...

And honestly, South America was not very high on my list of places to visit, but I may be changing my tune. I've been in Quito for only a few days, but I love the energy and vibe of the city. I am renting a room from a lifelong native and he does tours of the city so knows it well. We went to the downtown historic area, and I got educated and learned that Ecuador was the FIRST (see!) country in South America to be freed from Spain in the early 1800's. Simon Bolivar was a genius and in turn helped other countries do the same. At one time there was an effort to make most of South America part of COLUMBIA, and had that happened, our maps would be much different.

This area is also seismically active and there are two volcanos just outside the city: Cotopaxi, which is still active, and Chimborazo, which is Ecuador's highest peak at 20,548 feet (6,263 meters). I will be taking a motorcycle ride and a bus ride through them and look forward to that since volcanos have always been fascinated me.

Another first is the elevation where I am living, which is over 9,000 ft above sea level. So far, I have not felt it and the air is as crisp and clean as you would expect. The mountains surround the city and the view coming in from the airport was amazing as is the view from my room. When I went to bed the first night, I was awed by all the lights before me and the outline of the mountain peak. There is a cable car (Teleferiqo) nearby which takes you up the mountain called Pichincha (also active, last eruption in 1999) and I went to the cable car drop zone which is over 13,400 feet above sea level, the highest I have been. There is a path that goes to the TOP of Pichincha, and that is 15,695 ft., and I am giving that serious consideration...

I can't say that I was ever really attracted to Latin American countries, but I also never thought that I would find myself living in Mexico! Shit happens, right? There is a large expat community here and I was told that the city of Cuenca is the largest expat haven for Americans in the entire world. I plan to go there shortly.

South America is my fifth continent, and the first time in the southern hemisphere. The water in the toilet DOES flush counterclockwise, which I did not even notice at first. In a few days I will straddle the northern/ southern hemisphere line and let you know if I am in fact pulled in two directions! At the equatorial line a toilet flush SHOULD go straight down without swirling. Stand by for videos of that!

I need to be back in the US about September 12th for a trip to Dubai which seems to be taking place. Travel is very day to day, week to week right now but so far the event that I'm due to speak at is still moving forward.

Unfortunately, COVID is not over, and who knows if it ever will be. It will impact our lives and certainly our travel for the foreseeable future, but even with having to deal with face masks, sanitizing lotions, and COVID test with every new country I enter, I'm just glad that it's open to this point. Later this month I will join Kathleen and hit country #35: Peru.

My heart still lies in Europe, and I think that when this wanderlust is satisfied, that will be the base. Visa restrictions only allow 90 days generally, but I have no problem bouncing from one wonderful place to another every 90 days. And then there are a few safe havens like Albania and Georgia which offer a one-year visa. Like all of us, I am getting older day by day, and eventually we'll have to stop. Where and when that might be is unknown, but until then I will continue to Travel Younger!

Date: 08.15.21/ Next stop: Ecuador on Two Wheels

I have ridden motorcycles in Croatia; I have ridden in Romania; and now I have done the same in Ecuador. Until now, Romania was at the top of my "best roads" and "most fun" list, but they may be knocked off by my latest journey through beautiful Ecuador.

In all candor, I was not that enthused about South America when I started my nomadic journey three years ago, and I knew little about this country. I naively thought it was "hot" since it lies on the equator, and I never knew I'd be spending most of my time over 9000 feet above sea level! But I recently completed a 573 km (356 mile) bike trip over three days and saw some amazing things and enjoyed some of the grandest roads I have ever ridden. But there was a health hazard: my neck got sore from turning one direction to the next as every curve exposed more unique beauty. My jaw hurt after so many jaw-dropping vistas, but it was the never-ending grin on my face that brought sublime pleasure as I realized I was riding through some amazing country, full of history and some of the most geologically active terrain I have ridden through in my life. The smile was with me the whole time.

Thanks to my new best friends at Freedom Ecuador, I was able to see this country unlike most visitors, since they are usually in a tour bus or car. But the elevation changes from one minute to the next pushed my Suzuki V-strom to the limits and I reached the conclusion that that bike is ideal for me. Between the size, weight, torque and easy on throttle, the V-strom rocks! Freedom hooked me up with everything I needed, from protective (and warm) armored pants, to boots, gloves and jacket, so I was comfy and warm.

When I left Quito at 9000 feet and traversed into the 12,000-foot elevation of Quilatoa Crater, which is amazing, the roads were heavenly. From a few back roads to the extraordinary highways, it was smooth sailing almost the entire time.

I was lucky to have another friend, Edison Calvopina, who is also a tour guide and lifelong native of Quito, that made the trip even better. He's been riding these roads for a decade and mapped out the same route that Freedom suggested! Great minds do think alike.

We left Quito on day one and within an hour were out of the city and traffic. Not long after, the great Cotopaxi volcano showed up on my left, and we had to stop for shots. Often obscured by clouds, I find that mornings are usually best for clear viewing, and the almost 20,000 foot mountain was as spectacular close up as it was from Quito. Soon we left the major highway and took a mostly backroad to the "city" of Sigchos, which was quite small. But the route out was a biker's dream as the twisties kept coming and we handled them all with finesse. One of the great things about bikes is that signs like "road closed" does not always deter us. We asked some locals if the road was really closed, and they told us there was road work being done and we should give it a shot.

Which we did.

Ecuador is a majestic country with grandesque mountains and carved out valleys, and with that you get erosion and road damage. We had to slowly go through about 50 yards of narrow road full of rubble and saw the problem: half the road was gone- down the hill. But when we emerged the road opened up to a beautifully paved highway and I put the V-strom through its' paces as we went up one hill onto the next. For an hour it was one continual grin which plastered my face.

Our first major stop was the city of Quilatoa, which is set off the main road and to enter you actually pay a small fee! But it's worth it as we rode to the end of one of the streets and saw the park on the right side. I knew there was something over the rise, but I was not expecting a volcanic lake! Turquoise blue, shining in the sun, even with the howling wind, it was breathtaking. There are paths to follow all the way down, but time did not allow that luxury.

We had a terrific lunch at a local hostel that my friends knew about, and I had amazing trout and shrimp for all of $8.50 USD. But decisions needed to be made: do we stay there or venture on to the city of Banos, which we intended to hit on Day II. I asked, "Is it warmer down there?" and with a YES answer, off we went. It was only about 80 km, but with roads like this, nothing is quick- except us on our bikes.

Since it was about 2:30 when we headed off, Edison estimated arrival time into Banos about sunset, 6:30 or so, which worked for me.

Over the next four hours it was more amazing roads, and each corner revealed yet another magnificent view. At 6:30, just as predicted, we rode down into the valley of Banos, just 5900 feet above sea level, and much warmer. It is also the entrance to the Amazon, and I noticed the different heat, humidity, and vegetation, which was every imaginable shade of green you could think of.

Date: 08.24.21/ 12 Interesting Things About Ecuador

My 25 days in Ecuador were much different than I expected. When I started my nomadic journey, I made a list of places I wanted to go; Latin America was at the bottom. Nothing personal, but I guess I am more drawn to Europe than South/ Central America, and after living next to Mexico for decades I wasn't that enamored with the country. And here I ended up living in Mexico for 15 months and loving Ecuador- Go Figure!

Cool stuff to know...

Anyway, here's some things I didn't know before:

- They use US currency, mostly $1 coins, but they are only good in Ecuador and are different than the ones in the US. I saw just one $1.00 bill and I gave it back to him! Panama also uses US currency but, likewise, only between its borders.
- The Andes mountains are actually two mountain chains that parallel each other. Many cities fall in between them including the city of Quito. They go from north to south and converge right by Banos, the city that I visited on my bike ride.
- I naively thought that a country on the equator would be hot, especially in summer, but not so. This country actually goes from the high, high mountains to the plains, to the ocean. That gives it an incredible range of wildlife and vegetation and the most diversity in one country in the world in certain categories.
- Speaking of the Equator, this latitude intersection here between north and south is the highest elevation in the world, at 9,000+ ft. elevation. I have a video of the Coriolis force which shows water draining STRAIGHT, with no rotation, immediately on the line.
- The effects of being on the equator, Part II: when you live equidistant (more or less) from the equator, things don't change too much: weather, hours of daylight, etc... What DOES matter is elevation since that effects temps more than the latitude. BUT, one of the benes of being elevated is...no (or few) bugs! I have not seen an ant, mosquito, or cockroach since

- I've been in Ecuador. Mind you, at lower elevations and near the Amazon, scratch that rule!
- Volcanoes! Chimborazo, at 20,548 ft., which is just a few hours from Quito, is the tallest mountain in the world when measured from the center of the earth. It is currently dormant, has been for about 1500 years, and is taller than Mount Everest by 1811 meters. That is mostly due to what they call the equatorial bulge.
- There are 47 volcanoes in Ecuador, yes, I had to look that up, including 15 alone on the Galapagos Islands, which is a whole 'nother conversation that I'm not getting into.
- Food: lots of pork! They tell me that the beef is not as good as it is in other countries, but with great seafood and freshwater fish. It's interesting when you look at the carcass of the pork up on the counter, and they just cut pieces out of it. Guinea pigs of all things are a delicacy here, and they like their sweets like sugarcane and other nationally grown products.
- More food. Lunch, called comida, is the big meal of the day and you can get a standard setup which includes juice, soup, and main course, for as little as $2.50. They really don't take siestas here so most restaurants are open all afternoon.
- A special note about tacos and tortillas. In the US we know tacos, and in Mexico I certainly had my share, but other countries in Latin America do not do conventional tacos. Other parts of Mexico make them out of corn, and here, in Ecuador, they make them from potatoes, but they are not the same. I haven't seen a Taco Bell, but I'd be curious to see what they sell!
- Being relatively close to the US there are many expats from there living in Ecuador, and I understand that Cuenca has one of the largest expat community outside the United States. Even in Quito there is a solid expat community. I got to know many of them and heard many stories.
- Travel time: beauty verses time efficiency. From Quito to Cuenca I took the bus which took 8 hours. My return flight was less than an hour. So which is the better option? I think it's a matter of what drives you the most. In my case I wanted to see the beauty so endured the long bus ride, but there was no reason to do it again! So the one hour that it took me to fly made a lot more sense. Just food for thought..

Next stop: *Peru*

Date: 09.09.21/ Next stop: Peru Travels, Parts I & II

Part II of our journey started in Lima on a tour bus called Peru Hop at 05:30 in the morning. After several days of weighing options, we decided to take the bus south and visit several different cities which eventually would lead us to Cusco, the gateway to Machu Picchu. We did this so we could see different parts of the country along with acclimating to higher elevations from sea level.

Important Traveling Info

The first five days, part I, we spent in Lima, and they were fairly uneventful, and regretfully, we really didn't get around that much. Since Kathleen and I had to coordinate travel plans for the next week to several months, much of that time was spent doing that along with figuring out details about the trip to Machu Picchu.

We were at an Airbnb room outside downtown Lima, so we got to know the local area well, including the amazing restaurants that were abundant and very inexpensive. But overall Lima did not stick out in our minds.

One of the biggest topics of conversation was altitude sickness, since it is a real thing and we had to look at all the different cities and how high the elevation was. The net result was that we committed to staying hydrated, and just watching for symptoms.

We started our bus tour in the dark and a few hours later found ourselves in the city of Paracas, a small seaside village that is known for its access to the Ballestas Islands, about 45 minutes away by boat, which is a bird sanctuary. We were hoping to find sun filled skies to compensate for the overcast days we had in Lima, and as we were finishing our tour the sun did come out, which was a refreshing change.

After a nice lunch, we were back in the bus heading to the town of Huacachina, which is literally an oasis in the middle of the desert. This town is known for their enormous, and I mean enormous, sand dunes that you can buggy up, or hike, or do whatever you wish to do in the sand, but we chose not to partake. The air was extraordinarily dry and the idea of getting sandy and hot just did not sound appealing. We find our pleasures where we can!

The next morning was pleasant with a cool mist in the air, and during the day we visited a chocolate factory and a winery and got to sample both. Then it was back to town and back on the bus for our next leg to the town of Nazca, which is world renown from their lines/ pictures in the sand. There are about 70 of them, but most are viewable only from the air. After driving for several hours we got to the viewing tower which is about five or six stories tall and were able to see them from above. They were cool, no doubt, but I thought they would be much larger than they were. Regardless, they are an iconic part of Inca history. We got there just before closing and after a meal, prepared to take our first overnight bus trip to Arequipa, the second largest city in Peru.

It was due to leave at 9:00 pm, but got delayed till about 11:00, but inconveniences are part of life and of traveling. The seats were comfy, but still, a good night's sleep on a bus is difficult. We rolled in at 0900 and went to our nice $12 per night room where we stayed for two nights. A great breakfast and nap got us refreshed and the next morning at 0300 (that's a.m.!) I left for Colca Canyon, one of the deepest in South America. Wisely, Kathleen decided to skip that one since it was going into extraordinarily high elevations, which turned out to challenge me as well..

Sleeping on that tour bus was just not an option, so it was beautiful watching the night sky and the dawn as it rose over the mountains. On the way I kept monitoring the elevation and eventually at the summit hit the highest point I have ever been: 16,000 ft, then we went a bit lower, and over the next few hours explored the beautiful canyon, got to see my first condors, and also had my first exposure to altitude sickness.

I was not sure what was behind it initially, since I had been hydrating like crazy, and I ate a piece of fruit that made me a little bit queasy, but for several hours I felt like crap. Eventually I did throw up, which helped, and as we eventually got back to Arequipa, my stomach and head started settling down into normality. Here I thought I was immune to it, so I learned a very valuable lesson. Good health came just in time as a few hours later we departed for our second overnight bus ride in 3 days. BTW, this is not a schedule that I would recommend. Overnight buses are fine, but spacing them apart is a more wise move.

We left at 8:30 p.m. for Cusco, which is a 10-hour ride. This bus was much nicer than the prior one, but we found sleep challenging, and unfortunately Kathleen had some bouts with altitude sickness combined with motion sickness. Let's just say that bus rides need to be taken in moderation. At 11,000 ft elevation, our plan was always to stay in Cusco only as long as we needed to, which is exactly what we did. We found it challenging finding canisters of oxygen at 0700 on a Saturday morning, but a very cooperative taxi driver was able to help us. Rather than take a very crowded but cheaper collectivo, we hired him to take us to our next stop, Ollantaytambo, the city it has taken me a week to remember!

That city is one of the several gateways to Machu Picchu, and that will take us into part III.

Date: 09.13.21/ Peru Travels, Part III (Machu Picchu and Beyond)

I wish I could say that Machu Picchu was the highlight of our 12 days on the Peruvian roads and rails, but it was not. Hang on, I'll get to that...

Cool stuff to know...

We got to Cusco (11K elevation), and immediately hightailed it to Ollantaytambo, just 72 km (45 mi) away and a lower 8800 feet elevation, in about 90 minutes. This is one SMALL town and you can walk from one end to the other in about 10 minutes. With a population of about 10,000 people, (and that includes the outlying areas) the town thrives on two things: an amazing shrine, called The Sun Temple, in the middle of town, and the Peru Rail train stop which leads to Machu Picchu just 90 minutes away. The solitude was what we needed after an almost 12 hour bus ride the night before, and Kathleen having motion sickness problems much of the way.

Not fun.

After a few hours rest we explored and readied ourselves for the next day, when we would take the 0745 train to Machu Picchu, which BTW, is NOT the easiest place to visit. This is also not a cheap ticket and we opted for the "Vista Dome" which has glass wrapped around the top and afforded a very nice view and worth the money. It also allowed us to experience live entertainment with Peruvian music and dancing on the train. This was truly magical and getting to our destination came too soon. Even so, the ride was extraordinary, watching the high cliffs of Mount Veronica on one side, and the Urubamba River on the other.

After checking into our room in Aguas Calientes, we explored this charming, but very touristy town, for a few hours, got our pricey $24 bus ride tickets (it's only a 25 minute ride) and got in line for our 2:00 pm tour. We had a very difficult time finding ACCURATE and TRUSTWORTHY information on how and where to get tickets, but fortunately we had a good "inside man," Garret Geitner, a Facebook friend, who lives in Cusco. A 10 minute video call helped us a lot and we bought our entry tickets online ($38 each) and were ready to go. I will be providing an easy "Five Steps to Machu Picchu Guide" for you shortly, and it will walk you through exactly what WE did, and you can choose to follow if you want.

We hear about and read about Machu Picchu all our lives, and to see it there, in front of us, was a somber moment. Considering I never really traveled internationally until 5 years ago, and over the past 3 years have put on over 100,000 miles, I cannot say that this was the culmination, but it certainly put a mark in my mind.

The shrine IS breathtaking. To think of what it took to build such a structure at 8000 ft altitude is inspiring. Machu Picchu was not even discovered until 1911 and I have a picture below of what it looked like when it was shrouded in vegetation. Even though we are in the midst of Covid, it was still very crowded which took away some of the spiritual connection that I hoped to achieve there. Kathleen felt the same way. We were able to tour the entire facility in the two-hour time window that they provided for us, and even though there are other shrines in the area, most of them are still closed.

Kat and I talked quite a bit about our lack of connection to the monument, but a few days later after we returned to Ollantaytambo, we did in fact create a spiritual connection-- to a mountain.

We stayed in a hotel, on the side of a mountain. It is called the Vertical Lodge, and I have been reading about hotels like this for several years, but never in my wildest dream ever thought that I would stay there. Through the generous contribution of friends, we were able to make this once in a lifetime dream come true.

The lodge is built on a mountain, and there are 3 geodesic domes and 4 capsules that are literally hung on the side of a cliff. They just opened the beginning of August, and were still working out some bugs, so we got to be one of their beta testers. We had the choice of staying in either one, but because of the awkwardness of getting into a capsule and the fact that there is no room outside to really lounge, we went with the dome, and were very glad we did.

Imagine being inside of a dome with no real walls on the exterior, but just glass, and you can imagine what that night sky looked like at 11,000 ft! We got there about 2:30 in the afternoon and got a tour of the property. One of the amazing things about this location is the high quality restaurant on site, like a five-star resort looking at panoramic vistas all around.

We spent two days there, and they offered other treats, like zip lining, walking bridges, and repelling, but the mountain, as glorious as it was, is quite windy, and we did not feel comfortable doing any of those. That wind also made it mighty chilly at night! But as soon as that sun came up, the thermal rays warmed it up in no time.

Something else happened up there that we were not expecting.

When we got there and sat down in the restaurant for the first time, we felt an overwhelming sense of calm and emotions, and I was almost brought to tears. For several minutes I sat there, my mind was blank, and I just felt the grace and the gratitude of my life. Later on we found out that the owners of the mountain built this facility to share these exact same emotions. The lodge is family owned, and they believe that there is a spiritual energy there, and I definitely agree.

Across from Mount Veronica, which was to our right, there were three cathedral-like peaks on the other side that captured Kathleen's attention and she was drawn to them. When we mentioned that to Alan, the manager, he told us that the Incas believed that those three peaks were a door to another world and it reflected back on Mount Veronica. Some things defy explanation, and this is one of them.

We finally came back down to the city of Ollantaytambo, which, BTW, is part of the Sacred Valley, into our new room, and relaxed until our departure the next day to the city of Pisac. I knew nothing about the city, and the 90-minute taxi ride was absolutely gorgeous since we were going right through this valley. And the city had an interesting effect on both of us as well.

And that was a very cool energy which felt like a Northern California town from 1975. All the people were very mellow, and friendly, and the quality of craftmanship in that town from the different vendors was phenomenal. The town is a big draw for those looking for spiritual journeys, and ayahuasca, which I took last year, is a big attraction here. We never know until we visit a town whether we should spend more or less time there, and this was one that we both agreed we should have stayed for longer. But I guess that's a story for another day.

When we began our journey 3 years ago, our goal was to stay in different locations for 6 weeks and identify those that we wished to return to. Even though we did not spend 6 weeks in Peru, I think both of us agreed that we liked Latin America more than we thought we would and a return trip is definitely a consideration.

Our flight back to Lima was effortless, and the Cusco airport had probably the most easy security I have ever seen. Not only did we not have to remove our shoes or computers, we also did not have to remove the bottled water from our bag or Kathleen's canister of oxygen! That was a first. (Later we found the same ease at the Lima airport, so maybe allowing water is now a thing. God, I hope so). The return stay to Lima was only 24 hours long as we took the red eye at midnight back to Miami (on 9/11). I will be in the US for 2.5 days, and then on to another trip I never thought I would take: Dubai. I will be there for a business event and will share that in a future entry.

Date: 09.17.21/ Six Weeks in South America (Overview)

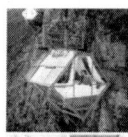

To borrow the title from a wonderful song in the play "*Hamilton*," my 6 weeks in South America were truly "Unimaginable."

When I left the US in February 2019, I had a mental list of where I wanted to travel in the world. Latin America, which includes Mexico, South, and Central America, were lower on my bucket list, but sometimes perceptions change hard, and my perceptions of South America have made a dent.

Being stuck in Mexico for 15 months due to Covid made me anxious to get back on the road, and since I had business events in the United States over the summer months, it made sense for me to stay *relatively* close. June 28 was my last day in Puerto Morelos, Mexico, and since I had heard so much about the city of Oaxaca, that is where I went for about 3 weeks. Like many times before, I used Oaxaca as a home base while I went to the cities of Mazunte and Zipolite, which I loved. They were very mellow beach towns and even though the water there was rough and it was an 8 hour bus ride away, it was absolutely gorgeous.

A few weeks later I found myself landing in Quito, Ecuador, my first footsteps in South America, and the first south of the equator. I had a vision in my mind of the Andes mountains and the west coast of the new continent was really the only place I wanted to go. High elevations never stopped me, and I had a vision of the mountains, the clouds, and standing at the center of the world, divided between the Northern and Southern hemispheres. I was able to enjoy them all.

I was very, very lucky that I stayed with a gentleman in Quito who turned out to be a very good friend. Edison and I hit it off from the very beginning, and though he was half my age, I considered him both a brother and a son at the same time. And we shared many philosophical and relationship conversations along with our love of motorcycles. I was able to rent a motorcycle for 3 days and he and I hit the road that he knew very well and enjoyed some of the most amazing scenery I've ever seen in my life. Even with the higher elevations and the colder temperatures, I had a grin on my face the entire time.

The only other town in Ecuador that I wanted to visit was Cuenca, which I had heard much about. The 8-hour bus ride through some of the most amazing roads I've ever seen was worth the inconvenience and the time, and I found Cuenca to be a charming little town. I connected with many fellow expats, picked their brains, and compared notes about why they settled there, and we all shared our experiences along the way. I did several awesome hikes to elevations I had never hit before, and overall, it was a beautiful time.

I later returned to Quito for a few days and then on to Lima, Peru, where I connected with my love, Kathleen. She and I took a two-month hiatus while she spent time with her son and grandchildren, and I executed the urge to travel by myself. As an only child and a very comfortable solo traveler, I needed to go through that experience myself, which was challenging in its own way on our relationship, but overall made us stronger than ever.

She, like many, were drawn to Machu Picchu, and though it was on my list, it was not a must do visit. Truthfully, I like things easy, and getting to Machu Picchu is anything but! It is way out of the way, and from Lima you must get to Cusco, then on Machu Picchu. Long story short, and you can check out my prior blogs, we did just that and Machu Picchu was pretty awesome, though not the spiritual aha moment that I was anticipating or looking forward to.

After our visit there, we stayed at the most amazing hotel I have ever stayed at before, the Vertical Lodge, and we enjoyed the brilliant starlight with a 180° night view through clear glass. Through the generous contribution of friends, she and I were able to stay at a place that would normally be beyond our budgets, but unless we ask, we never receive, right?

When we finished that leg, it was just a matter of tying up loose ends and getting back to Cusco, then Lima. Overall my 43 days in South America, which ironically hits the 6 week goal that I started with when I left United states, made me interested and more likely to return. I developed some friendships in Ecuador, and will almost assuredly go back, plus many people told me about Medellin, Colombia, and certain places in Argentina that are worth visiting. Now if we can only get past this Covid stuff ...

For those of you that followed my journey in South America and Mexico, thank you so much! Nothing pleases me more than when I hear people say that they are inspired to follow our footsteps, and I want you to know that I am here to help guide you if you wish. I have had several calls both seeking information and giving information, and if you have either to share, please let me know. Godspeed.

Seven things I learned about South America:

1) There is beauty there unlike anything I have experienced before. Mountains that rise up to the heavens, starting from valleys that are lush and green. As a lover of volcanoes, I was able to exercise that love, too.
2) Even though I only experienced a little bit, there is more variety of wildlife and insect life down there than anywhere in the world. Just the country of Ecuador has more species than many continents.
3) The cost of living and the price of food are insanely inexpensive. Same thing with taxi rides and most attractions.
4) Distances don't mean anything; it's time that matters. It can take you 8 to 10 hours to go just a few hundred miles! That shocked me when I first ran into it, but it became a way of life, and came to realize that buses are pretty much what moves most of the population.
5) The time of year is not always an indicator of temperature, either. It can be the equivalent of summer in the city of Quito, but within a 90-minute drive you go over a mountain and its winter. The two countries I visited are both active seismically, so elevations can be extreme and altitude sickness is something to always be mindful of.
6) English is usually adequate to feel comfortable in South America, especially in the larger cities. Once you leave those, it's hit or miss.
7) Some things are backwards down there! Aside from the fact that water flows down the toilet counterclockwise, sometimes hot and cold-water handles are reversed in the shower, too. All my life, which has been exclusively in the northern hemisphere, hot was always on the left. You cannot count on that down there!

MISC.: Traveling in South America (currently) can be challenging. As an example, to enter Paraguay, US citizens arriving by air may obtain a visa on arrival which is good for ten years. The fee is $160 USD, credit cards are not accepted, and border agents only accept crisp, new bills that are free of any ink marks, blots, or tears. If paying with $100 denomination bills, series CB and D are not accepted. (That is all verbatim from their guidelines)

Important Traveling Info

Supplemental: Five Steps to Machu Picchu Guide

I wrote a Special Report if you would like to download it from the link.

Date: 10.01.21/ Next stop: Amazing Dubai

I kind of knew it before I got there, but just being in Dubai for a week proved that they don't do ANYTHING normal or small. Everything is over the top, and bigger than life. Kind of like a real-world Disneyland, with lots of sand and tall buildings.

Important Traveling Info

My trip to Dubai was not part of my normal Travel Younger itinerary, but was an invitation to speak at an event. How could I refuse? They covered my plane fare (from Miami), but I took care of my room, which was surprisingly affordable, as was most of the town. Sure, you could get several hundred dollar a night rooms, but mine was about $35 in a nice business hotel, plus offered a terrific daily buffet for about $10. But I did find my share of $24 bar burgers and $14 spaghetti dishes.

I also knew it would be HOT, but I was not prepared for humidity! And we're talking upwards of 50 percent (or more), especially by the water, so that was a scorcher. Much of the town lives "inside," which makes sense, and that includes hanging out inside the biggest mall in the world. Let me start with the list of "LARGEST this and that."

The Burj Khalifa, at 2722 feet, is far and away the tallest building in the world, and holds 3.3 million sq. ft. It rises to 160 floors, but my observation deck was floor 124/125, (1500 ft) which was fine. You CAN go higher to floor 148, but the cost was $103-145, not quite in my budget. They also have several different price options, including sunrise and sunset tours. There are many world records at the Burj, including highest free-standing structure, most floors, highest occupied floors, and highest elevation that CONCRETE got pumped to make the darn thing! Plus, longest elevator ride to GET to the top, longest service elevator, and highest observatory.

And the view from the top WAS spectacular, though surprisingly hazy, which they tell me is flying sand from the desert. Not a surprise since there is desert everywhere, and as aggressive as they have been building over the last 15 years, there is still LOTS of land to build upon.

At the bottom of the Burj is the Dubai Mall, which, no surprise, is the world's largest mall, at 12 million sq ft, and about 1500 shops. It has waterfalls, an aquarium, an ice skating rink, and over 200 places to eat. I am not a fan of shopping or malls, but I was entertained by its sheer magnificence! Soon the "largest" category will include the Ain Dubai Ferris Wheel, which will be the largest in the world, due to open in October 2021.

The town is a high-tech marvel to some degree with a kick-ass metro which I truly enjoyed. The people were amazingly polite and even the taxi drivers were great to work with. Most were Indian, Pakistani, or Bangladeshi, and all spoke decent English. One took me to a better Metro station than I requested, and even though I didn't have enough cash for a tip he was cool and gave me a bottle of water.

Speaking of water, the water is safe and good to drink since it's all desalinated from the Arabian Sea. High tech, like I said. Plus, it left my skin really soft from the shower. Since English is as common as their native Arabic, I felt very comfortable there, especially after being in Latin America for 18 months. It is a highly Islamic culture, and many things are banned, but I was surprised that they allowed no WhatsApp video or Facebook Messenger video either. Some told me that was from telephone company pressure to increase usage.

The city has lofty ambitions and Dubai is so centrally located that the airport is getting to be one of the busiest in the world. The building cranes dominate the landscape, and the architecture looks like something from Blade Runner in places. If they feel they are short on waterfront property, what do they do? They build man-made islands right from the sand beneath them, which they have done with the beautiful Palm Islands, which holds a world-famous water park, Atlantis, among many other things. See what I mean? What they lack, they build. They don't have a lot of "natural" landscaping or greenery, but money can buy anything—including that.

Date: 10.15.21/ Next stop: Croatia Feels Like Home

In May 2019 Kathleen and I took a ferry from Ancona, Italy to Split, Croatia. In the months prior I knew little about Croatia other than that it was formerly Soviet held as part of the larger nation of Yugoslavia. In the mid-nineties Croatia, as well as much of Eastern Europe, finally regained their independence.

We sailed in overnight and rode into the harbor on a beautiful May 15th morning, and our love affair with Croatia—and Split—began. We stayed for 45 days then moved about a half hour south, then down to Dubrovnik area, and finally left the area the middle of July (2019). That September Kathleen returned for six weeks while I was in the US, and she had a lovely apartment in downtown Split which she loved. As soon as we left, we couldn't wait to return.

We had no idea that COVID would stall that for so long, but after two years we have come "home."

Weird as that sounds, there is something about this country, this area, that speaks to us. The beautiful water, scenery, weather, and food, plus the people, all help make us feel comfortable.

After a solid 90 days of summer travel for me, and Kathleen and I separated most of that time, we both connected on October 2 and took an overnight flight through Germany. BTW, many of the warnings and restrictions you read about concerning international flights is really, truly, not that big a deal. COVID tests are part of the routine now, and except for some occasional "locator forms" or "health affidavits," it's no big deal. Imagine our pleasure and delight when we landed at Split airport, had no problems with immigration, and found out that NO ONE was wearing masks. I'll bypass that controversial subject other than to say that they take things in stride here and except for a few random grocery stores, we've not had to wear masks anywhere.

Since our room in Split town wasn't going to be available for a few days, we got a short-term room for four days just north of town and relaxed and enjoyed the area that we loved so much. A few days later we moved into our 30-day rental right in Old Town, and we love it. We can walk to a dozen coffee shops in 5 minutes, same with the beach, and the weather is terrific (but chillier than we like...) and we're exploring the town. Again. We weren't quite sure how long we would stay here but having some "stability" was important for both of us, so we found a killer deal right on the main waterfront (the Riva), so will stay an additional 30 days there. As of now, Greece is next on our list. Gotta' find the warmth, you know?

I found a gym, Kat has several coffee/ writing spots, and we plan to unwind and get some much delayed work done. Along with some fun too! I got my first fiction book on Amazon, called "The World Series of OZ," both paperback and Kindle, and working on "COVIDstories," which is a collaboration with 19 other writers worldwide sharing their POSITIVE COVID stories. As I've read through my submissions it's reassuring to know that many people grew, learned, and changed their lives in a positive way. That book will be available before the end of the year, and the OZ book is live right now.

What's next?

Good question. As of now, Athens is the most likely port of call through Christmas and New Year's and then possibly Egypt/ Jordan/ Israel. We need to stay equator close till spring and then come north again.

Date: 10.26.21/ Decisions, Decisions: Where to Next? (Hint: Gobble, Gobble!)

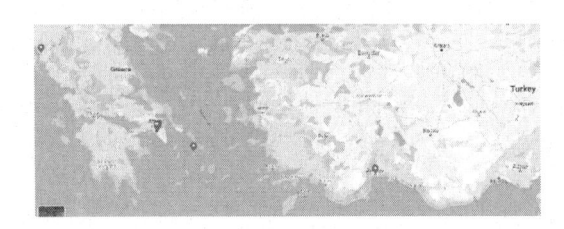

Even though we've only been in Split, Croatia a few weeks, we already started planning our next few months out. This is not the first time we went through this exercise. When we initially left the US in February 2019 we went to Valencia, Spain, and already knew from the beginning that Tivoli, Italy would be next. That took us through the first 90 days and we knew we'd have to leave the EU (Schengen rules...), but didn't have a plan initially. We eventually decided on Croatia, Split in particular, which is where we are now, and stayed north of town for 45 days and loved it. Croatia resonated with both of us so much that Kat later returned for some dental work, and here we are, two years later, back again. We had plans in 2019-2020 that may have kept us in Europe—or Asia--, so getting stuck in Mexico for 15 months was not part of our plan. Now we are back to "normal," or at least our version of normal!

We love Croatia and decided to stay for about 63 days or so, a bit longer than planned. But, what's next? Being cold weather wimps, we knew there was only one direction to go: South. Like the birds. To a warmer climate. Our initial plan was Athens, Greece since we only spent a few days there in 2019 and thought 30 days would be about right. From there we had the island of Crete as an option or Cyprus, or both. They are all EU countries so no matter where, we would be limited to 90 days.

As I started to investigate HOW to get from Split to Athens, the challenges started coming. Between costs and too many layovers, I began to rethink this. The only problem with this part of Europe is that trains are generally NOT an option, and buses can also be limited. We can take a bus only so far, ditto a train, but nowhere near to Greece. Kat also brought up the idea of skipping Greece and going back to Sicily, Italy, and to the island of Siracusa. Truth is, we both LOVED that spot, but flying to Palermo, the largest airport in Sicily, was pricey for our budget. So I looked at the map, specifically Turkey, and found the furthest city on the South coast: Antalya. And that is the new plan for about 40 days or so, maybe longer.

Antalya is warmish, has beautiful scenery and Turkey has one of the best railroad systems in that part of the world, including high-speed rails. That allows us to visit Istanbul and farther away cities without having to fly.

In this almost post-COVID world, some things are approaching normal, but most are not. Before we entertain any country as a destination, we have to investigate their entry and quarantine requirements, if any. We have learned how to follow the rules as well as bend the ones that can be bent. It is not "fun" in the conventional sense, but we feel that at least we can travel with our terms to some degree.

What happens after Turkey?

Good question. Initially it was Israel, Jordan, and Egypt over a 6 week or so period. They are all close, but Israel right now is still off limits to Americans. Without Israel being an option I'm not sure if Egypt and Jordan are enough of a draw. BUT, the pyramids are on MY Bucket List, so that carries a lot of weight. Funny, we use this term "Bucket List," and I can't say I had/ have one, but there still are quite a few things I want to do before I check out.

Anyone know how I can get a ride in a private jet??

Date: 11.06.21/ Are You Eligible for an EU (European Union) Passport?

What started as a quick catch-up call with a friend in Orange County (CA), my former turf, turned interesting when we discovered we both had Hungarian born mothers. The call was prompted by his curiosity and interest in moving to Europe with his family, and to share the world with his almost teenage kids. I supported that idea and told him I'd be happy to help in any way. I shared that the biggest limitation to Americans spending time in Europe is the 90-day visa restrictions, and what is known as the "Schengen Zone." You can read my special report from two years ago, but the short story is that there are 26 countries in the EU that, for passport control purposes, are considered ONE. That means if you stay 89 days in Germany, you can only go to France for one more, or you will overstay your welcome.

Cool stuff to know...

Before Kathleen and I left the US three years ago I studied this restriction deeply since I knew it would limit us, too. We started applying for residency in Portugal, then Spain, but neither worked out so therefore concluded, "we don't need no stinkin' visa," and off we went. One of the interesting options I have is to acquire a Hungarian passport through what is known as "Right of Descendancy."

As the son of a Hungarian born citizen, if I can PROVE that fact, plus learn a bit of their culture and language, I can get a passport—and in turn expand our options of staying in the EU for more than 90 days. My situation is challenged because my mom was born in pre-war Europe and had no passport since she was transported to Auschwitz, where she spent 3 years. After the war she may have had a French passport since she lived there for a while, but, alas, I never dug that far when she was alive. Her Hungarian hometown was not severely damaged in WWII from what I understand, so at some point I plan to visit and track down her birth certificate.

Back to you...The question is: Do you have a family line that goes back to Europe? Or Ireland? Or several other countries? If you do, you may be eligible for a second passport as well. Almost all countries will allow this for the CHILDREN of foreign-born citizens, but many will allow you to look to your grandparents or even further. The proof is the determining condition.

I share this because, as much as I am a fan and citizen of the US, for quality of life, life in Europe—and many other places—is much better. Safer; cheaper, more fun, etc...You pick your own motivation. If you do have familial lines that go back to a country you are interested in, Google "right of descendancy," and "your country," and you'll be able to get some solid information.

As for my friend, Jay, as soon as we finished our call, he contacted his mother and he now has her birth certificate in hand. Step 1: done. Now it's an application process and going through the motions, which can take a year or more. Some are faster and/ or easier. Generally, there is no or limited financial validation required, though many will require some language proficiency. So, start boning up on that now!

If you are interested in starting this process or wish to share you journey, I would like to learn and share it as well.

UPDATED: 2023

Since Athens had a Hungarian Embassy, I started the process while we lived there. I thought the most challenging part would be getting a copy of my **mother's birth certificate**, since she was born in 1919, but they were able to get one in just a few days. They also required an original copy of MY birth certificate, which I did not have, so I had to get one from City Hall in Philadelphia, and picked it up when I returned to the US in 2022.

Then, a glitch.

I was married in 1986, divorced in 2014, and common sense says that that would have nothing to do for me to obtain my Hungarian citizenship, but currently we are stalled until I get a copy of my marriage license... And I can only get it IN PERSON in Orange County, California, and that will happen later in 2023. After that is submitted we will see whatever roadblocks they put it...

Date: 11.21.21/ Our First Ferry Trip to the island of Hvar

Time moves so quickly it seems, and we never get to do everything we have planned. That may fit you, too, regardless of where you are. As permanent travelers we usually have a FINITE amount of time in each location, and our target is about six weeks. On this, our second stay in Split, we will be here for 60 days, and we still didn't go all the places/ do all the things we wanted. But we finally got to the island of Hvar for our four-year anniversary since meeting. And what an adventurous four years it has been!

It's 53.3 km, 33 miles, and takes about 1.5 hours via a regular ferry. I say regular because we could have taken a higher speed catamaran, made it in one hour, but we wanted to go to the city of Stari Grad since we heard so much about it, rather than Hvar City, the more popular destination. Ninety minutes on a ferry is a pleasure for me and I am SO glad I no longer get sick like I did years ago. After a week of somewhat overcast skies, we intentionally waited as long as we could before making the trek since sunny skies on a ferry across the ocean are much better.

Cool stuff to know...

The ferry was perfect, as was Stari Grad, and the weather was flawless. We only wanted to stay for one day so the 0830 departure time from Split got us there by 10:30 which gave us most of the day as well as the next. We weren't quite sure how far we were from the actual city or our room, but thank you, Google Maps, it was a 2 km walk, about 20 minutes, along the inland waterway, which was very nice. Since we had few smaller day packs, it was also easy. The actual "city" of Stari Grad is really just a few blocks long, with a "Riva" similar to what we have here in Split, along the waterfront. Since it is winter, most businesses and restaurants were closed, so our selection was limited. If we were there for a month, it might get boring, but we found a nice outside restaurant and had pasta and pork chops under sunny skies. Prices were comparable to Split, a nice surprise, and we explored a bit then took a break back at our room, which was another 15-minute walk up the OTHER side of the waterway. But when you're walking in such beautiful places, the time and the distance are less important. Since we had a later lunch, we went out that night for a coffee and dessert at a cute little spot, and we sat outside, bundled up, joined by a local cat who took the other chair and just cleaned him/her self the whole time. There is not much happening in this town at night, so the silence was welcome.

It was gorgeous the next morning and we found a great coffee spot, had our very typical breakfast strudel, then walked and explored the old homes and fortress in the area, then hiked outside town to what they call the Stari Grad Plain. It is several hundred acres of different crops growing aside each other, and at ground level it's hard to see the patchwork, but from a higher elevation it is visually stunning. As it was, there was a pleasant breeze, and we enjoyed the walk. A nice afternoon lunch of one of the best soups I have EVER had really surprised me, and normally I would not be a carrot/ ginger soup eater, but this was outstanding.

From there it was back to our room to pack up, and we were very lucky to have a great AirBNB hostess who let us check in earlier the day before and check out LATE on our departure time. We walked back along the waterfront as the sun was setting and got on the ferry just as a full moon was cresting over the mountains and shortly, over the ocean. Whereas I spent our ferry time topside on the first leg, I definitely stayed inside and warm for our return trip.

Thoughts about Hvar. There are 700 or so islands off the coast, and this was number three for us. Initially we planned to go to another island, Korcula, but the ferry timing didn't work, and many say that Korcula is even better (plus I love the name) but that will wait until our next trip back here, which will be next year. Meanwhile Hvar is definitely on the list of places to return to, and we spoke with a waiter who told us what to expect for a monthly stay there in spring. Un-friggin-believable, so that is now on the list of things to do.

One of the best things about this weekend, and the whole time here in Croatia, is that COVID is a non-topic. No masks were required or requested on the ferry, but people still stayed a bit apart. We haven't been thermal scanned since we got here and so appreciate that we can live life as "normal" as we used to.

In two weeks: Turkey.

Supplemental: The Coffee (Café) Culture of Croatia (published in the Croatia Weekly magazine)

https://www.croatiaweek.com/exploring-croatias-coffee-and-cafe-culture/

When I arrived in Split, Croatia for the first time in May 2019, after I got over my awe of the beauty of this place, something else caught my attention: there were coffee shops everywhere. I couldn't walk for more than a block or two before running into another one, and the majority of them only sold coffee, but no pastries, although some actually carried beer. *What's up with that*, I wondered?

I returned to Split this past October and was reminded again how many coffee shops there were. When I got here I put out a Facebook query and asked where I could get a LARGE, ie, American sized cup of coffee. That generated 54 responses and several great suggestions including many that said, "Get over it. It's not about the coffee itself, it's about the café experience. Go in expecting to have TWO cups and enjoy your time there." That feedback was echoed by my interview with Marin Rimac, who is usually called by his nickname "Dado," and since he owns one of the most popular java shops in town, 4coffee soul food, and has been in this business for eight years, I invited him for a coffee (!) to share what he could about the Coffee Culture in Croatia. He is not Croatian born, but hails from Germany and has been visiting Croatia for most of his life, although his parents came from Bosnian roots.

"Yes, they are correct in telling you it's not just about the coffee. But it's not just a Croatia thing, either" he said, "and covers most of the Balkan countries. Coffee here is a bit different than in western europe, though they love their coffee there, too. Many people here in Croatia own their property and receive income from it, so lots of them have time on their hands. Cafés are watering holes, meeting places, where people gather and catch up." He describes it as a "Southern Europe" thing.

Using a population of 178,000 per the 2011 census (which is probably higher now) I asked him how many shops there were in town. I was looking to determine how many coffee shops there were for each person. "Could there be 1780 shops in the Split area?" I asked, and he shrugged and said, "Who knows?" I used that number because it would calculate to one shop per 100 people, and that possibility blew me away. I mean, in the US there is a Starbucks on every corner, but the population difference is much larger.

"The problem, " he continued, "is that most coffee served is 'industrial' coffee, which is not that good a quality. When I arrived I saw that 'specialty' coffee was hard to find and that is what made me focus on that market. I wasn't intimidated by the number of shops since most of them were all the same." The people of Split, and presumably other areas as well, have learned to tell the difference, and the term "specialty coffee" came up in several of my Facebook responses.

But what IS specialty coffee? "Let me put it this way," he said. "I get my own green beans from agencies I trust. I roast my own beans, which are all handpicked. I have notes about when it was picked, how it was washed, and I can follow the whole timetable until I get it here. The way that specialty coffee is treated is more like a fine wine or quality whiskey or scotch, and that has a huge impact on the final product." The good news is that the good news has spread and there are half a dozen (and growing!) specialty coffee shops in Split, with surely more to come.

As an entrepreneur for decades, I have met many of my kind and one thing I recognize is passion, and Dado had that in spades.

The problem with coffee is that the industry has become too "Americanized" if I can use that term. If we look back a few decades, there weren't a lot of JUST coffee shops in the sixties and seventies. There were some that also offered entertainment and other nighttime activities, but pure coffee shops were rare. The institute of coffee came about with massive numbers, and just like other fast-food chains and other businesses like that, they were solely driven by quantity, not quality. That probably works better in America where people get much of their coffee "on the go," but here in Croatia and much of Europe, coffee is not treated as a pick me up, quick caffeine jolt, but instead, more of a lifestyle enhancer. And that is certainly the case in Split and Croatia in general.

Dado echoes that thought and describes what is happening today as the "third wave." The first waves, maybe a half century ago, grew into the massive growth of coffee shops in general during the 70's, and now people are balking at "boring" coffee and want something different; something better. The coffee drinking public pays attention and they have developed a more refined palate.

"What really changed things was the invention of the espresso machine," he said, which surprisingly took place over a century ago. But espresso machines did not really become practical—or affordable—until just a few decades ago. That simple machine is more compact and efficient than it was in the beginning. In my travels the way they drink espresso in other countries, like Italy is NOT like we do here in Croatia! The average enjoyment time of an espresso shot in Rome can be measured in minutes, not hours.

In Croatia people love their cafes-- drinking beers, coke, an espresso with milk, smoking and talking. Being in the cafe is the draw, which is why they linger so long, but a good java makes the experience even more enjoyable.

Coffee is a very unusual bean. It is a tree but has characteristics of a bush, and the coffee bean can be affected by the types of trees around it. It can be roasted in many different ways, too, and of course, it can be brewed perfectly—or not so good. Regardless, the Croatian Coffee Culture has it right. Enjoy the bean. Enjoy the company and enjoy life.

Date: 12.10.21/ Next stop: Goodbye Croatia, Hello Turkey

I remember about a decade ago I was watching a TV show with my (then) wife in my very comfortable living room, in my very comfortable chair, in very comfortable Orange County, CA. A TV commercial came on advertising the country of Turkey, possibly from their visitor's bureau. I recall thinking, maybe even aloud, "Who the hell wants to visit Turkey?"

A few years later a friend of mine, Sara, told me she was visiting Turkey and I expressed the same thoughts, maybe even to her: "WHY Turkey?" I don't recall her answer, but she was amazed, impressed and so were the pictures she shared.

Important Traveling Info

I am IN Turkey, and a few weeks back I was on a call with my cousin in Portland, and when I told her where I was going she posed the same, "Why Turkey?" question. What is it about this country that made/ makes Americans ask that question? I admit I had preconceptions and imagined a primitive country more Morocco-like than European-like. Over the course of Kathleen and my travels since 2019 we planned to visit the country TWICE, and we even had tickets but had to cancel them at the time.

Tunisia in 2019 was our first Muslim country and both of us were unsure how that would feel, but it was lovely, as were the people. It took about a day to get over the attire, the 5 times a day "call to prayer" which sounded over loudspeakers, and the language which was much different. Regardless, the food was delicious, and the people were as curious about us as we were about them. Turkey has the same prayer calls, but is VERY contemporary, with more selections of food, clothing, jewelry, and anything you wish to buy. At insane prices...

Since she and I are cold weather wimps, and it is now the start of "winter" (per the calendar) we kept searching for warm or warmish weather. We looked into Greece and their many islands, plus Malta, and Cyprus and then one day I looked at the map and found the furthest south place we could stay before running into Africa or having to trek to Asia. That city is called "Antalya," –in Turkey--and that is where we are.

We did some research on the country and found it to be remarkably tourist friendly with one of the best railway systems in this part of the world, which was a very nice surprise since our usual haunts in Southern & Eastern Europe have poor rail systems, and per wiki, "an active network of 12,532 km (7,787 mi) of railways, making it the 23rd-largest railway system in the world."

We've been here less than a week and every day we discover new "AHA" places, events, and views. For instance:

- The town is located in a bay on the Mediterranean and it has loads of history. Hadrian's Gate was the entrance that the emperor entered in to back in the time of Christ. Likewise, there is a Tower, Hidirilik, which is undergoing renovation and that is also 2000 years old, plus some of the most beautiful mosques I've ever seen. Very close is the amazing Duden waterfall (look it up), plus within a view hours bus ride there are towns like Cappadocia, with unbelievable landscapes, and Pamukkale, with thermal pools flowing down travertine terraces.
- The difference between the US dollar and the Turkish lira (TL) is at an all-time low, which is hard on the natives, but means our dollars go far. Breakfast for two, including omelets, bread, and two cappuccinos are about $5.50. Last night we had a huge burger, which came with fries and a small salad, plus I added a Mediterranean salad and a glass of wine, and the total was $10. This also means our rent is cheap...Our planned AirBNB visit did not pan out so we are staying at an apartment/ hotel which is in "Old Town," 2 minutes to an amazing viewpoint, and within 5 minutes' walk to more restaurants than we need.
- Residency. One of our biggest hurdles over our three years of travel has been the common 90-day visa limitations. Albania and Georgia were possible destinations for us to get around this (12 mo. visa), but Turkey has the easiest residence process than anywhere we've been. Our plan is a one-year visa which easily transitions into a two-year permit and if we do that for eight years, we are full time residents. That is very tempting!
- It's almost Christmas and I am writing this at a café with no jacket on and 63-degree temps. It IS rainy season, but it's been warm so far and we don't expect weather to be restrictive.

So if you share this blog and someone asks, "**WHY Turkey?**" you can tell them why!

Date: 12.28.21/ Settling Down, but not Settling: 2021 Review

Three years ago, when we left the US and decided to travel the world and stay for six weeks at different locations, our plan was to eventually "slow down" and have access to two, three, or more locations that we loved and could return to. Somewhere we had a relationship for lodging and maybe even had friends.

That is now happening.

As the beginning of 2021 unfolded, like many, we were still "COVID stuck," unable to travel freely, so until June we remained in Puerto Morelos, Mexico, just south of Cancun. We recognized it was a good place to "hunker down," since we had great winter weather, inexpensive cost of living, and were just minutes to the water. Kathleen and I were both anxious to get back on the road, but we had a detour—the birth of her first grandchild—in January. So she spent the summer in Ohio with her son and family, and I traveled solo throughout Mexico, Oaxaca, and Mexico City, then Ecuador, spending most of my time in Quito and Cuenca.

I was never driven to visit Latin America, but Ecuador captured my heart due to unbelievable beauty, great weather, lots of amazing mountains and canyons, and a good friend I met as my AirBNB host. The idea of returning to Ecuador is still possible, though I remain drawn to Europe, specifically Eastern/ Southern Europe, and the Balkan countries.

Kathleen met me in Peru in September, and we travelled throughout much of the country via bus, went to Machu Picchu, saw some amazing places, and stayed at a hotel literally on the side of a mountain, called the Vertical Lodge. Our 21 days in Peru were magical, then we both returned to the US where Kat went back to Ohio and I had a business trip in Dubai, another first for me. My 10 days in Dubai were better than I expected, and I was overwhelmed with the architecture and over the top attitude of the city. Would I return? Probably only by necessity.

After Dubai I was back to the US (Nashville) for a business event, then Kat and I met in Newark, NJ for our first adventure back to Croatia, formerly our favorite country. I'll get to that in a moment. She had some dental work to finish and since we knew the area it was a place for us to hang out, enjoy good food and weather, and just BE for two months. We were in Split from the beginning of October until the first week of December and then flew to a brand-new adventure—Turkey—which is where we are now. Neither one of us had Turkey on our radar, even though we almost came here twice before. No, what drove us here was weather, and the approaching winter, and the charts that showed the winters here in Antalya are mild.

In Croatia we developed relations with two different landlords and arranged to return in the off-season, when prices were better. That was the plan until Turkey…We thought we'd spend six months or more in Croatia (but only 90 days at a time) and the rest of the time traveling.

Turkey kind of took us in a new direction.

One of our biggest concerns during our travels was the normal 90-day visa limitation which was always in our minds since we knew we'd have to exit where we were. With some research we found Turkey's residency laws to be quite lenient and we are in the process of getting a visa for one to two years. It does not FORCE us to remain here, but gives us a great home base. It's a big country with lots to explore, and that is our plan. We are strategically located on the border of Europe and Asia, which is great for going east or west. We can also go north to the former Soviet countries and Scandinavia, too. And just south is Africa, Jordan, Egypt, Israel, etc…so we are literally perched at the center of the compass for this part of the world.

For now our plans are uncertain, but we know we will be in Antalya until May 1 or so, then it gets more crowded, hot and expensive—the unholy three! But between now and then we will explore other parts of Turkey to determine where to enjoy the summer months. The plan is to get a (motor) bike and check out the west coast of the country, which offers many options to suit us for several months. And not having to worry about "leaving" is a blessing.

Our travels are far from over and my list of "must visit" countries has about 20 more left. But unless things change, we will probably call Turkey our "home" for the foreseeable future. We can maintain temporary residency for five to eight years and then be eligible to become official and legal full-time residents.

We are not close to settling, but we are close to settling down. As 2022 unfolds we have many things in mind, and monitoring the traveling COVID-related complexities and the challenges of international travel are at the top of our list. Keep your eyes on us as we continue to Travel Younger.

Date: 01.10.22/ Checking Off the Boxes in Turkey

Whether we do it consciously or not, when we make decisions on certain things to determine if we "like them," we go through a mental checklist and check off the boxes of what works and what doesn't. The simple act of walking into a new restaurant would prove this out as you determine if it's clean, quiet enough, smells good (or not), makes you feel welcome, etc... If an important box is unchecked, you may just check out yourself. When you dated (or still do), when you meet/ met someone, you did a mental box checking act to see if you liked them or not.

- ✓ Too tall or too short? Check
- ✓ Heavy, skinny? Check
- ✓ Right color hair, clothing, voice? Check, check, check.

Important Traveling Info

As Kathleen and I explored 24 countries and countless cities over the past three years, we also went through a checklist to determine if we liked it, thought about returning—or even live there. We loved and still love Spain, Portugal, and especially Croatia and we have had countless discussions of whether we wanted to return or if we wanted to stay "long term." For several years Croatia, and Split city in particular, were at the top of our "Yes, we could live there, conversation," but now Antalya, Turkey has replaced it as number one. That is just one of the many reasons we have applied for residency here in Turkey, and that will allow us to stay for one to two years and not worry about visa issues.

What does our checklist look like?

- Weather: check. Very similar to Orange County, CA, where I lived for four decades, and one of the best climates in the US. Chilly (mostly 50 degrees range, lower at night) and a bit rainy in winter, and hot in summer. From what we heard this town gets TOO hot in summer, so we plan to go north or to higher elevation to be comfortable.
- Scenery: as nice as Orange County and California are, this place kicks its ass. The cliffs and Mediterranean Ocean here are breathtaking, and considering we can see walls and buildings that are 2000 years old, it can be humbling. Having the ocean just 10 minutes away by foot is also very convenient!

- Food: plenty of it and all good. Heavy in the fish and veggies and that fits since the Mediterranean diet is considered to be the healthiest in the world.
- People: so amazingly cordial and friendly in a very real way, and most speak English so there is no language barrier here at all. There is also a decent, but small expat community of English speakers from many countries (mostly UK), but not many Americans.
- Cost of living: one of the biggest draws since our lifestyle is about 25-35% of what California was and we can live and eat for a fraction of what we used to spend. For the next several months we are in an apartment/ hotel and on the roof is a full-on pano view of the ocean and marina, and our rent is not even double what my car payment used to be...
- Access to other areas (domestic): Turkey is about 8% of the size of the US, and 16% larger than Texas and there are 5000 miles of coastline split between four different oceans: Mediterranean; Aegean; Sea of Marmara, and the Black Sea to the north. That means lots to explore just inside this one country, plus they have a good domestic rail system as well as here in the city of Antalya.
- Access to other countries (international): on the compass dial we are situated to the east of Europe, but we can get there in just a few hours. We're just north of the middle East and Africa and they are also accessible. If we choose to go further into Asia (Turkey IS considered Asia, which I did not know before) it's easy, plus airline costs are much cheaper than in the US.

When we compared Turkey to any other place we've been (or thought to go), no place checks off that many boxes.

If you're curious and would like to visit or want information, please let us know, we'd love to introduce you!

Date: 01.20.22/ Tea! For all the Tea in Turkiye??

It's a cliché: we use the expression, "all the tea in China," to indicate that you would not do something "for all the tea in China," which means you definitely will not do it. I think I can amend that to read, "for all the tea in Turkiye," too.

Cool stuff to know...

I remember walking into a grocery store when we first got to Italy a few years ago and being awed by abundant displays of pasta on the shelf. I mean, it took up an entire aisle! It may be a stereotype, but it's still true: Italians love their pasta! But so do many other countries.

Meanwhile, here in Turkiye, their style of eating is unlike others we have encountered in the world, especially pertaining to breakfast. It is a Muslim country, so bacon and eggs are uncommon. A traditional Turkish breakfast is more like a European buffet spread: cold cuts, hardboiled egg, and then they add other more native delicacies. Nuts, figs, dates, and a whole collection of cheese. And don't forget the bread! Pita of course is very Turkish, but you can get bread anywhere in many flavor choices. As the New Yorkers have their bagels, here they have what is called a simit, which is a little skinnier version of a bagel with lots of sesame seeds, and is very, very good.

And the point to this entry is that as the Italians love their pasta, here they love their tea, and it comes in many different assortments of flavors and styles. Turkish tea, also known as chai tea, is served anywhere and everywhere, and just walking down the street we see the merchants and vendors sitting outside enjoying their tea. Hence the reason for this picture of an entire aisle of tea!

I have grown to like their tea and have at least one cup every day. As a matter of fact, if someone asks you if you would like some, it is rude to decline. And of course, I don't want to be rude! Turkish coffee is a "thing," and it is very thick and dark, though not as strong as some regular ground coffees. I like it but not enough to drink it regularly, and prefer tea, which is the national drink, not coffee.

If you have read any of my blogs over the last 3 years you know that food is an important topic of my conversations. From the initial foods we discovered in Spain, then Italy, then Croatia, followed by different parts of Eastern Europe. Later it was onward to Greece, the Far East, Thailand, etc, and finally on to Mexico where we were stuck for 15 months. Yes, food is important although I do not call myself a foodie. You wouldn't know that considering that I have dozens if not hundreds of food photos on my Facebook feeds!

So far no food has been a total turn off, though what they call Turkish delight, is too sweet for me, and their ice cream is too thick. I do miss my strudel and my more western style breakfast pastries, but overall, the food here is much healthier.

Supplemental: Our YouTube profile from Travels with Warren and Julie

Kathleen and I were given the opportunity to share our "Travel Younger" journey with Warren and Julie Knox, fellow nomads, who educate others about nomadic travel through their YouTube channel. This video gives a small overview of how we started our adventure, how we afford to travel the world, and why we love what we do. We hope it will help inspire others who have always wanted to do the same, but were too afraid to take the leap... please check us out.
https://www.youtube.com/watch?v=CBsVeeLmm4Y

Date: 02.03.22/ Residency in a Foreign Country: Yes or No?

After 67 years as a citizen of the US (I still am), and three years on the road and calling 25 countries "home," we finally leapt into a new opportunity as Kathleen and I are officially "temporary residents" of Turkey for two years. That means we are not restricted to the normal 90 days visa limits, and we can come and go at will with no requirements of how long we need to stay here at all. The "ikamet," which is what it is called, can be renewed annually, and if we do it for 5 to 8 years, we can become official citizens of Turkey. We can still retain our US citizenship, but being permanent gives us added benefits, including health care.

Important Traveling Info

Before we came to Turkey, we looked into this and pretty much knew we would do it. Of all the countries we've lived in, or thought about residency, this was the easiest by far. We did not have to supply income documentation, fingerprints, or security background, and it cost us a few hundred dollars. Aside from being able to stay longer, we are also able to bypass the "visa on arrival" regs we dealt with when we got here, plus we get discounts on museums and other cultural offerings. From beginning to end the process took us about one month: sweet.

For Americans, or citizens of other countries that wish to travel, a nomadic life may seem like an unrealistic dream. It was not even ON my radar most of my life, and the thought and desire to do it never crossed my mind until 2016 when I was invited to speak at three different events in Europe. For 19 days I was on my own and hit six different countries and all the while appreciated the way that Europeans lived; they did NOT live to work, they worked to live, and they did that very well. I'll not rehash my entire history since it's part of my Traveling the World Six Weeks at a Time story and encompasses two books, and the next volume is about 2/3 done. But one of the realities that Kat and I faced when we hit the road in February 2019 was the time restrictions that most countries have for visitors. Some are more onerous and strict that others, and some are more lenient. Some require a special visa either before you GET to their country, or upon arrival. But regardless, no country will just allow you to ENTER and stay.

That brings up the whole residency conversation, and since Kat and I loved Europe, they have their own deal there which is called the Schengen Visa, which encompasses 26 countries. The EU, or European Union, decided to make passport control more easy by grouping most, but not all, of Europe under one agreement. That agreement allows non-Schengen residents to stay for 90 days total within the entire region. It's complicated and you can read my [special report to know the background](#) and how it works, but in short, if you stay in France for 88 days, you can only stay for 2 more days in Spain. To restart the clock you must leave for 90 days.

You can probably see the problem here, right? If we dug Spain and wanted to stay for four months, we could not. If we stayed for two months and wanted to go to Portugal for two months, we couldn't do that, either. There are two countries with unusually lenient visas for Americans, and they are Albania and Georgia, which both allow up to one-year visas. That is very inviting. Another good thing is that there are several non-Schengen zone countries that share borders with those in it, so you could literally drive across borders every 90 days if you choose. Many countries are not cool with that and are making it more difficult.

While in Mexico we had a six-month visa and considered residency there, but we couldn't see ourselves living there full-time, so decided against it. But NOW, in Turkey, we could easily see ourselves here for years, and with our close proximity to so many different options, we can have our cake and eat it too.

That's the long and short of the residency conversation and we feel very lucky that we added another country to our options list. If you're interested in learning more, get a hold of us via TravelYounger.com.

Date: 02.17.22/ Three Years & Counting (part I)

"What a long, strange trip it's been," or so said the Grateful Dead band, and that is what they titled their second compilation album in 1977. They may have been talking about another type of trip, but since it's been three years since Katheen and I left our US homeland and have been on the road ever since, I thought a brief recap might be nice in case you're new to Travel Younger.

We left Los Angeles airport Feb 17, 2019, and our plan was to travel the world, seek out Mediterranean temps, and stay in different locations for about six weeks at a time. We started in Valencia, Spain, and picked an amazing time to be there since one week after arrival they started their annual celebration called "Las Falles," or The Fires. For thirty days fireworks went off every day and massive statues made of Styrofoam and wood were constructed on street corners. You can read about them here. (https://travelyounger.com/chapter-10-las-fallas-in-valencia-get-ready-for-the-chaos/) We had no idea how big this was, but over a million people come from all over the world to attend the event which concludes by, get this, **burning all these magnificent structures on the last night**. A-mazing! Aside from that, the city was beautiful and full of wonderful architecture and museums along with being a good hub to take a train somewhere else. I am happy to report that after a two year absence, Las Falles will return this year.

Our second leg was Tivoli, Italy, a small medieval town about 20 miles east of Rome. And full of history since it was 700 years OLDER than Rome, and our teensy apartment, which we called "The Cave," was over 500 years old. The city has three major parks/ attractions and we visited them all, which you can read about here.

Since we pushed our 90-day EU visa to the max we had to leave the Schengen region, and so ferried to Croatia, which we knew little about before we got there. By now it was mid-May and summer was coming and we enjoyed our stay near Split, a major Croatian city. The food, the people, and the cost of living was very inviting, and after two motorcycle trips around the country, we proclaimed Croatia as being our "Favorite," since everyone always asked which one was at the top. We used our six weeks there as best we could, and then it was time to hit the road again.

We had a Eurail pass to use so (foolishly) tried to cram as many trips in as possible over a 30-day period, but finally took a break after relocating about every three days. Romania was our respite and we loved it. We're talking early August and the weather was magnificent, as was the geography. That got enhanced with a motorcycle trip which allowed us to ride some of the best roads I've ever ridden. Again, great food, nice people, and even cheaper than Croatia! Along with Romania we hit Serbia, Poland, Slovakia, Hungary, and the Czech Republic, so that was a busy, busy summer.

Since I had some business in the US shortly thereafter, I did that for six weeks while Kat went back to Croatia, which she got to know even better since she was right in Old Town. When I returned, we went to Sicily, Italy, and lived in Syracusa, a small southern city, and had a great time seeing other parts of Sicily, too. We had a bike for a month so took advantage of that and explored much of the island. Then it was off to Athens, Greece for just a few days, and we have committed to going back since it was much better than we expected—and had been told about. Such history! That short visit was enhanced by the islands of Naxos and Santorini, and even though it was around Christmas, the weather was mostly tolerable.

That brings us up to New Years, 2020, when our lives changed, as it did for many others, and I'll cover that trip to Singapore, Thailand, Cambodia, Vietnam, and eventually, Mexico, in Part II.

Date: 03.01.22/ Three Years & Counting (part II)

This is part II of our three-year recap since leaving the US on Feb 17, 2019. If you haven't read the first part, here it is:

https://travelyounger.com/chapter-132-three-years-counting-part-i/

Back in the day...before pandemics...

Like most of us, Kathleen and I entered the year 2020 with great excitement. After almost a year on the road, we left Europe and headed to Asia, a first for both of us. We had a last-minute weather scare getting out of Greece, but we left on New Year's Eve and looked forward to yelling "Happy New Year" over the ocean in an unknown time zone. We landed in Singapore at 0300, it was dead, and killed time till our room was available. It was HOT, HUMID, and very different than what we were used to. As it was, we only spent three days in Singapore and, like everyone who visits, we were overwhelmed with the architecture, tall buildings, and very comfortable English-speaking environment. Then it was off to Thailand, where we committed to for 60 days.

Bangkok, the most visited city in the world, was a shock to my system. Crowded, smoggy, very energized, and I did not take it well. We had a beautiful room on the 38th floor of a 42-story building, and even with the infinity pool, gym, and lounge, it still wasn't comfortable for me. We decided that we would use Bangkok as a BASE and visit different places, which is what we did. Chang Mai, Chumphon, Vietnam, and Cambodia visits made it more worthwhile, and overall we had a great time. But then that C-word messed everything up, as Kat got COVID very early, the second week of January, before anyone even knew what it was. But that was just the first domino as the virus spread worldwide and affected most of our travels, even up to now. Our return trip to the US did not come off as planned, nor did Kat's son's wedding, scheduled for the second week of March, just as things were getting crazy.

As it turned out, our visit to the US was cut WAY short since we were fearful our two-week break in Mexico would be jeopardized. That was the least of our problems as our intended quick visit turned into 15 months since we could not return to Europe, the US, or venture any further south. We made the best out of Puerto Morelos, a small seaside fishing village with about 10,000 people, and we liked being close to the beach, meeting new friends, and the highly affordable lifestyle.

Like most of the world, our color coding and the effects of the virus went from extremely dangerous, to light, then back and forth, and we never knew when we'd be able to move on. That finally happened in June 2021 as Kat went to Ohio for the summer to spend time with her son's family—and new grandson-- and I traveled solo through Mexico and Ecuador. We reconnected in Peru for 17 days and visited much of the country, including Machu Picchu, so that was a unique experience. Then it was hurry, hurry, rush, rush, as we both made it back to the US and I jetted to Dubai (a first) for a business expo, then returned 10 days later. A quick business event in Nashville, and then, finally, we reconnected AGAIN, ready to return to our favorite country-Croatia.

October started there and we spent two months in Split, and it was the first time we felt almost settled for quite some time. We stayed in two different locations, including an amazing room right on the Riva (waterfront), which we got for a sweet price. We were able to get out to the island of Hvar, and really enjoyed that, but otherwise, it was more relaxation and writing than anything else. After about 60 days we came to Turkey since we were chasing warm weather and avoiding our 90-day visa limitation. And that brings us to where we are now, Antalya, Turkey.

Turkey has replaced Croatia as being our favorite but just by a very small amount, primarily due to the scenery, the cost of living, and the ease of gaining residency, which we now have. For two years we are "secure" and not forced to move, and as a nomad, that is a HUGE advantage. We will be in Antalya until July 1, then hit the road—on a motorcycle—up the western coast, and our plan right now is the country of Georgia to the east, or Greece and Eastern Europe to the west.

Which way will our brave senior nomads go? I guess you will have to continue watching our journey here at Travel Younger.

Date: 03.23.22/ 1600 Kilometers (994 miles) from Bucharest, Romania to Antalya, Turkey: on a Motorcycle

If you have been following my personal Facebook page, you might know that after many years of not owning a bike I picked up a BMW in Romania and rode it "home" to Antalya in five days. Let's just say that this Younger Traveler didn't feel so young, especially since the weather was in the forties (Fahrenheit) most of the time, and the blustery wind never let up over almost 1000 miles. I enjoyed the hell out of it, but it did take its toll on my legs, neck, and arm muscles!

Kathleen and I have been nomads since Feb 2019 and visited 26 countries. We have rented bikes (usually scooters), in many of them, and many times shared the dream about getting our own. As a non-EU citizen I was unable to buy anything unless I got creative, typically by creating a corporation. I didn't want to go that route but two American friends did that, one in France and one in Bulgaria. We were lucky in that we rented a bike in Romania in August 2019 and had a wonderful experience with the BMW 750GS as well as with the rental company, motorentals.ro, owned by Sergiu Stoica. When COVID kept us out of Europe we still knew we would return, and I posed the question to him about renting "long term," probably a year, maybe more. He was open to that, but he sold that particular bike but had a smaller BMW 310GS, and we structured a deal with that.

So now we have a bike and a large country to explore! Part of that exploration was my journey back since I came down much of the western coastline of Turkey and we will reverse that trip when we leave Antalya on July 1. But here's a quick overview of the route I just completed.

Day I took me out of Romania and all through the country of Bulgaria (country #39 for me) from north to south, about 330 km. A fun fact: Bulgaria is the oldest country in Europe and the only country that has not changed its name since it was first established. Who knew?

After riding about 250 miles, 7 hours, I re-entered Turkey, had to go through THREE checkpoints, and stayed the night in the city of Edirne. It was initially just a pit stop but Kat sent a write up showing the amazing mosques in town, so the next morning I checked them out along with the Great Synagogue, which is the only one in town. The mosques were some of the largest I've seen and were quite beautiful, but then I hit the road which started at a brisk 40 degrees F and went through some mountain passes which had snow just a few days before. I was watchful of snow on the road and finally hit sea level late in the day and stayed in the city of Canakkale, which I truly loved. It had a great vibe and required a 15-minute ferry ride across the Dardanelles Strait, taking me from Europe to Asia, a weird concept when you think about it. After all, it IS a manmade construct...

The city was very cool in that it had a nice waterfront area which held the Trojan Horse from the movie "Troy." No one REALLY knows where the city of Troy was, but it is not just a legend and they claim it's about 30 miles from Canakkale. I didn't have time to take that side trip, but I did stay in a great hostel for about $7.00 USD. THAT is how I can afford to do this.

The following morning my destination was Izmir, the second largest city in Turkey, and riding into town I felt it. It reminded me (too much) of Los Angeles, and fortunately the weather turned nice, so after gassing up I decided to press on, and made it to Ephesus in the city of Selcuk. If you know your Bible and history that name may be familiar and it has deep historical and religious meaning. And it WAS magnificent the following morning as the day started bright and crisp but still very, very cold. After an hour exploring Ephesus it was back on the road to Fethiye, which I knew was within a one day ride home. That city had been mentioned many times by expats and locals and everyone suggested I check it out. Conditions were not ideal as it was still cold there, and when I left the morning of Day V the wind was worse than ever. Regardless I was able to hug the coast and ride along some of the most magnificent water and cliffs I have ever been on. A biker's paradise! That last day was 173 miles, but they were some of the toughest as the wind was borderline scary, buffeting from the cliffs inland and the ocean from the other direction.

All this is highlighted in much more detail on my Norm Bour FB page and I have been commissioned to write two stories for a touring bike site called RevNTravel.com. If you are interested I will send you a link when they go live.

Date: 04.02.22/ The Affordability Factor of Traveling

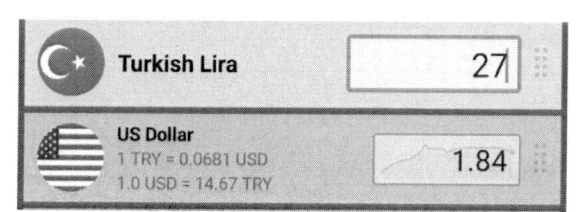

Being a permanent nomad is fraught with misunderstandings; usually from those on the OUTSIDE who see how we live. So many times over the years people have asked, "Did you win the lottery? How can you afford to do what you do?"

The answer is easy, since the cost of living is lower than what we had in California and probably would be similar throughout most of the US. Who knew?

Important Traveling Info

It wasn't until Kat and I visited Barcelona (Spain) and Nice, France in January of 2018 that we realized how reasonable prices were in Europe. Our room in Barcelona directly ACROSS THE STREET from the most iconic landmark in that town, the La Sagrada Familia, was about $55 per night. We were looking at the towers of the Gaudi cathedral from our bed. And a few days after that we left for Nice and stayed in a small studio just two blocks from the marina, which was about $35 per night. Mind you, it was January, off season, and this was a few years ago, but there are still bargains to be found.

Generally, Western Europe, Great Britain, and the Nordic countries, are more expensive than Eastern Europe and Asia, likewise with most of South America and Mexico. We have learned to avoid the "Big Cities," and instead stay outside them, or go to the suburbs. Staying in Paris or London or Stockholm is a budget stretcher, but if you are 15 minutes outside of town (by Metro!), that makes the visit affordable.

I just returned from a 1000-mile motorcycle ride from Romania to our home in Turkey, and over five days I stayed in five different locations. The most expensive room was about $18 USD, and I had a great room in Canakkale for 100 Turkish Lira (TL), which was $6.69. I had to take a ferry across the Dardanelles Strait and that was 21 TL which is $1.43. Crazy. In Turkey they have a breakfast pastry called a "simit," which is a small version of a bagel, but without all the different types of flavors. The going price for a simit is 3.5 TL, or 23 cents. Add in some Turkish (chai) tea, some cheese, olives, and a hard-boiled egg, and I get a great (and healthy) breakfast for a little more than a buck. Even though they've had horrendous inflation here, the $5 carmel macchiato from Starbucks is still about $1.60 here.

A few days ago I went to the theater to see The Batman. That ticket in the US is about $12 unless it's a matinee or senior rate. My ticket was $1.84, and some popcorn and a drink cost about the same. Those little things add up!

Kat just went to the hospital to get some medical tests done, and this is what they did for $89 USD:

- Complete eye exam
- Ear specialist
- Dermatologist
- Internist along with complete abdominal ultrasound
- And a complete blood panel...

There was minimal paperwork or hassle with insurance and, as an American, they gave her priority service since they know we pay on demand. When I first got to Turkey I had an eye exam to get an updated prescription, and that was under $9.00 and new frame and progressive lenses was about $300.

Public transportation is cheap overseas, but there is one thing that is pricey: gasoline. But when I was in the US last month my friends were posting pictures of almost $10 per gallon gas, so it's all relative.

Would you like to Travel Younger? It is not just a dream, but can become your Reality if you wish. Three plus years later we are still learning...and teaching you!

Date: 04.17.22/ Our 21 Day Beta Test Road Trip

After four months in our apartment/ hotel, Villa Tulipan in Antalya, we checked out, and we move into our new apartment May 1. That means we had 21 days in between, so what do we do?

Road Trip!

This will be a Beta Test for our much longer bike trip coming up in July, when we will ride back up the coast of Turkey into Bulgaria, then head west into Greece, where I will be hosted by several resorts, hotels, and visitors' bureaus while I write a travelogue on their behalf. Very exciting!

Meanwhile, every journey starts with the first step/ mile, so here is what happened before and during.

Cool stuff to know...

Day I, April 9: We had several options, including heading south and hitting Cappadocia and possibly taking a ferry to Cyprus, but when I saw the beautiful coastline coming south from Fethiye, I wanted Kat to see it, too. Day one was beautiful and the hazy air from a Sahara windstorm that plagued us for the past two weeks was finally clearing. The amazing Taurus mountains, that we used to clearly see every day, was back, after being concealed behind a curtain of brown.

On the way north I saw the off ramp for the Olympus ruins, which we were at in December, but were unable to see it due to a swollen creek. I asked if she's rather see it NOW, on the way out of town, or on the way back, and the response was, "Now...my butt needs a break!" so we rolled down the back, windy roads to Olympus.

It was different than I expected, and the most noteworthy thing (to me) was the location at the ocean's edge. What a beautiful setting! Unlike several of the ruins we visited lately, this one did not blow my mind. We stayed for a few hours and had an amazing trout dinner at one of the neighboring restaurant. The entire trout, fries, and some veggies for $4.75 which we even shared with the very polite cats, and headed back out.

The ride from there to Finike took us along the waterfront and some amazing scenery near a park called Mavikent Plaji. (Plaji is beach in Turkish). The road climbed up, down, and both directions and we enjoyed some magnificent shots from on high.

For day one I rate it a solid 7 on a ten scale and look forward to the next 20 days.

Day II, April 10: A lesson was learned today: even with an ocean view room, DO NOT get one fronting a major highway! There was noise most of the night and truthfully, we weren't here long enough to really appreciate the view. We had a decision to make over breakfast; stay one more night, chill, and NOT have to pack it all up, OR take off. We decided noise or no noise we would head north to Demre, the next city on our journey.

The ride from here to there is only 17 km, but they are some of the most majestic miles along this coast, and the same road I hit a month ago on my way back from Bucharest.

The weather was picture perfect, and even though Kat had a bit of fear (still getting used to being a bike passenger...) we got to Demre and found the road that paralleled the beach. Since our hotel breakfast offered no coffee, we found a nice coffee spot right on the water and started digging into room options for the following nights. After researching AirBNBs and hotels, we walked a few hundred feet and checked out some right there, since we knew we could at least see them beforehand.

We found this less than 4-star pansion run by a lovely lady who spoke no English. She had two room options and we negotiated $19 a night for two nights, $38 total. Mind you, it's nothing special, but it did have a kitchen and the ocean was two minutes away. We were good with that decision so decided to explore more and found an amazing beach, Suluklu Beach, and a funky hotel with one apartment right on the sand. It was a one bedroom wooden cabin that was more than we wanted to spend, but hey, you only live once, so after our two days at the other place, we planned to go there. It also adjoined a restaurant just as funky, so we thought we'd have three days to explore the area.

When we returned to our prior room in Finike I notice that Limyra was there, a major and significant historical site just a few miles away. So the start of day three included that and another amazing ride up those amazing 17 km along the beach.

Day III, April 11:

The Limyra ruins was a letdown so we rode by and moved on. The wind was gusting pretty hard and luckily the distance to Demre was not too great, but even so, as we got on the road the buffeting wind off the mountain cliffs was troublesome. Luckily, we were not in a hurry so we took it very slowly and even though we ran into some light rain we made it to Demre with a great sigh of relief. Small, light bikes are good for some things, not so good for others.

We got to our room, called Turkmen Boutique Hotel, paid our reasonable amount, and got mostly unpacked. Since we carry everything in two backpacks and a gym bag, efficiency and logistics are paramount. Fortunately, Kathleen is a super packer and more organized (and conscientious) than I am. The lodging, which has a living room, kitchen and two bedrooms, is very spartan and when Kat pulled a blanket out of the second bedroom armoire, four eggs fell out. We suspected the chickens around the house got inside and laid them, and we felt bad that we broke them. And we believe the Momma chicken knew what we did...

One of them was able to get inside, we had to chase her out, and it was a truly laughable, memorable moment.

It was time for lunch so explored the smallish downtown, had a great lunch for less than $7.00 (for two) and discovered that the Myra ruins we just a mile outside town, so we headed there, spent an hour exploring and it was one of the more noteworthy places we have been. The necropolis (crypts) are actually built into the side of the mountain several hundred feet up, and it was a chilling and amazing site. The stadium was just as memorable and in great condition. Even though the entire area is not as large as many we have visited, it is a definite "must see" if you are in the Demre area.

The wind never did let up the whole day, so we are hoping tomorrow dawns with sunshine and calm air.

Day IV, April 12:

A very, very cold night, but the 4th day was beautiful and much warmer. After a light breakfast we decided to check out Kaleucagiz, the ferry port to the island of Kekova, which everyone recommended we visit. It has (more) ruins, plus a sunken city, which we look forward to seeing. We really liked the very small port town so checked out some rooms and found one where we will stay for the next few nights. Again, amazing prices, and off season is definitely the time to travel.

When we got home I told Kat we really needed to check out the Cathedral of St. Nicholas, the true man behind Santa Claus. It was under renovation, but quite lovely with nice murals and the final resting place of the man who supposedly performed miracles and was the protector of children.

Tomorrow we have one more local museum to check out on our way to the next stop, and for two days we plan to kind of chill...

Day V, April 13:

We arrived in Kaleucagiz and the reality of staying in this room was even better than we thought, so plan on maybe five days or more. From here we can veg, catch up on writing, hike, visit Kekova Island, check out Kas (our next destination), and play it by ear. Truth is, we have four windows in our room plus a door to the balcony, and every room overlooks the water. We can't do much better than this so decided to take advantage of it.

Day VI, April 14:

It was insanely quite last night and the nasty wind finally stopped blowing, which means it got nice and WARM (66°F)—finally. Our room includes breakfast, which was a great traditional Turkish buffet, and that suits us just fine. Afterwards we hiked a bit of the Lycian Way (540 km the entire way), and what little we did was lovely.

Day VII, April 15:

We "found" Kas, and it truly IS amazing. The view from atop the hill was as breathtaking as the place we are staying now. We traversed around the perimeter of the peninsula and checked out a few rooms. Kat found this amazing place with an infinity pool and in most parts of the world it would be 4 star, but here: about $50. It was further outside town than we wanted so we checked out the downtown area, had a bite to eat and found a nice pansiyon for half that. We decided that we'll return next week for one week and use Kas a new base to look beyond.

The weather is finally really nice, it hit 70 today, and even though the water is not QUITE ready to dive into, it's close! Regardless, Kat and I are enjoying the hell out of our journey and we're just 1/3 through it.

Day VIII, April 16:

When we got here in Kaleucagiz a few days ago I knew we had to get over to the actual island of Kekova. There are boat tours, but the owner of our hotel, Ibrahim, also has, in addition to his restaurant, a boat, so we took that over for all of 800 tl: that's $54 for two people and we were the only ones on it.

First stop was a 10 minute ride to the island of Simena, and the Simena Kalesi castle on top. The hike was moderate and the views from the top were spectacular. I swear, sometimes coming up with new superlatives is a challenge! After we were there for about an hour we continued on to the actual island of Kekova and the "sunken city," which is more an oceanfront area where buildings used to be. We could see sunken Roman baths and evidence of buildings along with archways and such, but regardless, it was very cool. A bit later we pulled into a beautiful cove and anchored there for about an hour, soaking up the sun, and even jumping into the Mediterranean, which was very cold! We had the boat to ourselves and felt like we were living a fairy tale.

We are grateful every day, especially when we can enjoy such luxury for such a low cost.

Day IX, April 17:

Happy Easter, and a day to relax. After breakfast we took a short hike up the Lycian Way in the other direction and explored the sarcophagus along the waterfront and stumbled into a dry dock where many boats were undergoing renovation. This is our last day here, the sky has been overcast since early, so we're catching up on work and messages and things like that. Tomorrow we check out to Kas where we will spend seven days, possibly more. And as of tomorrow we will be halfway through our 21 day journey.

Date: 04.25.22/ What Makes a GREAT AirBNB/ Hotel Room Great?

There are rating systems used worldwide for hotel rooms, and they usually rate from 1 (or no) stars to five stars, sometimes six. They use criteria like location, amenities, room quality, views, etc...and that works for "tourists," but not necessarily for TRAVELERS. We travelers are not in rooms for a day or a week, but sometimes for weeks or months at a time. Our criteria is much different since we don't need room service, concierge, or valet parking; we need pure, basic usable amenities of LIFE--not luxuries.

Cool stuff to know...

We recently stayed in a room (a pansiyon they are called in Europe; in America we normally refer to them as a hostel), and they have come a long way from what they used to be. Some who have traveled may remember them as dives (and some still are!), but generally they are nice and you can get private rooms, not just dorms. The Isinda Pansiyon in Kas checked off so many boxes I wanted to do a deep dive between this unit and many/ most others that may miss some marks.

- ✓ Great location: that is all relative, of course, but aside from being water or ocean close, great location can also mean quiet streets or access to public transportation. This unit is a 5-minute walk to town and 10 minutes to the marina.
- ✓ Good price: again, all relative, but in Turkey, where prices are very low, this one hits the mark. The longer the stay the better you can negotiate, and we stayed for 7 days so got a good deal
- ✓ Soft bed with clean sheets: Ah, life's little luxuries! We run into hard beds often, so a nice soft bed with great linens and sheets is nice.
- ✓ Modern shower with good shower head and hot water, also one that does not have odors and has the ability to seal the bathroom sink to wash clothes. Speaking for me, the two things I REALLY need is a good bed and a good shower. That means hot water fairly quickly, good pressure, and enough room to move. The showers in Turkey are overall much larger than in Europe, which is very appealing. We have also run into many that have nasty odors coming from the drain, usually from old pipes, but this one here, no problem. This sink actually has a stopper, so extra points there!

- ✓ Bathroom storage, shelf: Sometimes minor details are important! Some bathrooms have no place to put anything and rarely do we find a medicine cabinet, something we take for granted in the US. This unit has a shelf for a bag or supplies...score 1.
- ✓ Refrigerator with adequate room and not obtrusive. We have fridges about half the time, and even though we don't cook, it's nice to keep things cold. This unit here has a nice size fridge with an enclosure around it which enhances the look of the room. Sweet!
- ✓ Good lighting, not just an overhead, either with side tables or indirect lighting. Some rooms have NO personality at all, and many just have a singular light overhead, which we both hate. This room has mood lights behind the bed, a switch to turn them off and on, plus indirect lights on the wall which casts more than enough light.
- ✓ Nice balcony: THAT is something we always relish, and this one is large enough for a table and two chairs, PLUS there is a security fence that would keep an intruder away from our slider door. This was well thought out.
- ✓ Sliding door with high quality windows/ double pane. Along with that balcony a decent sliding door (with screens) is something we don't take for granted. This unit has a high quality, heavy door, AND screen
- ✓ A kitchen or access to a kitchen or restaurant, and or grocery stores. Most of our units don't have a kitchen, but many have hot water boilers, which is great for making coffee or tea. In lieu of that if there is a decent food place—or coffee place—that makes up for the lack of a kitchen and adds points to the location category above.
- ✓ Good internet! NOT to be taken for granted, but always appreciated! Most of our units have satellite internet which has been surprisingly quick! We can both watch Netflix with no buffering, so we'll use that as a benchmark.
- ✓ High quality door. Along with the slider doors, a good FRONT door is nice, along with an easy to use and secure lock. We have both.
- ✓ Storage space and/or drawers: We have stayed in rooms with NO extra space at all, and that sucks. This room has racks to hang stuff plus several drawers and cabinets, so we have enough room for everything! Ditto on electrical sockets, which this place has everywhere.
- ✓ Hooks for hanging jackets, shirts, etc: A minor detail, but adds to the score for sure.

What kind of room do YOU like? We have been very lucky and have the process down almost to a science. We depend on AirBNB, Bookings.com, and Google Maps and rarely do they let us down.

Date: 05.03.22/ Our 21 Day Beta Test Road Trip (part II)

Day X, April 18:

(If you missed part I of the story, <u>here it is</u>)

Our last night in Kaleucagiz was unique in that we had lightning and thunder! It never did rain, but it ended our perfect five nights there. I paid our bill, and considering we were there five nights, had one meal and the three hour boat ride…and the bill was about $250, I was good with that. After breakfast we rode into Kas and we dug that room, too! We were close to everything, and it was cute and pretty large. We had a balcony (which we love), and a really nice bathroom and shower. The bed was soft and we stayed for seven nights. After we unpacked we strolled downtown, found some restaurants pricey, others better, and had a nice meal for about $10.

Day XI, April 19:

Our first full day in Kas and we were surprised by an early morning rainstorm! There was nothing predicted, but by 0900 the sky was clear and we started our exploration. That usually means two things: 1) a good coffee shop and 2) ditto on a good simit spot. We lucked out on both!

Afterwards we walked a bit and explored and found a really nice campground, of all things. We have no camping gear, nor a traveling van, but they did offer bungalows for 600 lira: $40 USD. That is a lot for a bare room with no amenities, but the location of this place was extraordinary, so we may return at some point down the line. Meanwhile we found an almost as good location in a restaurant where we could hang out for the entire day. They had no "minimum purchase" (yet), though they will starting in May, so we worked, sunned, and relaxed for several hours.

Both of us got really good vibes there in Kas and plan to return in October (after Greece) for maybe two months. Subject to change, of course…

Day XII, April 20:

I guess we don't need to document every day in paradise…and today was just that: paradise. Nice breakfast on the balcony, went to the beach for a few hours, and researched rooms for later this year…Yes, we plan to return for a month or two. And by the way, once again we were the only residents of this pansiyon. There's about 8 rooms, but very, very quiet, which was fine with us.

Day XIII, April 21:

On my way from Bucharest home to Antalya in April, I covered much of the western Turkey coast. One of the towns that caught my attention was Kalkan, about 40 km north of Kas, which is where went. Riding through that town was beautiful as it starts along the state highway and slowly slopes right down to the ocean.

Today we checked it out, and it was VERY steep!

I can't say I was as impressed as I expected to be, but it's worth a visit, and we did get an invite from a local expat to stay at her resort next week, so we'll see if that comes together (it did). As it was, we did not stay in Kalkan (yet), but we went 20 minutes further to Patara Beach, one of the longest in Turkey. It's about 11 km and is pure white sand from one dune to the next. And there was hardly anyone there.

Kathleen and I have been so enjoying these two weeks and each day is as good as the last.

Day XIV, April 22:

What do you do when you wake up early, maybe from the FIRST "call to prayer" at 0450? You get dressed and catch the sunrise at the 2000 year old Antiphellos Amphitheater! So that is what we did, walking along the mostly dark street at 0545, but it was beautiful. There were a few stray cats hanging out, and they were joined by two street dogs who hung out with us. A good way to start the day!

Day 15 (and more):

We have been digging into Kas, looking at possible living places, and getting to know the town. There is a section of town called Cerciler which one of the local British residents told me about. It is more of a "locals" neighborhood, rather than a tourist-centric part of town. It's up at the very top of the hill surrounding the town and some of the views are pretty spectacular. It's also sparse of restaurants and feels a bit run down.

How much is it worth to live in an area you really don't want to live in?

We faced that same question in Mexico, and lived in Colonia side rather than Portside. The difference in rent was considerable, and Colonia, though not as "nice," was also not as crowded or expensive for food as well as rent. It looks like we can get something more or less "in town" for maybe $800 USD, which fits in our budget, so I decided that unless we could save $300 or more, we'll look to move into the town proper.

Meanwhile, we found amazing beaches and coves, and though the water temp is still a bit cold, it won't be long now! We stayed an extra day at the current pansiyon and have been invited to a very nice resort from the Welsh owner who appreciates our lifestyle. We always appreciate the universe taking care of us! It's 15 days since we left and we'll be heading back to Antalya next Sunday.

April 26

Reluctantly we finally left Kas and had an interesting offer: In the local Facebook page for the city of Kalkan I posted that we were looking for a room for a night or two. A very nice Welsh lady, Elle, has a six bedroom retreat/ spa that is she is just readying to open, and she invited us to stay for a few days. Which we did. It was magnificent with a full on ocean view and amazingly comfortable bed. We had full run of the house and chilled for two days plus went into "town" for a meal and to explore. We were more impressed than on our first go-round so decided that maybe this town does deserve a further view.

April 29-May 1

We had a few choices of how to route our last leg home, so we stopped in Demre (again) for a quick snack and trucked on down to Adrasan, a small, out of the way, beach town that was very laid back. Kat found us a great pansiyon for a good price, so our last few days were spent there, enjoying the little stream outside our window along with the ducks quacking over there. We had a great fish dinner, very inexpensive, and the room was nice, as was the coolish night temperature. Since we are already "packed" Kat wanted to visit Istanbul before leave for the US in four weeks, so we will rest for ONE day, then fly to Istanbul. Oh, well, I knew we'd get there eventually, so why not now?

This 21 (actually 23) day Beta test did actually what we wanted it to do. We were able to pack the bike and take with us what we needed to live. In 60+ plus days we will do it again, but that trip will be about four months. Most of the time we'll be in warm temps, but towards the end it may get chilly so we have to incorporate that into our packing plans. We will "end" in Northern Greece and we have several options of where to go from there, but it looks like south to Athens then ferry back to Turkey is the most likely case. Stay tuned...

Date: 05.14.22/ Istanbul!

If a picture can speak 1000 words, a word can generate 1000 pictures, and the mere name of the city we just visited—Istanbul- conjures up many thousands of images! One of the oldest cities in the world, it was founded almost nine thousand years ago, and initially called Byzantium, then Constantinople, and it has been under the rule of Greece, the Roman Empire, and the Ottomans. It is one of the few cities that bridges two continents, and it's magical, crowded, full of history, a gourmand's pipe dream, and a traveler's fantasy; Istanbul is many things. It has one of the busiest airports in the world and is easier than ever to get to.

In past blogs I shared the surprise I had when we arrived in Turkey in December 2021 and how the thought of visiting this country—let alone living in it—was never a thought in my head. But after 6 months and visiting just a fraction of the western coast, it is truly a jewel of the world. Since Kat and I are returning to the US for the month of June she suggested (insisted??) that we visit this town of 15 million people and almost 20 percent of the population. "When someone asks us if we got there, I'd like to say yes," was her pitch, and I didn't fight it. It wasn't a big deal to me, but it was to Kat. I didn't care, but we went to Istanbul...and here's what happened.

Important Traveling Info

The flight from Antalya was cheap, about $62, which is typical of most flights outside the US, where domestic flights are expensive. We found a nice AirBNB in "Old Town" which is where we were recommended to stay. It's near the Golden Horn, the Bosporus straight, hell, pretty much everything we wanted to see, including several major mosques, Topkapi Palace, Galata Tower, and more. As it turned out we got there the second day of a three-day holiday called Eid al-Fitr, which marks the end of the 30-day celebration of Ramadan. Now that the faithful can return to normal activities, including eating, drinking (even water), and other assorted activities, they celebrate. During Ramadan even sex is forbidden, so that's pretty committed to their faith.

Our flight was easy, as was the 90-minute journey from Sabiha Gokcen Airport, the newer one, which is waaaay outside of town. It required one bus and one metro, so that wasn't horrible. The town was active, but well within reason, and when we arrived on day one, it was surprisingly quiet—until we got to the tourist area. Two of the major mosques are within a 10-minute walk of each other, so that is where the crowds were. We were told that after the three days were through things would get more "normal," whatever that means.

Day II we got an early start and walked over the Galata Bridge, which was very cool in that the top deck was covered with fishermen and their lines hanging over the sides, and below that level was all restaurants. On the other side Kat spotted a very cool tower, Galata, so we climbed a very steep incline to find it. Packed, that's what it was, so we didn't go in, but enjoyed the area. The tower was built in 1348 and over the centuries had damage, rebuilding, fire, add-ons, and now it is a tourist spot. This was the big day for walking—12 miles—and that includes lots of hills since Istanbul was built on seven hills, following the example of Rome. Of course, back then it was called Constantinople and it was the gateway between Europe and Asia as well as the bridge between Christianity and the Muslim faith. I do have to add that as used to being in and around "old buildings" as we are, Istanbul was humbling. We spent several hours in their archeological museum and were face to face with statues, sarcophagus, coins, and other relics that were seven, eight, even ten thousand years old. Their statues were particularly impressive and since they had the entire country to get them from, they were probably the best of the best. I was particularly enamored with a huge exhibit dedicated to Troy, the real city, which they determined was in northern Turkey. It also was a city that was covered repeatedly with dirt and new constructs, and they had to dig through ten different levels to get to their origins.

We took it a little easier the next day, only 6.5 miles, and visited the Hagia Sophia, Suleymaniye, and Blue mosques, each different and spectacular in their own way. That left 3227 that we did NOT visit, since that is the estimated number of mosques in this very conservative, devout town. We saw far more Hijabs (head and body scarves worn by Muslim women), and everyone blended right in. The crowds in SOME areas were better, like around the tourist spots, but the Grand Bazaar and others like it were pandemonium. Most vendors were courteous, a few were pushy, but since we are very particular about what we buy (being nomads), we held our own. Dinner was at a great buffet where you pick your food dishes when you enter and it was terrific.

Our last day was a full one since we didn't fly out until 8:30 p.m., but the roads everywhere were a mess and we had concern about getting to the airport, even though we left four hours early. It ended well due to a shared taxi ride rather than the city bus, and by the time we got home we needed a day to just recover.

Istanbul is what I call a "city on overload." Busy everywhere, though SOME streets were barren of traffic, and others were a parking lot. There wasn't much in between. The buses and subways we saw were usually jammed, I mean sardine jammed, and made us both reluctant to use them. On top of the 15 million residents, I suspect that that number increases 20-30 percent with visiting tourists. As the largest city in Turkey, and in Europe, we heard scores of different accents, and far more English than we did in Antalya. It seems that Americans and Brits visit THERE before they go anywhere else. We found the affordability reasonable, as in "Turkey reasonable," and imminently affordable. The weather and crowds must be factored in if you plan your trip since it gets quite cold in winter (they had snow this year) and pretty hot in summer, but the determining factor is more the crowds than the weather. We were there for four days and we could go back for a month and still not see "everything," but for us, personally, since "cities" and crowds are not our thing this might be a One and Done.

Date: 05.22.22/ The BEST Ruins I Have Ever Visited

In March I rode our new BMW bike down from Bucharest to Antalya, about 1600 km, 1000 miles. One of the stops on the way was in Ephesus, which is not the name of the city, but the names of the ancient ruins. Those ruins are at the top of my Best Ruins list as I reflected upon others I have visited. In the past four years I have been to 26 countries and collectively I'm at 39 over my lifetime. Most of those countries are in Europe where so much history took place. Between Greece, Italy, Croatia and now Turkey, I have lost count of how many ruins I have been through. Add in Asia, South America, and Mexico and the numbers grow. And we still have Egypt, Jordan, and Israel on the list, hopefully in 2023.

When it comes to picking the "best" ruins, it almost sounds like an oxymoron. Are the BEST ruins the ones in the best condition NOW, after renovation, and make it welcoming and inviting? Or are the best the ones in the most "natural" condition that reflect the way it looked initially?

I don't know. My list is personal and biased of course, and if you have been to any one of them, I welcome your thoughts! And if you have any other recommendations, please let me know.

Cool stuff to know...

Many listicles like this have the top five, top seven, the top 10, etc, so rather than focus on the numbers, I went back and went from less impressive to most impressive, but regardless they are ALL amazing! I'll not go into all the details for each of these, but share the highlights.

- Ephesus, Selcuk, Turkey: Of all the ruins I have been to, the Library of Celsus in Ephesus was the only one that has two entire floors and it was magnificent. This town of Ephesus was founded in 10th century BC, which is mind blowing to ponder; we're talking 12,000 years ago. The city has been restored to what it

once was, with beautiful marble streets, coliseums and stadiums, and many fully restored buildings and statues.
- The Acropolis and Parthenon, Greece: Anyone who recalls their history classes in junior high is familiar with the Acropolis, which is the hill that holds the Parthenon along with two other significant temples: Erechteion and the Temple of Nike. They are all magnificent and to be in Athens is a humbling experience.
- Angkor Wat, Cambodia: It's the largest religious monument in the world at 402 acres, 163 hectares. It is a sprawling complex that requires long walks or hiring a guide to ride from one ruin to the other in a tuk-tuk, a three-wheeled motorcycle with a carriage. Angkor is swarming with monkeys, so that adds to the mystique of the complex and the better physical condition you are in, the better, since you can climb many of these. Also, the tree growth throughout is unique and is actually part of the structures.
- The Valley of the Temples, Sicily: The valley is not really a valley, but sits on a rise outside the city of Agrigento in the south of Sicily. I had never heard of the Valley until we stayed in Sicily for six weeks, and it required an overnight trip from our room in Siracusa. Worth it, every minute. These temples have been built and rebuilt several times and are considered a shining example of Grecian architecture, though they are in Italy.
- Aspendos, Turkey: This site has the best stadium renovation I have ever been in. It looks like it could have held a play or musical event last weekend, and it may have: they use it today for outside entertainment, and it can hold 7,000 people. Along with the theater you can wander around the several hundred acres and explore entry gates, houses, and cathedrals, many of them in great condition.
- Machu Picchu, Peru: it's the Big One, the one everyone aspires to, and is probably on more "bucket lists" than any others listed here. And it is magnificent. Set high on top of the Andes mountains at 2430 meters, almost 8000 feet, it can take your breath away in more ways than one! Machu Picchu takes effort to get there and it is known for both the construction techniques which used no mortar or concrete, as well as the unknown astrological purpose behind the construction.
- Hadrian's Villa, Villa Gregoriana, Villa d'Este, Italy: I called Tivoli, Italy, the "City of the Three Temples," and some are older than the city of Rome, which is a 45-minute train ride away. All three of these are different and unique. Gregoriana is more of a natural temple that is folded inside of a breathtaking valley, with waterfalls and lush greenery. Hadrian's Villa is more similar to other "ruins" in that there are buildings, walls, and statues in varying condition, and they are all part of this several hundred-acre complex. Villa d'Este is the newest of the three, built in the 16th century, these Renaissance villas take you back through time and the many hundreds of fountains are all gravity fed with no pumps.

- Side, Turkey: Yes, Turkey has a lot of ruins, and this is one of my top three. It is almost like a Hollywood movie set, in that it is fully restored, and you could almost imagine a "Universal City" billboard on the lot. It is set apart from the rest of the "real" city and ends at the beach, where the Temple of Apollo is the main draw and is inspiring.
- Termessos, Turkey: another one I never heard of until we lived in Antalya, about 30 minutes away. This city was built 1000 meters up in the mountains and required some effort to visit, but worth it. It is covered with ruins that have NOT been restored, which truly takes you back thousands of years. This city has a wonderful amphitheater that is rustic and natural and with views that go forever. This city is also renown in that Alexander the Great was unable to conquer it.
- The Coliseum, Italy: Yes, THE Coliseum. Sure everyone who ever went to school or watched a Roman movie knows the Coliseum. It was built to hold brutal and spectacular events from lion fights to chariot races, and at one time had a water feature for ship fights. It is in downtown Rome, five minutes from the Forum and countless other relics of the past. The Coliseum is amazing and many would put it at their number ones—until they see what else is out there.
- Perge, Turkey: as you can see, Turkey is abundant in ruins, and this one is just a 20-minute metro ride from Antalya, so easy to get to. Hundreds of acres that took us by surprise since we had little knowledge beforehand.
- Myra, Turkey: Almost done with Turkey—for now, but this ruin in the city of Demre is quite small, but the necropolis built inside the mountain is so eye catching it made the list.

I left one or two off, so we'll call that list my Top 12.

In July we head along the Turkish west coast, into Greece, and traverse from east to west. How many ruins will replace these listed? I guess we'll both have to find out!

Date: 06.05.22/ One City, Two Airports

With hundreds of thousands of miles behind us over last 4 years and God knows how many cities, our recent trip back to the states was the first one where we had to not only switch planes, but we also had to switch airports.

And we had no idea what to expect.

Important Traveling Info

London is one of the busiest cities in the world with one of the busiest airports, Heathrow, but they also have a smaller airport that you may be familiar with called Gatwick. It's primarily used for regional flights and for many low-cost carriers. We have seen many large cities, including Istanbul, which has had to expand into a second airport due to increasing volume.

COVID restrictions for the US are very specific, and you must get tested "within 24 hours." But does that mean 24 hours before you leave, or 24 hours before you arrive in the United States? We were not sure. Would we need to do a second test in London? That was a question soon to be answered!

We left Turkey at almost 10:00 p.m. and landed in London about midnight their time. Our flight to the US was not until the next afternoon, so we had 15 hours to kill, including trying to find a place to sleep! This was not the first time that we had to crash out in an airport, but it was 50° outside and chilly throughout the entire building. As it turned out we found several different spots including a warm one that was part of a cafe which was closed for the night. It felt like a hippie crash pad because people were strewn out all over the benches and the floor! We fit right in.

We had no choice about going to Heathrow early since the shuttle from Gatwick did not start until 0500, so we ended up taking it about 8:00 that morning, a 40-minute ride, and about $25 per person. Now the cost savings was lessened...

Long story short, we spent most of the day at Heathrow airport, which was quite lovely. Plenty of food options and places to hang out, and we got on our US flight mid-afternoon as planned. So what are the takeaways here?

- If the cost savings to switch airports is substantial, find out what it cost to get from one to the other, since they may offset that savings.

- If you think that you will be crashing out at an airport be sure you bring something warm to wear. Fortunately we had a blanket with us (thank you British Air!), but regardless of the outside temperatures, most airports are kept very chilly. Bring a hat.

Kathleen and I look at experiences like this as being part of the adventure. We don't get the most restful sleep, but we do end up with a great story to tell!!

Date: 06.16.22/ 14 flights, 31 days (part I)

Starting May 30 and until July 1, I will leave from Antalya, Turkey and visit London, New Orleans, Miami, Dominica, (with ALMOST a "side trip" to Puerto Rico...), Columbus (OH), Salt Lake City, Chicago, and return to Turkey. I counted how many flights that will include: 14 flights in 31 days. As of this writing I am just over halfway there.

No question, travel is NOT what it used to be and some flights were smooth while another flight was missed by FIVE minutes due to a late arrival in Miami, mostly because of a tropical storm. That was minor, but it did cause us to stay at Miami airport for one entire day (and night) and sleep on the floor. Not the best of strategies, and the SECOND time we did this in one week, but we deemed it the most practical and affordable solution. Our most stressful leg was in trying to LEAVE the island of Dominica, which was a mess since they cancelled our flight out. American Airline's app—and a telephone call—showed the flight being on time and scheduled, but our driver told us, "The plane is not HERE (Dominica) from Puerto Rico, so you aren't able to leave as planned." That meant waiting until the ONLY other flight out, which was later that afternoon, along with having to get a motel room, but it worked out. Overall, even with COVID protocol, it was pretty smooth. We find that while we are IN the moment of distress it's a mess, but afterwards you realize it could almost always be worse.

Visiting New Orleans for a few days was a bit surreal and as much as I enjoy the food, I did not enjoy the touristy areas of Bourbon Street and such. I was not lamenting leaving after being there three days.

Meanwhile, the island of Dominica (NOTE: different than the Dominican Republic) was a gorgeous, primitive, and pure island of waterfalls and green, plus 365 rivers and nine active volcanoes. None of which we saw...

As much as our lives LOOK like a vacation from the outside, our travels are truly part of our day to day lives. So visiting an island resort (I won a trip through my writings) and lounging by the pool for five days was pretty much what we wanted and needed. We explored the town, Roseau, the capital, but unfortunately "lost" two days since we got there on a Sunday (Deadsville), and the next day was a national holiday (ditto). For the three days that things were more normal, we liked the town. It felt very Caribbean and though English was their official language it was infused with Creole and their own native dialect and was tough to decipher. The younger people there, especially at the Fort Young resort, spoke slower and enunciated better, so we were able to communicate.

For those that are into nature, I highly recommend you check this island paradise out. They say that if Christopher Columbus—who "discovered" the island on a Sunday, hence the name, was to come back, he would probably recognize it as much the same. We found it peaceful and except for the crazy windy road from the airport to the resort, we really didn't go anywhere except for a whale watch. That was worthwhile and we got to see pilot and sperm whales, along with dolphins.

As I am writing this midway through our trip, I offer some suggestions:

- Many smaller Islands have limited flights each day, so it's a good idea to have a plan B in case of weather or other delays. Be sure that you get to your departing airport on time both coming and going, since you may only have one shot per day.

- In the Caribbean, and in many parts of the world, small islands are different and unique countries which means different currency and visas, and though these are becoming less important, COVID requirements. Right now the US entry COVID requirements have been REMOVED and many countries are doing away with them, too, plus Passenger Locator Forms.

The world is not normal by our old definition, but it is settling down. Delayed and cancelled flights, especially domestically, are an epidemic, so be patient and plan ahead. My next entry will cover my trip to Salt Lake City and then back to Turkey via Chicago and London.

Date: 07.05.22/ One Missed Bus Can Mess up Everything!! (14 flights, 31 days, part II)

Kathleen and I returned "home" to Turkey after 30 days in the US and the island of Dominica. I am also happy to say that we got married while we were in Ohio and ready to start the next chapter of our lives. Together.

I posted part I of this trip a few weeks ago which took us from Antalya to London, switching airplanes AND airports (Gatwick to Heathrow), then on to New Orleans in the US, Dominica, then back to Columbus, where we stayed for about 10 days. I left for Salt Lake City for business while Kat stayed with her family, and we met up again at O'Hare in Chicago and back to Antalya via Heathrow-Gatwick once again. The return trip was not so easy...

Important Traveling Info

But 14 flights in 31 days, came with some good news: COVID restrictions are mostly past, but flights are busy, delays are the norm, and cancellations are way too common.

The airline industry is understaffed due to many layoffs and early retirements in the aftermath of COVID, and predictions are that it will take another year, maybe two, to balance out. Meanwhile, flights are pricey and those incredible bargains from the past two years are gone for now.

Some thoughts about going "home" again to the US. As is always the case, price sticker shock was even more shocking this time since gas is at an all-time high, and inflation pushed up food prices as well. An Uber ride I used to take for about $50-60 USD was over $90 in Salt Lake, and it was difficult to find a decent meal for less than $15 per person. We KNEW that Turkey would spoil us with their low cost of living, and once again we were reassured that we could, and never would, live in the US again.

There were/ are some things that I "missed" in the US, including being able to read and listen to everything—and understand the language! Sometimes being the odd man out when everyone around you speaks a different language gets uncomfortable. I also missed bacon...tough to find overseas.

Back to our return trip: One wrong bus can mess things up, and after almost 4 years on the road and two dozen countries, we still make mistakes! As we were ready to return, Kathleen and I met up in Chicago, me coming from Salt Lake City and her coming from Columbus, and our trip overseas to Heathrow airport in London was effortless. Unfortunately, we had to change not just planes but airports--again. (note to self: don't do that again), but since we had done it on the way over, I thought we had it dialed in. So easy, but a boneheaded move later (by moi) we took the bus supposedly to Gatwick airport, only to find out that we got the wrong bus and went almost an hour in the wrong direction. With 3 hours left until our flight departed back to Turkey.

We got to the first town, a beautiful little berg called Winchester, and went to the bus/ train station and asked quite excitedly, "How fast can we get to Gatwick airport?" He suggested a 3-train combo and unfortunately after the very first one, we missed our connector train by about 1 minute. That meant we had to resort to an emergency plan, and fortunately there was another young gentleman, Dylan, who was also going to the airport and had done it before so we followed on his heels. Long story short, we got to Gatwick 40 minutes before our flight left, and of course our luggage was flagged because we did not remove our liquids, so we hauled ass down the walkway and did get there in time. Then of course the plane sat on the tarmac for 90 minutes because there were too many planes in the sky per air traffic control and we ended up getting to Antalya just as the last tram was shutting down before midnight.

After that we had two days to ready ourselves for our four-month trip up the coast, and that will start with my next entry.

One question that everyone asked in the US was, "Where are you going next?" and we have several options starting in October, including taking our little BMW back to Romania, or keeping it. One option has us going to Albania for a few weeks since we'll be close, and I am also a candidate for a travel writing trip to Jordan in October, so that affects our plans, too.

We may return to Turkey, probably to Kas, and stay the winter, OR we may go to Tanzania or somewhere close, since we are hosting a safari there in February. When we started our journey in Feb 2019, we planned things out 3-4 months ahead, and we still like to do that. With 26 countries visited since then we have a pretty good idea of where we'd like to return to and those that we don't. We spoke to many people in America about our adventure and some were inspired and some thought we were nuts—or a little of both. We've gotten that same feedback since Day One, so, to each their own.

Date: 07.21.22/ A Travel Younger Reality Check: Traveling Older

We are at the beginning of a 4-month journey up the coast of Turkey into Greece on a motorcycle. Everything that we need is packed onto the motorcycle. There are some who admire us for what we do, and others who think we are a bit insane and we actually feel that way about ourselves too...

We had a little bit of a reality check after just a few days on the road as Kathleen got sick for several days and we stayed put in the lovely city of Kas in a comfy hostel/pansiyon hosted by a lovely couple who brought us a few meals and a thermometer. It was a wonderful place to convalesce. Finally, after six days, we hit the road again with our destination of the city of Fethiye. Unbeknownst to us, we were traveling during a major holiday so finding a room was a challenge. We found a cheap little hostel for three days, but it was not in the best location, and did not want to stay any longer than necessary. We moved up the hill to the city of Hisaronu, about 1000 meters higher in sea level and about five degrees cooler. We had very strong feelings and good energy there, so stayed for six days in a lovely hotel, and now it was my turn to get sick! I got the coughs more than anything, and fortunately it passed after a few days.

The major highway along this part of the Turkish coast is called D400, and is a relatively easy motorcycle road, but with a few twisties in spots. As we explored some of the more rural roads here, they became more treacherous, very windy, and lots of switchbacks. I had to face the reality check of traveling on a motorcycle at my age of 68, and doing that with a partner on the back. Truth is, I am not 48, and not even 58, so some of these roads can be challenging. I must face the reality that I have lost some of my skills, and some of my confidence. That is a sad reality check.

We also have the problem of excessive heat, which has complicated our journey, exasperating it. The temps in the area are in the mid-nineties, and we have been searching for higher elevations, but didn't see much respite there. We even considered heading into Greece earlier than scheduled, but the temperature's there are not much better. Actually almost ALL of Europe from north to south is sweltering. Along with the heat we also encountered high winds, but so far, no rain...so not ALL the elements are conspiring against us!

As we looked at the road going forward, physically, and metaphorically, Kathleen insisted, and I agreed, that we stay only on major roads. I think the age of wanderlust adventure is behind us. Those half our age can carry their backpacks and sleeping bags with them and sleep anywhere, but we want a bed, a shower, and air conditioning. I don't think that makes us spoiled Americans; I think that makes us mature adults. Our time of carrying our possessions on our back and sleeping in a park or on a beach are behind us. Going forward I have promised her that we will stay only on safe roads and if I do not feel capable of them then we will not go. If she feels afraid, I will honor that and not dismiss it.

My "motivation" to start Travel Younger was to be inspired by Millennials and pass it on. I will still do that, but may tamper it down with maturity, wisdom, and a bit more precaution.

Date: 08.05.22/ A Funny Thing Happened on the Way to Greece: Government Bureaucracy

We hear all these stories of being caught in the complexity of customs and immigration and other types of legal issues when you travel, but we have been very lucky. Until now. We had some friends who literally had to leave Turkey within 24 hours with their car since they overstayed their welcome. When we got our two-year residency in Turkey that went amazingly well and we rarely had issues. But we recently tried to leave Turkey to go to the Greek island of Chios, and found out that we owed a steep penalty because we did not notify Customs about our motorcycle which remained behind in Turkey when we went to the US in June. It seems that even though the bike sat in a secured garage and was not ridden, we were supposed to notify Customs that a vehicle was left behind.

Who knew?

We had a ticket for the ferry, but were unable to leave until we paid the penalty. The problem was no one knew how much it was! It was a Saturday, generally a non-working day for the government, so we started with one person, then another, and eventually three or four people actually worked on the problem, while we waited all day trying to understand what was happening, and no one could explain it properly. The 0900 ferry left and we were finally told that the fine was 7615 Turkish Lira: $425 USD. GULP! All because a bike sat unattended for 30 days while we were out of the country. There was no battle to be won here, they required cash, so I had to hit two ATM machines, and then we had to decide to take a later ferry or shine it on; we took the later one and killed time until 7:00 p.m. after being there for about 12 hours.

We would have encountered this problem when we left Turkey eventually, it just so happens that we experienced it now. This is just part of the trials and tribulations of dealing with the multiple regulations in different countries along with language barriers, and we had our share in the US, too. Between city, state, county, and the IRS, there are a multitude of government regulations that have no common sense. Our situation was complicated since we are US citizens with a US driver's license, driving a RENTED motorcycle from Romania, and having temporary Turkish residency.

Chios was nice, we found a nice room near the ferry, and explored as much as we could over a few hours. The next morning at 0820 we caught another ferry to the island of Lesbos (still in Greece), so that was easy. Our few days on Lesbos were very pleasant and we got to explore some of the island, plus found some nice coves to relax in and float on the salty Aegean waters.

We started our four-month bike journey on July 4, so we are one month in. I've lost count of how many rooms we have stayed in and for the most part the trip has been great. Kat and I both got COVID, one after another, and we took a small spill on the bike, with (fortunately) no serious injuries, other than my ego and her fear of having it happen again.

If someone asked us to write an essay on "How I spent my summer," we have one hell of a story to tell!

Date: 08.15.22/ A Sense of History

I've learned to appreciate history a lot more over the years we've been traveling, and I found out that this town of Canakkale (pronounced Chan-a-collie) played a major role in World War I. I'll get to that in a second, since one of the most significant cities in history, the Ancient City of Troy, was one of our stops on the way here. Admittedly, it was much smaller and lower key that I expected it to be, and it was really just a series of ruins connected by wooden walkways. Along the way there were signs stating, "Troy I, Troy III, etc...," and they indicated the various levels of Troy that were built on top of each other. That is not a new thing and in most major cities, like Rome, London, and New York City, whenever new construction or excavation is started, they usually find old relics. What is cool about Troy is that for many years they did not know if it was a real city or just a myth, mostly because it was buried under dirt. They had a reproduction of the Trojan Horse at the ruin, but the one in Canakkale marina is much cooler, and was used in the Troy movie.

Across the Dardanelles Channel (about one mile) is a castle that neither of us ever heard of, but we both agree that the Kilitbahir Castle is undeniably the COOLEST one we have ever been to. THAT says a lot! It was massive, with four-foot-thick walls, and the footprint of the structure is like a three-leaf clover, with three sections and a huge tower in the middle. We were able to climb INSIDE the center section and it was mind-blowing! Of all the castles we've visited, this one beats them all. It was built in the 15th century as the Ottoman Empire was gaining strength and the sultan, Fatih Sultan Mehmet, recognized that the straits were critical to the defense of Constantinople, now Istanbul. Even though it is 300km along the waterway, the mouth of the Dardanelles is the weak link to get to the heart of the former capital via ships. He built this castle and one on the other side, Cimenlik, which is nice and now houses a naval museum, but is nowhere close to Kilitbahir. Over the centuries both castles played a part in defense of the Dardanelles, but about 100 years ago is when it really came into the spotlight.

Like many, I was familiar with the name Dardanelles Strait, and I also was familiar with a battle (and movie) called "Gallipoli," but I did not know it was the name of the entire peninsula that extends from Istanbul out to the Aegean Sea. It was also one of the deadliest campaigns in military history during World War I, with almost 350,000 soldiers killed.

Back in WW I, the so-called "War to End all Wars," the Turks were allied with Germany and Austria-Hungary, and collectively called The Central Power. The Allies included France, Great Britain, Russia, Italy, Japan, Australia, New Zealand, and the US. In March 1915 the Allied Powers tried to open the Dardanelles for their ships to get through to Istanbul, and they started an almost yearlong campaign which failed. The Turks held strong and the army of 70,000 soldiers were turned back. It was a very high casualty battle and within a few miles of here are dozens of cemeteries honoring the dead. This was a very personal, very bloody war, and if you've seen the pictures of soldiers in foxholes, hunkering down with nowhere to go, you might get an image of how frightening and deadly it was. There were many Allied soldiers that died on Turkish soil who were never identified, and what bodies were left were not claimed until the Armistice in 1918. I visited some of those battlefields and memorials and it was sobering, and also very sad to see how many innocent lives were lost at such young ages.

Kat and I have been to countless churches, castles and other "old ruins," but these were the first memorials I ever visited that were in relatively recent times. I have yet to visit any World War II or more recent battlefields and I'm not sure if I want to...

Date: 10.11.22/ My Many "Firsts" in Greece

Now that our 31-day Urban Centers of Northern Greece tour is done, I thought I'd review the many things I experienced along the way. Aside from spending 88 days on a motorcycle and traveling through four countries, plus sleeping in 35 different beds, there were some other noteworthy items, like...

Cool stuff to know...

(1) My first real caves. While in Turkey, Kat and I visited a small cave outside Antalya called Karain, but it was nothing compared to the Aggitis Cave, one of the few river caves in the world, and Alistrati, which was a fairy wonderland of stalactites (top down), and stalagmites (bottom up), and they blew our minds. Alistrati even had a robotic tour guide for the first few hundred yards called Persephone, who speaks 33 languages and was a totally unexpected surprise. It was also nice that even though photos were "forbidden," the tour guide allowed us to take some.

(2) I had never been to a monastery, so visiting a small one outside the city of Serres, was a treat. It was like stepping into a medieval movie, walking down steep driveways that were nothing but inserted rocks and stones. The building itself was painted such vivid colors they were almost fluorescent, and the chandelier was as extravagant as any I have seen. But, when we went to the city of Meteora (coming up), that was a whole other story! Monasteries at the top of one quarter mile pinnacles was beyond belief.

(3) Ok, this one is not quite so jaw dropping: I had never been "off road" before in a four-wheel drive vehicle, but I did that at Lake Kerkini. This was not what I expected and I was underwhelmed, but it was blistering hot and since we went looking for wildlife, they were all hiding during the heat of the day. If I never go off-roading again, I'm OK with that.

(4) I have gotten quite fascinated with Alexander the Great and have read two books about him while we were traveling. He was one of the legends in history and even though he died at age 32, he left a legacy that will never be equaled. Much of what he learned about life, came from Aristotle, but what he learned about

commanding an army and about warfare, he learned from his father, Philip II, one of the most significant Macedonia leaders in history. He put Alexander in the field before he was legally able to buy a beer (age 20), and Philip was murdered by one of his own bodyguards, so things haven't changed much over the years. Keep your friends close, and possible assassins, even closer. I share this since I visited the King Philip II tomb, which was UNDERGROUND (called a tumulus) and was breathtaking and not even discovered until 1977 in Vergina. A definite "must visit" if you come to Greece.

(5) We traveled much of the Via Egnatia highway (A2), which was the first across the country interstate highway in the world, built by the Romans over two millennium ago. It used to start in Albania and extend to Istanbul, but now it stays within the Greek borders. It also has 76 tunnels, and within a few hours we went through about 45 of them, including the longest cave I've ever driven, 6 km. Some of these tunnels were surprisingly elevated and curved inside, another first for me.

(6) I am fascinated with really, really old ruins and such, and up near Vikos Gorge there were ruins that were built in 9000-7000 BC, so we're talking about 10,000 years ago. No question, the benchmark of "old things" changes when we think of thousands of years of history. Growing up near Philadelphia, PA in the US, that town was noteworthy since it was where the Declaration of Independence was signed: 246 years ago. Puts things in perspective. In Greek, Roman, and Egyptian timetables, that is like last week!

(7) I never knew what an Oracle was, but we visited Dodoni, which is an oracle even older than the famous Oracle of Delphi, which we will visit while we are back in Athens. This is where many types of people came for advice, and that includes major leaders who asked about how to run their cities and even military people who looked for guidance before going to war. There were archeologists working there when we visited and it was interesting watching that process.

(8) Meteora was in a class by itself and was the most impressive pinnacle park I've ever seen. It was even more impressive since we were able to drive up to them and visit the monasteries at the top, which were build 600-800 years ago by monks risking their lives—and dying in the process. However, in the US we have Zion and Bryce National Parks in the state of Utah, and they were and are impressive as hell.

(9) On a personal and less history based "first," I did a bike ride from the city of Litohoro to the base of Mount Olympus. At the ending point was a town (though too small to even BE a town) called Pereia. It's a launch point for hikers but the road up there, all 18 km, was the twistiest mountain road I have ever ridden on a bike. Eight 180 degree turns and lots of great vistas put it on my list.

(10) And on another more personal note, I had my first mussels and octopus meals...Yea, not that significant, but the taste and texture of oysters never worked for me, so I was never attracted to mussels. They used to sell them on the street in Turkey and since eating "bad" seafood is not a good idea, I never wanted to risk it. But Kat and I joined a cooking class, which was really just a "watching" class, and Loulou made steamed mussels and octopus. I loved them both!

There are probably even more firsts or seconds or AHA events or moments over the past few months, so I'll come back to them later.

Date: 10.26.22/ The Differences Between Turkey, Greece, Bulgaria, & Romania

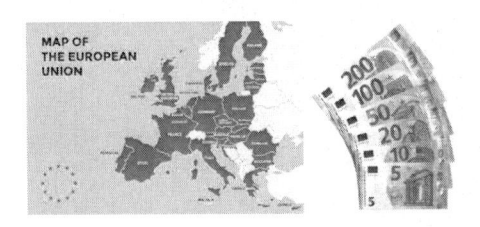

Over the past five months we have spent a significant amount of time in Turkey and Greece, along with two side trips to Bulgaria and Romania. We were in Turkey from December 2021, until July 4th and feel we know it pretty well. We lived in the southern city of Antalya, and for 88 days traveled northward by motorcycle up the Turkish Coast and into Greece, where we toured the northern regions for 31 days in partnership with visitors and convention centers. The most amazing thing about Europe, at least from an American's viewpoint, is how CLOSE countries are, and it is remarkably easy to travel from one to the next, and literally feel like you are in another world. The US, with 50 states and 3000 miles of land east to west, has variety, but except for Mexico to the south, there is no significant change in cultures. Even if you venture north into Canada, except for some nuances, it's almost like being in America.

Now that we are settled into Greece (for now), I wanted to offer some examples of the differences between those four countries: Turkey, Greece, Bulgaria, & Romania.

Important Traveling Info

One of the big determining factors that give countries some identity is if they are part of the European Union, the EU, since that influences their immigration policy, their financial strength and cost of living, and their money. Along with that is the Schengen Zone factor which determines how long you can STAY in each country. If you want to know more, here's a report I did several years ago:

https://documentcloud.adobe.com/link/track?uri=urn%3Aaaid%3Ascds%3AUS%3A e6665968-5467-45b4-85cc-d13cff4bcb7f

EU vs. Non-EU:

Greece is EU, which makes it part of a vast interconnected and interlocked community. Twenty-six (soon to be 27) countries all share a common "Schengen" passport which makes it easy to cross borders, whereas Turkey is an island alone and shares none of that. Turkey has its own individual culture and is predominantly Muslim, while Greece has commonalities with a few countries, like its neighbor, Italy, which is reflected in their foods. The two things they both have in common is a vast and impressive history, though most of the world knows Greek history much more than Turkey's. Romania and Bulgaria are EU, but non-Schengen...

(Written) Language differences:

The world shares many different types of written language, from the variation of Asian/ Chinese Han symbols and icons, to the Cyrillic of Russia and the Arabian text. Turkey employs "English" letters which makes it easier for us to understand (somewhat), but Greece uses a variation of Cyrillic letters which is very difficult for us to interpret. Over the months we drove on the roads we were used to NOT being able to read the signs, but most had English translations, too. Romania uses Latin letters, whereas Bulgaria does not.

Money:

Greece uses the Euro currency, which is predominant throughout the EU, and currently the Euro/ dollar ration is almost 1:1, which makes calculations very easy. We've been in Greece for several months and our buying power is good, but not great. Turkey uses the Lira, which has been very depressed and offers us some of the best buying power in the world. The Euro is supposedly the currency of the EU, but Romania and Bulgaria are both members, but have their own currency; Bulgaria with the Lek, and Romania with the Lei. Buying power in both countries is better than Greece, but not as good as Turkey. BTW, our favorite country, Croatia, will become an EU member on January 1, and convert to the Euro from the Kuna. That does NOT make us happy, but even worse, they will be part of the Schengen, which curtails our residency powers.

We won't go into conversions since they change and the bottom line is that ALL these currencies offer a lot of buying power in their respective countries.

COFFEE!: This almost deserves a separate post since finding the RIGHT coffee in each country takes real effort! You would think that something as universal as "cappuccino" would be the same, but even though most countries are similar, some are made with one shot of expresso, some with two. Some like them lukewarm, others (not enough!), make them hotter. The milk they add varies from cream to whipped to blended, and have all sorts of fat content. There are way too many variations of a simple cup of coffee, and finding the RIGHT coffee with the RIGHT atmosphere, with the RIGHT prices, is a chore.

Food:

In Turkey you don't have to go very far to find a shop selling "chai tea," and almost any street you walk down will have merchants out on the curb drinking it. Along with the tea, the breakfast "meal" I fell in love with included a simit, which is like a sesame seed bagel, usually very soft, and incredibly inexpensive. Some tea, a simit, a pack of black olives and cream cheese, and I was a happy man. But cross the border and what happens?: NONE of that!

It's strange that something as man-made as a border crossing would change the world of food, but it does, and we found food in Bulgaria different than Greece, which was different than Turkey. The Greeks make really good salad and even have a salad named after them: Greek Salad, which is usually served with a healthy block of feta cheese on top. That salad is rare in Turkey and unfortunately, we rarely found crispy, crunchy, tasty salads there. Bulgaria and Romania also had good salads.

In the alcohol world, Turkey has raki, Greece has ouizo, Bulgaria has Rakia (similar), and Romania has Țuica. Beer is also highly popular in all four countries, and each one has their "country favorite," and it always amazed me how we would see people drinking beer from early in the morning until whenever. But they were almost always under control.

Vive la Difference is a French expression which says we should appreciate the differences. As we have traveled over these past four years we have seen many differences, but one thing was almost always a commonality: most people are kind, pleasant, and wish to be friendly and courteous to these English only speakers from a Strange Land.

Date: 11.09.22/ Are You a Tourist or a Traveler? Plus Residency Vs. Citizenship

I saw a post recently from a friend who was in Athens, and she shared a few things that showed that she is traveling as a tourist, rather than a traveler, which is perfectly fine. Here's the tells...

- she's staying in a boutique hotel...which is great when you are on vacation, but usually not practical--or affordable---when you are a traveler. For those that have deep pockets and good cash flow, a boutique hotel is great, but sometimes not practical for 2, 4, 6 weeks or more.

- she is near music everywhere (and wanted to be)...which is GREAT for a few days, but when you LIVE somewhere, music--especially late at night--gets annoying. In Antalya, Turkey we had a great room which unfortunately was close to a nightclub. About 6:00 pm the music started and went into the night and thankfully the city required music to END at midnight. We have stayed other places that have no restrictions, and music would drone on until 3, 4, even 5 o'clock into the morning.

I have written about this distinction in the past, but now that Kat and I are going on 5 years as nomads I thought it worth a revisit. Travelers live a whole different lifestyle because for them/ us, travel is not a holiday, but part of life. After 26 countries in four years we still have many more to go, and will be in number 27, Albania, shortly.

Another term that can be confusing concerns the difference between Residency-- both short term and long-term-- and Citizenship. As a general rule, and certainly throughout most of Europe, most visitors can stay for 90 days. If you are familiar with the term "Schengen," it is a collective of 26 (soon to be 27 countries) that all share common border guidelines. That means you can travel back and forth between those countries a little easier than crossing most borders in the world. The bad news is that these collective/ countries are tied together as one so most visitors can only stay for 90 days out of a collective 180 days: three months out of every six-month period. If you stay in France for 89 days, you can only stay in Italy for one more. There is more to it than that, so here's my old Schengen Chess Game report.

If someone wanted to stay beyond 90 days, the easiest step is to gain residency. That gives you the legal right to stay longer, usually one year, sometimes longer. It does NOT grant citizenship, nor the right to a passport. That residency process can be very cumbersome, and we started it in a few countries, and got it in Turkey, which was quite reasonable.

The other option, which is harder to get, and only under specific circumstances, is citizenship. Many people do this through their family bloodline, called Right of Descendancy, which I also covered a while ago. That rule book is also very fluid, but worth considering if you have parents or grandparents from a country you would like to live in. Details of all these are available online, but remember that rules and requirements change, and many who post information are legal firms looking to be hired by you to do the work. Which may be worthwhile.

Date: 11.19.22/ Our 87 Days in Greece

Since 2019 we have stayed at several places for more than 45 days at a time, including Valencia, Spain; Italy (two different places); Croatia (3 different places); Turkey (9 months), and of course, Puerto Morelos, Mexico, where we were in COVID lockdown for 15 months. But we just finished almost three months in Greece and got to know it better than the other places since we toured the northern section for 31 days, then spent six weeks in Athens. Along the way we hit four islands, Naxos, Santorini, Chios, and Lesbos, and found it to be an amazing country, full of as much history as anywhere we have been, along with wonderful food, scenery, and lovely people.

If you didn't follow our two-wheeled bike trip this past summer, we visited 15 different regions and cities in partnership with the respective visitors bureaus and convention centers, and rode the bike about 1500 miles. You can visit some of our archives or my personal Facebook blog has almost day by day reports as well.

Now we are in Albania (country #41 for me) for 63 days, and we have been wanting to visit Sarande since 2019, but it never quite worked out. So far, first impressions are great and we have a wonderful waterfront location with a view of Corfu, and our plans/ hopes are to make this an annual destination. For Americans reading this, Albania offers us something very unique: a one-year visa for tourists. That is very lenient by EU standards of 90 days, which is the same for most other countries, too. As non-EU residents, we have to be mindful of Schengen limits, and our 87 days in Greece pushed right up against that wall. Now we must exit the EU for 90 days to "reset the clock," but if you plan it properly, you can bounce back and forth for years. Which is exactly what we are planning.

Athens took me by surprise and I liked it more than I expected, but Kat REALLY liked it better, especially as she learned her way around the town, the metro, and all her favorite coffee shops and shopping places. And you cannot ignore the history of the country, and especially Athens, since it surrounds you in a very comfortable way. On our last night there we met a friend for dinner and right above us the Acropolis was bathed in their nighttime lighting scheme. After dinner we took the metro home and walked by the various sites we passed by throughout out time there, like Hadrian's Library, the Agora, and many more. We have heard some say that Athens was not a favorite place, but I personally think it's how you view it. It IS crowded, especially during the busy season, but just as we were leaving, the crowds we noticeably smaller. Yes, there is graffiti, but you find that in any major city, and some is junk, but much of it truly is "street art."

We found the affordability very good; much less expensive than most Western European cities, but not as cheap as Turkey or Asia. The food was overall AMAZING, and generally the people spoke English and were very cordial. Greece does not have a big rail network, but Athens offers a few train options, including two destinations that we recommend: Thessaloniki and Meteora. Meanwhile, busses can take you from one end of the country to another, but let's not forget ferries! With 227 inhabitable islands you have many choices, but realistically only three dozen or so are on anyone's radar, and between all that, you have more than enough options to enjoy this amazing country.

Date: 11.28.22/ Next stop: Getting Situated in a New Place

I estimate we have probably stayed at 15 or more places for longer than 30 days since starting our nomadic life in 2019. We are now in Sarande, Albania, and after all this time, we understand the process. For those who might be thinking about traveling to different places for longer periods, here are some of the steps we take.

Important Traveling Info

The first thing we do is check out the neighborhood. Having a local intimate coffee shop is important to us along with (close) places to eat. Ironically, where we are right now lacks those things! But that's okay, there are compensating factors that make up for it, including probably our favorite room we've ever had, and a view that cannot be beat of the island of Corfu and the sunset. The closest coffee shop is about 10 minutes away, and it's quite lovely, and there are plenty of restaurants just a little bit further. When we were in Athens we were initially dismayed because we had the same problem; nothing was close. But once we realized how easy it was to take the Metro and go exactly where we wanted, that took care of that. This town is much too small for a subway, and we think that there is a local bus, but not even sure of that!

After we get the lay of the land, it's important that we stock up on provisions and supplies. That means food and investigating all the options, since we don't want to eat out every meal, and sometimes that requires getting things over and over again, like spices, plastic storage containers, paper supplies, etc. That's just the cost of doing business, not much we can do about that.

We also look into public transportation, and here in Sarande, we already knew that there wasn't any. Taxis are abundant, and cheap, and since there is no rail infra structure here in Albania, buses are the way to go, and we recently took the bus to the city of Tirana, the capital, since we needed to get new passports. After 4 years I ran out of empty pages! The 4.5-hour trip was quite beautiful, but it was a small minibus, fully crowded, and unfortunately this is the rainy season—and it did on our ride-- so we could not enjoy the views. We surprisingly enjoyed Tirana, and may go back again, but haven't decided. I need to return to pick up our passports, but that's going to be a quick turnaround trip.

For me, a gym is one of the first things I seek out, and hopefully one I can walk to in a reasonably short time. The gym here is pretty awesome with a great view and very quiet, which works for me!

One of the most important things to think about when moving to a new location is what type of weather you can expect. Since its winter here in the northern hemisphere, we try to stay as close to the Mediterranean belt as possible, and even though we have cold weather clothing, our choice would be to not need them! So far the temperatures have only gotten down into the 40s, not much different in my old home in Orange County, California, but the good news is that our apartment is extraordinarily well insulated, and the windows are well sealed. No wind blowing through, which has been a problem in several of the older rooms we have stayed at.

This type of lifestyle may intrigue you, and you do not need to jump in with both feet and leave where you are permanently. But if you feel so inclined, and would like to go visit a place for a month or two, we think it's a tremendous experience. We constantly run into parents of younger children who travel with them, and the kids get a terrific cultural experience that they could not duplicate in schools.

Date: 12.11.22/ Medical Expenses Overseas

The two most common questions Kat and I get:

- What's your favorite country?

- What do you do about health care?

First I'll speak to the second one, and the reason I said "overseas" rather than Europe is because some of you may be traveling to other places besides Europe, which is our favorite hangout. But regardless of whether you are in South America, Mexico, or Asia, most of this insight is pretty close. The only exceptions would be for travelers who want to live in the more "cosmopolitan" (ie, pricey) areas, like London, Paris, Stockholm, Australia etc... Those areas are not our thing (fortunately), but what IS our thing is eastern Europe, especially the Balkans and south into Turkey.

If you aren't sure where the Balkans are, or what they include (and there is uncertainty there) generally it would be the area from Slovenia south along the Adriatic/ Ionian Sea, and east to the Black Sea to Romania. That encompasses (generally): Albania, Bosnia and Herzegovina, Bulgaria, Croatia, Kosovo, Montenegro, North Macedonia, Romania, Serbia, and Slovenia. We have been to seven of them and hope to hit the others next spring.

We recently decided that since we'll be in Albania for several months it was time to get a medical checkup. That included a dental cleaning, and since we ain't getting any younger, some blood tests and maybe an ultrasound would be a good idea.

The local expat community offered strong recommendations for the dentist we went to, and we were pleased to find a husband/ wife team who spoke great English and had a nice clean office in a good location. Kat needed to have one of her teeth ground down due to some past work, it probably took a half hour, and the first time we were there they did it at NO CHARGE. A few days later we went back for a thorough exam and cleaning: the price? 2000 lek, about $18 each.

Our visit to the health lab went flawlessly since they spoke great English as well, and when we asked, "Can we get tests done without seeing a doctor?" the answer was, "of course." THAT is something we could not do in the US.

First things first, a full blood panel workup with about 30 basic tests, AND the results were printed out in English, plus they were able to interpret the results and offer feedback. Kat was a nurse, so this was familiar turf for her, and they were able to speak professionally since they had similar skills. The ultrasound tech was upstairs, and he spoke moderate English and shared while doing the tests, "normal, normal, normal..." No waiting to get results, which he printed out on the spot, and gave us copies. They included kidneys, bladder, liver, spleen, stomach, pancreas, and whatever else is in there!

I know, how much did all this cost?

The best for last: 8800 lek total for both Kat and I, so that was about $40 USD each. There was no insurance required, minimal paperwork other than asking our names and ages, and we were in an out in less than an hour.

Over the past four years Kat has had two occasions to require a paramedic ride to the hospital and a visit of several hours. One was 106€ (euro), the other about 250€.

Two questions about health that come up quite a bit, besides the ones I mentioned, include, "What about travel insurance?" and we have talked about it many times, but have declined so far. With medical costs being so reasonable we believe we spend less on visits than we would on insurance. The other query is, "What happens if you have something 'serious'?" and for that the answer is less clear. Since we are over 65 we have Medicare, but using that would be a logistical nightmare and cost us more in travel and lodging back to the US if that were required. Even if we DID have to pay out of pocket, it would probably still be cheaper. We can only speak for ourselves, but so far, this is what works for us.

Any questions?? Oh, and the answer to the other question is probably Croatia, Turkey, or Albania! The list of "favorites" is growing, which is great since it eliminates the many that we have less interest in visiting.

Date: 12.28.22/ How SAFE Are Other Countries in the World? (beside the US)

As Kathleen and I have traveled to almost 30 countries in the last four years, many times we get asked, "Is (country name) safe?" or "Are you afraid?" Those came up when we lived in Mexico and Turkey, and Mexico mostly felt safe, but I DID feel uncomfortable with some aspects of what I call the "bandido mindset," and that stopped us from renting a motorcycle down there.

The US embassy puts out safety warnings of every country and the potential safety issues. They tend to take a VERY cautious approach and err on the side of safety, and there's some places you just DON'T go, and some places you just shouldn't or can't go, but most of the world is open and very safe. When we went to Tunisia several years ago the embassy gave a level IV warning, and they cautioned us to stay away from the border of Libya, which only makes sense. We had an amazing time in Tunisia and the people were lovely. It was our first Muslim country so there was some culture shock, and Kathleen felt a little bit awkward because men were looking at her, mostly because they just aren't used to seeing Americans, and most women over there are not dressed like she is, ie quite fashionable! Now we are in Albania.

Three years ago Kathleen was going to stay here in Sarande on her own for a month while I went to the United States, but we did some research and neither of us felt comfortable with that. There were rumors of drug traffic, gangsters, and a host of other things right out of an espionage movie. After a month here we feel more safe than the majority of cities in the United States. When I went to San Antonio Texas for business 2 years ago, I felt very uncomfortable walking down the streets with homeless people all over and tweakers asking me for money.

The media, TV, and movies certainly skew our views of the world. How many movies have you seen where there is a footrace along the rooftops and fruit markets in the streets of Istanbul and Morocco? International intrigue is entertaining, but I have never seen anyone racing through the markets in the streets where we were!

I was curious how many "mass shootings" there were in the US this year, and even though there are several definitions of what those entails, the number is over 600 and the final tally may exceed the record from 2019, when it was almost 700. THAT is scary and we have met several Europeans who do NOT want to go to the US because of numbers like that.

The other morning I had breakfast with another American expat who has been here in Sarande for 4 years. He said that the city and country caters to tourists and they encourage their citizens to be cordial and certainly not cause us any harm. He shared a story of a restaurant owner that was rude to a customer a few years ago as he followed the patron outside, jumped on their car, and broke their windshield! That's what I call a violent temper. A few days later the city bulldozed and leveled his business. The city made a big deal out of it and made it known they wouldn't tolerate that from their people. Here's the story:

https://timesofmalta.com/articles/view/albania-bulldozes-restaurant-after-owner-attacks-tourists.730258

Can you imagine that happening in America or most of the world??

Is it safe? If we use common sense we can avoid most areas prone to crime against tourists, the most likely being pickpocketing. For anyone who clubs until 0300, well, that's just not a smart idea. Especially for female/ solo travelers. Again, common sense. The answer is yes, overall we feel very safe. We have left credit cards, money clips, telephones and even my passport behind somewhere and each time they were returned. Just before we left Turkey I left my wallet and credit cards at a nut shop and realized a few minutes later while walking away. Before I had the chance to return, a young man ran out with it, fully intact, and when we tried to give him a thank you reward he declined.

After so many countries and meeting so many different people, we are firmly convinced that most people everywhere are good and try to DO good. It's the few bad seeds that muck it up for the rest of us.

Date: 01.18.23/ Indispensable Items to Carry when Traveling

In today's parlance of social media, we use the word, "hacks," which implies shortcuts or easy ways to do things. We've all seen hacks of things you can do with duct tape, plus scores of ways to "pack a bag properly," and they are usually terrific pieces of advice. When I started traveling I learned a lot about HOW to pack, and WHAT to bring from videos like these, so the tips I mention below are things that Kat and I carry with us—and find indispensable. She is the queen of innovation and sometimes I am in awe of how she uses some of the items below. I hope you get some pointers.

- Shower head holder: Have you ever used a shower where the shower head was NOT attached to the top, but was at the end of a long-corded wand? Yea, well that is the norm in Europe, and we hate it! One hand to hold the wand and the other to wash your hair—with one hand. Somewhere on the road we found these suction cup holders that attach to the shower wall and the clip holds the shower head in place. Simple, brilliant, and oh so lovely! We have left a few behind along the way so I picked up two of them via Amazon when I was last in the US. If you are irritated by showers that are not connected at the top, find this sucker!

- Power pack for power on the road: Phones are indispensable when traveling and even with stronger batteries they lose power throughout the day. Video and Netflix are power hogs and even having your phone searching for wifi signals eats into it. Many of these small portable power packs have cords to power up TWO devices, and now that USB-B is a relic, almost everything is USB-C, at least for Android people. You iPhone lovers have your own version. Kat's portable unit works on Chromebook, which is terrific, but my Lenovo laptop requires its own plug-in cord. I am amazed at how many travelers do NOT have one...

- Fast dry underwear: I did an interview a few months ago with a fellow nomad named Rax, who hails from Singapore. We had a great conversation which you can listen to here, and he asked me a question that stumped me. The question was, "what items do you always carry with you?" and after coming up with just a few (like these listed), I asked him what OTHERS came up with. He said, "quick drying underwear," and I laughed and said, "hell, yes!" I guess I take them for granted, but on the road, socks and underwear are the two things we need to wash the most often. Many times in a sink. When they are quick drying you can wash them at night and they're dry by the morning. SCIENCE! Thank God for it.

- Buffs: The Survivor TV show introduced me to buffs many years ago and they are fantastic for their many uses. I wear it around my neck since that area is exposed between a jacket and hat, but, since I am bald, I also use it to keep my head warm by wearing it as a fashionable sock! If you Google "buff" videos you can find about a dozen ways to use them. This was something I took for granted until Rax's conversation brought it to mind.

- Double stick tape: This is Kat's thing, and whenever I go back to the US, it's a "must buy" request. She uses it for many things and that includes hanging hooks on the walls, securing loose cords out of the way, and a host of other ways. This product is not easy to find on the road, so if you have a chance to get one wherever, I suggest you do.

- Clips: Clips, clips, clips; they come in various sizes but we use the relatively small to medium sized ones. They can be used to secure a cereal bag, keep cords together, hold curtains open or closed, and lots of other places.

- Hooks: like clips, they are small and come in many variations. We've stayed at over 100 places since 2019, and some are "equipped" better than others. Some bathrooms are tiny with no shelf for anything and sometimes having a simple hook to hang a shirt or towel is like heaven! Simple pleasures sometimes require simple resources.

- Faucet head for kitchen: This is one of our newer toys, and it came about because the kitchen faucet in our Athens unit (for 6 weeks) sprayed all over. We've had that problem before and in Mexico we had a great faucet head and it made things easier. We never thought to keep it since the stuff we carry has to REALLY make sense or make our lives better, but going forward this may qualify for that.

These come to mind now and others may come up in the future. What about you? Do you have your own travel hacks to suggest? Let us know.

Date: 02.06.23/ 27 Days in Israel, part I (Jan 23-Feb 1)

Since we have been in Israel for just less than one month, and since this trip is so significant in history, both my own, and world history, Kat suggested that I post my personal blog posts here on Travel Younger in case you do not follow me on my Norm Bour Facebook page. I hope you enjoy it.

Jan 23, 2023: Tel Aviv

Shalom and welcome to Israel! I've been wanting to visit most of my life, but truthfully, it was not at the top of my list. But here we are in the capital, Tel Aviv, after two very, very early morning wake ups to get here. One was for a 0600, 9 hour bus ride from Albania to Athens, and then a 0730 flight to Israel. We had two great surprises in the short time we've been here. ONE, was the EASE of getting through the airport and the "lack" of security! I expected a search of our luggage when we landed and soldiers with guns everywhere, but neither happened. We zipped through passport control with ease. MAYBE it's a way to make visitors feel more welcome and secure, not sure.

The second surprise—no SHOCK—was the food prices here! Mind you, we HAVE been spoiled between Turkey and Albania, but $8.00 for a bagel floored me, along with $23 for a Sweet and Sour Chicken at a Chinese restaurant. A small ice cream was $5, and compared to many countries, including the US, they are not outrageous, but by our skewed standards they were. Kat and I shared a large chicken salad for dinner which was reasonable. We DID luck out and have a room directly across from the beach for three days, so we're liking that, along with temps pushing close to 70°.

Jan 24, 2023: Tel Aviv

7.6 mi of walking, plus one bus ride, and we hit the Sarona food court, where they had about 100 different food courts and eateries, then we bussed to the city of Jaffa, and hit the flea market, the historical clock tower, and the marina, and finished up at the Carmel fruit market, where we shared an amazing lunch pita platter with Syrian bread. There were hundreds of vendors there, including one of the most impressive bread & pastry shops we've seen, and we also stored up on my nut supply for my treat bag. Amazing! Overall Tel Aviv is a cool town, but I think 3 days is about the right amount of time to spend here-- almost like what we should have done in Bangkok! But it was SO nice to be in a t-shirt all day.

Jan 28, 2023: Jerusalem

We've been in Jerusalem for about 48 hours, and yes, we are safe. There was an incident yesterday which we had no knowledge of until friends asked about us, but all is good.

It's a dynamic town with a much different feel than Tel Aviv. Getting off the train we noticed that the buildings were older and very authentic and the people much more conservatively dressed, with more covered clothing, and more rabbis and Hasidic Jews with their signature hats, long coats, and hair curling from their heads. Our apartment is just a few minutes from a huge food bazaar called Machaneh Yehudah, both a blessing as well as a curse! So many temptations, lots of pastries and ethnic foods, as well as a good selection of fresh fruit and veggies. Prices seem just a bit less expensive that Tel Aviv, but certainly the highest we've experienced over our four years of travel.

Yesterday we walked to the Old City about 25 minutes away, and they have dedicated boulevards for just trams and pedestrians, so it was a pleasant walk. Viewing the wall as we approached was surreal and we strolled the entire perimeter, passed by all the eight gates, and absorbed as much of the history as our minds could handle. Seeing the Dome of the Rock, Damascus and Lion's Gate, and walking into what is reputably the site of the Last Supper and King David's Tomb, was a lot to take in. Kathleen and I took lots of pictures but we both agreed that they do not come close to capturing the feel and the presence that we felt. We intentionally did not go INSIDE the walls since that is a day in itself, but will do that this week. Inside is the Western Wall, the Church of the Holy Sepulcre, the site of the burial and resurrection of Jesus, and much more.

As we left the Old Town and returned to our apartment we noticed that almost all businesses were closed, and that was a little past 3:00 p.m. We knew that things close at sunset for Shabbat, but most close much earlier, so we had to scramble to get some dinner and food supplies for the following day. Our AirBNB host invited us to Shabbat dinner this afternoon so that will be very special and demonstrates the kindness of people we have met all over the world.

The city is a true magnet for Christians, Muslims, and Jews, and of all the places we have visited over our travels, this is unique in many ways. More to come.

Feb 1, 2023: Jerusalem

Here in Israel, and surely here in Jerusalem, Shabbat, their Sabbath, which starts Friday night at sundown and continues till Saturday at sundown, is taken very seriously. This is the only place we have been to that is ruled by religion, and starting from Friday night everything shuts down. Businesses are closed, no public transportation, and no cars on the street. There are some exceptions, but its eerie quiet and except for not having access to restaurants, grocery stores, or coffee shops, it's kind of refreshing. We walked through the normally bustling marketplace/ bazaar, and instead of stands with products displayed, we were able to view the graffiti on the metal doors in front of them. The citizens spend the day at home with family and enjoy a Shabbat dinner after sunset on Saturday when all returns to normal.

We did find the Israel Museum open and found it fascinating. I am drawn towards ancient history and archaeology museums, and this one had displays starting way back, 10,000 BCE, with exhibits showing everything that happened after that. They also had something that is iconic and something I never thought I'd see: The Dead Sea Scrolls.

These scrolls were written mostly on animal hide between 300BCE-100AD and document Jewish and Hebrew manuscripts that were incorporated into the Bible. They were discovered inside caves between 1946-1956, and at the time their historical significance was not fully understood and they were sold multiple times for peanuts. The clay jars that held them protected them from the elements (somewhat), but it wasn't until technology allowed them to be unfurled and studied under specialized scopes that they were able to decipher them. Some of the text is in Hebrew, some in Aramaic, and almost every chapter of the Old Testament is incorporated into the Scrolls. The room that holds them is very classy and in the middle was a large circular display case with the scrolls behind glass, but we found out that these were copies, and the REAL ones were in smaller cases around the room.

No question, this was a visit that stood out from many others and there is still so much to see here.

Date: 02.14.23/ 27 Days in Israel, Part II (Feb 3-Feb 11)

After almost one month, we are in our last week in Israel. This has been one of the most unique and special places we have visited, both from a historic and cultural perspective, as well as a personal voyage of my own religious history. These are daily blogs from my Facebook site which Kat suggested I add to this one, too. It starts when we finally got inside the Old Jerusalem city walls until our trip to Jordan for two days, to visit Petra.

Feb 3, 2023: Jerusalem

Over the past few days we were able to dodge rain drops, overcast skies, and wind, and we finally got inside the walls of the Old City of Jerusalem. This hotly contested area for centuries is an amazing mix of cultures, religion, and ethic focus, and is actually like several cities inside a perimeter. We entered one of the main gates, the Damascus Gate, which led us into the Muslim quarter, which was very reminiscent of Tunis, Tunisia, and Istanbul. Lots of beautiful clothing, dishes, and tons of eateries, and as we walked along the road suddenly it changed.

"Welcome to the Jewish quarter," and just like that, the signs changed, along with the flags and the merchants inside the shops. That led us over to one of our primary goals to visit that day: The Western Wall, also called the Wailing Wall, since it is known as the most coveted piece of land for Jews, and until the 7-day War in 1967, was off limits for thousands of years. For many years this was in Jordanian territory, and the boundaries in that area are still open to opinion. It is the only remaining wall left from the Second Temple period, one of the highlights of Jewish history, and is also known for holding the prayers written on pieces of paper that visitors insert between the rock.

The inside sections are a maze of shops, walkways, and how they can supply all the businesses inside is a mystery! But from the Jewish quarter we were able to find the Christian quarter and to one of the most revered sites in Christianity: The Church of the Holy Sepulchre. This name was not familiar to Kat and me, but what it held inside was: it is claimed to be the site of the crucifixion, burial, and resurrection of Jesus. To see the supposed site, called Golgotha (Calvary) was humbling, and the church itself was amazing to walk through and find little nooks and historic locations.

We both decided that another visit to the Old City was due, that way she can shop without my resistance, and I can tour and seek out history, which is more up my alley!

Feb 5, 2023: Jerusalem

As much as we enjoy the sights and the places we visit, we also get to meet some amazing people along the way. That is one added benefit of being a traveler rather than a tourist. We normally connect with expat groups in each place we live, and some are more active and outgoing than others. Over the past two years we have especially enjoyed being part of these groups and have made some lifelong friends. One of our fellow travelers, Paul, has followed our path to Turkey and we followed his to Albania. We also met while we were both in Romania, and next month he will return to Albania, and we get to hang out once more. Sometimes we also make friends with our hosts, and that is what happened yesterday.

When we first arrived at our room, our AirBNB host, Shlomi, invited us to Shabbat dinner, which takes place Saturday afternoon. We did that yesterday and had an amazing time. We joined his wife and two kids, plus two grandkids, and had a great meal and wonderful conversation. He educated us about Jerusalem and answered some questions we were wondering about, and his family asked us about our travels and experiences, so it was a great exchange of cultures. He has been involved with philosophy and humanities for many years, and we all shared deep questions about "The Meaning of Life," and once again we were shown that people everywhere—regardless of religion, nationality, color, or age—all wonder the same things.

Feb 11, 2023: Jerusalem

This has been an interesting week, as the rain and extreme cold kept us closer to home than we would like. We were able to dodge raindrops a few days ago and visited the David Museum, as in KING David, the slayer of Goliath. Like most ruins we have seen, it was humbling to walk among such history. There was a section that still had the original walls from 2000 plus years ago, and considering the Old Town of Jerusalem was destroyed and rebuilt several times, that really rolls back the calendar several dozen centuries. We've seen innumerable ruins in so many places, but to have so much history contained in such a small area says a lot how about the significance of this town.

Today we went to their Holocaust Museum, called Yad Vashem, which was fascinating. Many of my new friends did not know, but I am the son of a Holocaust survivor, and my Hungarian born mother spent three years in Auschwitz. The first time I went to a Holocaust Museum, in Washington DC, was just a few years ago, and it was an emotionally charged day. I'm not ashamed to say that I cried throughout and since that was my first time, it hit way too close to my heart. Visits after that to similar places, including Auschwitz itself, have become less impactful, but no less important.

It is now (Friday night) the beginning of Shabbat, the Sabbath, and tomorrow hardly anything will be open, so it's a great day to relax and get ready for Sunday, which takes us to Petra, Jordan for a two-day stay, which includes sleeping in a Bedouin camp. This is part two of what I call the Triangle of History tour, and THIS will be one of the most unusual places for Kat and me yet!

Date: 03.01.23/ 27 Days in Israel, part III (Feb 12-Feb 18)

Feb 14, 2023: Jerusalem: Petra, Jordan, part I

They don't call Petra one of the Seven Wonders of the World for no reason: it is beyond magical. It is beyond jaw-dropping, and every type of exaggerated expression you could come up with.

Our journey started at 0730 on morning one, as we were picked up in Jerusalem and headed southeast to Jordan. The trip started rough since we spent about five hours at the border crossing and we initially didn't know the cause. It was a simple human error as one of our fellow tourists fell asleep on bus #1 and was not awakened at the border to exit! He finally did, and even so, the process of border crossing was one of the most challenging ever, since we had to pay a FEE to exit Israel ($52 per), and another to ENTER Jordan, as well as leave a day later ($70 for both). That involved two different stops, but we lost half of day one, which made everyone, including our Jordanian guide, a bit testy...

We stopped along the way at Mt. Nebo, which was, according to the Bible, where Moses was granted a view of the Promised Land before his death. The views were beautiful and the ride up to it was staggering and windy, which really brought home how mountainous the country is, as well as having a lot of NOTHING desert. Another side trip to the city of Madaba was next, and their claim to fame is their Byzantine mosaics, especially the 6th century map of Jerusalem and the Holy Land. Since we still had another three plus hours ride to our overnight camp, most of our bus was anxious to get on the road.

How do you visualize a "Bedouin camp?" Kat and I each had our ideas, and because we arrived in the dark, we weren't able to fully appreciate it until the next morning. But we got there about 8:00 pm, had a nice dinner, and were shown to our "room," which was a cabin/tent with enough room for a bed and one side table. Oh, and it had no heater, which did not thrill us, with 35 degrees (F, about 2 degrees C) outside temps, not enough to freeze water, but enough to make those five layers of blankets quite necessary! After dinner we went to a nice entertainment room, a much larger "tent," with cushions and pillows strewn about, and we hung out with some new friends, a family of three plus a friend, and we all had a chance to enjoy some much-needed rest and some terrific tea. The camp had several dozen rooms, including some which were geodesic domes, and it was nestled into an amazing mountain wall with lights all along the face. They were like little fireflies which made the cold tolerable, and the experience memorable. Along with no heater, we also had no bathroom, but I'll not share the joy of an overnight visit to THAT room!

An early (leave 0700) morning followed, and we were just 12 minutes from the Petra entrance along a road that was so curved and hilly it even had me worried! But it was worth it as we got to Petra and started our tour just as the sun was coming up about 0730. And to see the sunrise glowing against the illuminated rock faces was something I will always remember. We had all of six hours to enjoy what can take several days, but we made the best of it.

Those next six hours takes a whole focus, so will have that posted tomorrow, and I will share the majesty of the Nabataeans who built Petra in 3000 BC, plus our donkey ride through half the park, the 850 steps we did on the backs of them, plus Kathleen's amorous male who lit out for a cute little filly!

Feb 15, 2023: Jerusalem: Petra, Jordan, part II

Words cannot do Petra justice, nor can photos; it is truly something you must see to appreciate, how a tribe of what we now call Bedouins, which we originally called Nabataeans, built this thousands of years ago. They do not know exactly when the construction started, but it prospered about 1000 BC and was a major trade hub of frankincense, myrrh, and spices, the same gifts we think about when referencing The Three Wise Men who came to visit Jesus' birth. Later it was taken over by the expanding Roman Empire, and was significant until 363 AD when it was severely damaged by an earthquake. That, plus trade routes that went through alternative roads, caused the city to flounder, and by the 7th century it was mostly abandoned. For 1100 years.

In 1812 a Swiss explorer found it, but it was off limits to "outsiders," so he masqueraded as an Arab and thereafter shared the city with the world.

The sandstone rock is quite soft which makes it easy to carve, but also prone to damage from wind and water erosion, and as you enter the park it is mostly flat with a few carvings on the rocks. The "Siq" is where the fun starts, which is a narrow gorge about a mile long, and over the centuries it has been flooded and carved into. Channels run along much of the length, as well as damns, which slowed down more water entering the narrow alleyway. With every 100 yards the views change, and we had our guide for this first part, as he explained the history behind it. Towards the end you can see just a view of something BIG, which is the Treasury.

It is spectacular at 40 meters/ 131 ft high, and intricately carved, and includes six pillars with lots of different figures and symbols. Rumor was that there was a treasure inside, but that has never been proven either way. The large area in front is a mega bazaar, with camels lounging about, just waiting to be ridden or have their photos taken. We were told of the possible routes to take from there, and generally they recommend going to the Qasr al-Bint, which is a huge almost square monument, with a still-standing archway. From there you have a few options, but the most popular one, is up to Ad-Deir, also called The Monastery. And that is almost straight up 850 mostly natural stairs, carved into the rock face.

When we were told this we had to decide: do we walk it, ride it on a donkey, or not go. We opted for the donkey, and we were introduced to Abdollah, who told us to call him, "Why Not." He went on ahead to the stable where we had to pay, and he cautioned us that we would be solicited by others offering the same service and we should just tell them we are "with Why Not." Cute. It's a name you cannot forget.

Getting on the donkeys was awkward since neither of us were experienced in donkey riding, and fortunately the first several hundred yards was mostly downhill, so it was just a matter of keeping our balance. All was well and good until we got to the bottom of those 850 steps, and we asked, "We aren't going up on the donkeys, are we?" and the answer was, "Of course!" So picture this. Steps that vary in height, width, and smoothness, with a deep ravine on our right side. With each step we got jostled and were told to lean forward. Faith, baby, we had to have faith, that these animals know this path and have done it hundreds, maybe thousands of times. With each step we held on, Kat's bridle actually broke on the way, so Abdollah had to twist the wires together and do a jury-rig repair on the slope. (It's in the video)

From there it was up to the top, The Monastery, which was larger and more impressive than the Library, and we hung out there for 30 minutes or so, then had to make a HUGE decision. We took the beasts UP the steps; do we take them down?

Honestly, I said NO, I was not comfortable, but Kat wanted to try, so I joined her. That lasted about 8.5 minutes when both of us decided that the DOWN was much worse than the UP. Our guide waited at the bottom of those 850 steps and we got back on, ready to exit the park and join our group. I had in my mind that I wanted to interview a Bedouin, so I did that, side by side, donkey to donkey, with him sitting side saddle. And then, another dose of excitement!

Kat's donkey decided to take a side trip, thinking he was going to "The Church," another stop, which we did not have time for, and she was several yards along that reverse path and heard the Call of the Wild, in this case a female donkey braying at the top of that slope, with her ride responding. Like any healthy male, he took off, with My Lovely hanging on for dear life. "Pull back," I cried out, but Abdollah took off up the hill to save them both. She was shaken, stirred, but carried on until we had to leave them both.

From there we joined our group, had a delicious lunch, and started on our too long trip back to Jerusalem. We had more, but different problems at the border (our bus and driver went to the wrong place!), but made it back, a bit tired, a lot sore, and glad for the experience.

Feb 18, 2023: Jerusalem: Petra, Jordan

This was probably the most unique and fun interview I have ever done! Please enjoy, especially Kathleen's runaway love struck donkey. *Interview with a Bedouin*

And feel free to share: https://youtu.be/LUUmNhoOlwo

Date: 03.01.23/ From Israel and On to Egypt (Feb 18-Feb 26)

Feb 18, 2023: Jerusalem

As we finished up Israel, we also celebrated four years on the road, and on to country #28...

Yesterday was our four-year anniversary since Kat and I left the US, and it's been a hell of a ride! We marvel at how much has happened since then, and on one hand it seems much longer than four years, but yet it seems like it was just a short time ago. We are now in country #29 since we left, and we have both been to about 45 countries in total. Egypt is coming up next, and later this year many more will be added in the Far East and Southern Hemisphere.

I have taken 69 flights since 2019, and I think a few layovers are missing. We have met some amazing people on the way, including several who we now consider lifelong and dear friends. Unfortunately, we have lost some old friends as well, but that is inevitable just based on distance and different lifestyles. Along with 29 countries, we've stayed at more than 100 Airbnb rooms and hotels, in hundreds of cities, and seen an insane number of churches, cathedrals, castles, ruins, and museums! Some of the novelty has worn off, but we are constantly amazed to STILL see something new and exciting. That has certainly been the case over our past month in Israel.

For those who have stayed in touch, and new friends we found along the way...THANK YOU. It's less fun doing what we do if we don't share it, and when people tell us that they started their journey because they were motivated or encouraged by us, well, that makes it all the better.

Feb 20, 2023: Jerusalem

We are at the Tel Aviv airport with just a few hours left before we depart Israel for what may be the last time. It's been a pretty terrific visit, and we had a lot of time to kill on this, our last day, since we had to check out of our room earlier in the day, and our flight did not leave until 0500 the following morning. I collected some random shots just for memory sake.

Feb 26, 2023: Egypt!

This has been one of the busiest weeks we have had in a long time! To encapsulate the last few days, the day after we arrived in Giza, we visited two pyramid sites, including the Saqqwara Necropolis, which is the site of the very first step pyramid. This was the first attempt at MAKING a pyramid, and that took some trial and error, followed by the second one at Dahsur, which was made at a 54° angle, and they soon discovered that it was too much angle. The bottom corners fell off very quickly, so they decreased the angle to 45°, and the rest of them followed suit. Some pretty amazing mathematics! But at Dahsur we went INSIDE the red limestone pyramid, climbed down 163 steps into the open burial chamber, which was quite cool. THAT was an experience!

From there we visited the Egyptian Antiquities museum and saw our first mummies, I mean, real mummies! They were very tiny and small since that was part of the process of the mummification, and the shapes of their heads were very elongated, almost freaky. Unfortunately, we were unable to take photos.

The next day we hit the big guns: Giza, with three pyramids, plus the Great Sphinx. But before those icons we went to Cairo one more time to the Cairo Museum and saw the original King Tut exhibit. Again, no photos allowed...

It's hard to really describe the experience at Giza. I don't really have a bucket this per se, but if I did this would be on it. Kathleen said that if we were ever going to rent camels this was the place to do it and she was right! We took a camel ride from the top of the hill down to the Sphinx at the bottom, and it was a memory that will stay with us forever.

Three days of non-stop was exhausting, but the fun was not over yet! The next day we flew to Luxor and met up with some friends from Albania. Stay tuned!

Date: 02.24.23/ Egypt: Luxor

Before we started working on our Egypt trip we had to make many decisions. How long did we need in the country; where were we going, and how were we traveling?

We kind of knew we wanted just a few days in Cairo/ Giza since it was so busy, and after researching the other spots to visit, Luxor was our next spot. We decided to fly there since it was just one hour away and fairly cheap, plus, we met up with some American friends we met in Albania at the airport, and the four of us shared a flight together. This was a first after so many years of traveling since with it is usually just the two of us, but Steve and Kathy were great partners and we all got along well together.

Luxor is a small town, especially compared to Cairo, and the Nile River splits the town in half between the east and west bank. We stayed on the east side and there was a great selection of rooms, plus it was more "rural", and not within a crowded town.

Our room at the Oasis Guest House was terrific at just $16 per day—including breakfast on the roof patio. When we arrived we met with our host, Abraham, and talked about tour options, and like in Giza, decided that a tour made sense. Also, since we now had two other people to share it with, we were all able to save a bit of money. The Valley of the Kings was a must-see, and our tour guide showed us around, shared the history and insight, plus took us to the Temple of Hatshepsut, one of the most significant Queens in early Egyptian history, and a monument we had never heard of, called Medinet Habu. All were spectacular!

The next day we were on our own so took the ferry across the river and visited the Temple of Karnak and viewed the Luxor Temple, which is visible by just driving or walking by, and the next morning, our last, we all did something we had never done before: a hot air balloon ride for $50 each, which was outstanding. We left just after sunrise and sailed over the places we had visited, plus saw other sites from a 2000 foot perspective. Money well spent!

There is much more detail that I shared on my personal Facebook page if you'd like to read it.

Date: 02.28.23/ Egypt: Aswan

Three days in Luxor was about right, and the following day we moved on to our next destination, Aswan. There was really only one place we wanted to see there, and that is the Great Temple at Abu Simbel, which I had seen in photos since I was a kid, but I was not familiar with the name. But this is the 4000 year old temple built along the Aswan Lake, which was formed by building the Aswan Dam in the sixties. The rising water put Abu Simbel at risk of being covered, so they dismantled and moved the entire structure about 200 meters up the hill to a higher elevation. This was, and probably still is, the largest archaeological project in history and cost about $200M in 1960's dollars.

The problem we had was twofold: the "town" of Aswan was dirty and polluted with not much there, and the ride to Abu Simbel was 3.5 hours ONE WAY out, which left just two hours to visit, then another long ride back. To facilitate this we left the hostel at 0430 and that made for a long, tiring day. In hindsight, the visit to Aswan was one we could have passed on, and that would have allowed a shorter trip or more time in Luxor. Again, the beauty of hindsight is clear, but at least we can share it here with you!

The next day it was time to leave, and that involved an overnight 12 hour train ride to Cairo, and then leaving the following day. That part follows.

We are in Egypt for our final night, and it has been one hell of a ride! From camels to hot air balloons, from taxis to trains, tomorrow we are heading back to Albania, and not a moment too soon. We have been gone for 41 days, and most of that time was spent in Israel, but the last 10 days or so have been non-stop. Tonight is our fifth night in a different location, and that includes last night, on an overnight train, and tonight, when we will be sleeping more or less at the Cairo airport. Tomorrow night we will be on the island of Corfu for the first time.